Education in the Asia-Pacific Region: Issues, Concerns and Prospects

Volume 43

Series Editors-in-Chief

Professor Rupert Maclean, *Office of Applied Research and Innovation, College of the North Atlantic-Qatar, Doha, Qatar*
Dr Lorraine Pe Symaco, *Zhejiang University, Hangzhou, China*

Editorial Board

Professor Bob Adamson, *The Education University of Hong Kong, China*
Dr Robyn Baker, *New Zealand Council for Educational Research, Wellington, New Zealand*
Professor Michael Crossley, *University of Bristol, United Kingdom*
Ms Shanti Jagannathan, *Asian Development Bank, Manila, Philippines*
Dr Yuto Kitamura, *University of Tokyo, Japan*
Professor Colin Power, *Graduate School of Education, University of Queensland, Brisbane, Australia*
Professor Konai Helu Thaman, *University of the South Pacific, Suva, Fiji*

Advisory Board

Professor Mark Bray, *UNESCO Chair, Comparative Education Research Centre, The University of Hong Kong, China*; **Professor Yin Cheong Cheng,** *The Education University of Hong Kong, China*; **Professor John Fien,** *Swinburne University, Melbourne, Australia*; **Dr Pham Lan Huong,** *International Educational Research Centre, Ho Chi Minh City, Vietnam*; **Dr Chong-Jae Lee,** *Korean Educational, Development Institute (KEDI), Seoul, Republic of Korea*; **Ms Naing Yee Mar,** *GIZ, Yangon, Myanmar*; **Professor Geoff Masters,** *Australian Council for Educational Research, Melbourne, Australia*; **Margarita Pavlova,** *The Education University of Hong Kong, China*; **Dr Max Walsh,** *Secondary Education Project, Manila, Philippines*; **Dr Uchita de Zoysa,** *Global Sustainability Solutions (GLOSS), Colombo, Sri Lanka*

More information about this series at http://www.springer.com/series/5888

Jing Liu

Inequality in Public School Admission in Urban China

Discourses, Practices and New Solutions

Jing Liu
The University of Tokyo
Tokyo, Japan

ISSN 1573-5397　　　　　　ISSN 2214-9791　(electronic)
Education in the Asia-Pacific Region: Issues, Concerns and Prospects
ISBN 978-981-10-8717-2　　　ISBN 978-981-10-8718-9　(eBook)
https://doi.org/10.1007/978-981-10-8718-9

Library of Congress Control Number: 2018935898

© Springer Nature Singapore Pte Ltd. 2018
This work is subject to copyright. All rights are reserved by the Publisher, whether the whole or part of the material is concerned, specifically the rights of translation, reprinting, reuse of illustrations, recitation, broadcasting, reproduction on microfilms or in any other physical way, and transmission or information storage and retrieval, electronic adaptation, computer software, or by similar or dissimilar methodology now known or hereafter developed.
The use of general descriptive names, registered names, trademarks, service marks, etc. in this publication does not imply, even in the absence of a specific statement, that such names are exempt from the relevant protective laws and regulations and therefore free for general use.
The publisher, the authors and the editors are safe to assume that the advice and information in this book are believed to be true and accurate at the date of publication. Neither the publisher nor the authors or the editors give a warranty, express or implied, with respect to the material contained herein or for any errors or omissions that may have been made. The publisher remains neutral with regard to jurisdictional claims in published maps and institutional affiliations.

Printed on acid-free paper

This Springer imprint is published by the registered company Springer Nature Singapore Pte Ltd.
The registered company address is: 152 Beach Road, #21-01/04 Gateway East, Singapore 189721, Singapore

Foreword

Since the 1980s, the Chinese government has promoted the principle of nine-year compulsory education with exam-free, cost-free entrance to public schools based on proximity to place of residence. Under this principle, children are supposed to be assigned to lower secondary schools by lottery. However, in urban areas, severe competition pushes parents to use various means to bend the system to access public schools with better objective conditions, such as better school facilities, more qualified teachers, superior students and leadership, and greater support from above. Parents do so by making use of connections with power, by using resources, or by manipulating the criteria for special selection based on academic excellence or special talents. It is not only parents but also schools who want competent students, and private tutoring institutions driven by commercial interests play roles to create different channels for school admission and the ways to utilize them.

Zexiao, which is the main theme of this book, means the diversified mechanism of competitive admission to lower secondary school and the practices of stakeholders related to it. The literal translation of it in English is "school choice," but its actual meaning is very different from its generally accepted idea of offering alternatives to the students and parents to better fit their educational needs. *Zexiao* is like a giant elephant. One may be able to touch a part of its body but it is difficult to grasp the whole shape of it, because it is largely hidden under the surface of formality. While *Zexiao* is a social phenomenon which has caught the attention of the media and the public in the urban areas, it is more likely to be discussed in a superficial and sensational manner. There is still only limited academic discussion based on critical and comprehensive analysis of *Zexiao*, its ethical implications, and effects on the increased gap of educational opportunities among social classes.

In this book, Dr. Liu successfully uncovers the social, structural, and economic dynamics behind *Zexiao* and specifies the elements which constitute the whole mechanism, through the analysis of discourse surrounding it. For this purpose, he reviewed newspaper articles (professional papers on education, national papers, and local papers of major cities) dating back over thirty years, in addition to policy documents, reports, and education-related regulations. To match the analysis of discourse with that of practices on the ground, he also conducted a case study of schools in one school district of Beijing, interviewing administrators, school principals, teachers, and parents. By combining these two sets of analysis, he presents the complete picture of this giant elephant from the macro policy level to the micro level of schools and individual actors involved in its practice. It is a major strength of this book and a potential area of contribution to academic and political discussions.

In addition, Dr. Liu considers *Zexiao* not only an issue of manipulation of the school admission system among the urban well-to-do families, but also in relation to the restricted educational opportunities of the poor and migrants from rural areas. By adopting the theory of social closure, he tries to explain the phenomena as mutually enforcing processes of reproduction and exclusion. The uncoordinated but collective acts of people who try to maximize their own profits by monopolizing the limited resources and opportunities have accompanied the practices of exclusion. Dr. Liu points out that it was actually the strong control by the centralized state which caused such practices to emerge and deviate the admission process through informal means, and thus systematically exclude those without power, regardless of the formal arrangements to ensure equality.

Dr. Liu Jing was among the first group of students whom I supervised in Nagoya University and the first Ph.D. who flew from my humble nest. He is one of the most hardworking students in my memory and always tried to do all and even more than what was suggested to him. Looking back, I feel that he has proven himself by devoting his best efforts to the field of his choice. As he writes in the Preface of this volume, *Zexiao* overshadowed his own earlier life. The elite secondary school which he managed to enter as a "special talent student" was not necessarily a comfortable place, restricting him in the pursuit of his own curiosity and assessing his capacity for something for which he did not have passion. After being treated as an unsuccessful student, he came to Japan to restart his tertiary education, with a deeply held unyielding spirit under his softly smiling face. The major he chose was education.

The steps he took to untangle the sociopolitical structure of *Zexiao* was, I believe, also a journey to make sense of his adolescence. The rewards he received for his hard work, such as dissertation awards, must have boosted his self-esteem and confidence gradually. Now, Dr. Liu Jing publishes his comprehensive analysis of the school assignment mechanism in the capital city of China, which is largely invisible from the eyes of international observers. I have no doubt in its academic value, particularly for being published in English, and I am proud.

Congratulations, Liu Jing.

Applied Social System Institute and Graduate Shoko Yamada
School of International Development
Nagoya University
Nagoya, Japan

Preface

It has been eight years since I became keen on investigating how people interact in admission to public junior high schools in urban China and why they had to do so. I could not clearly tell why I was so interested in this topic until I realized these are all growth paths that I experienced. As a primary school student in 1994, I experienced abolishment of entrance exams to junior high schools in Beijing. Also, I felt how my parents became worried about my schooling in a "bad school" based on the principle of proximity-based school admission to junior high school. Moreover, I observed how they were forced to visit my class teacher and school principal with gifts for their "help" with a recommendation of my promotion to "good schools." Moreover, the experience of playing the violin as a hobby also let me understand that knowledge is no burden right after I was successfully enrolled into a "good" junior high school as a "special talent student" who just knew how to play the violin. In addition to these, I learned many other alternative ways of going to good schools from my buddies in the same class. Some of them went to good schools by paying additional fees. Others gained enrollment by partnerships between the good schools and the work units of their parents. More than 20 years have passed, and I recognized that students and parents had more difficulties and challenges to access good schooling in urban China from media, research papers, stories of friends, and conversations between passengers on the subway or buses. And I knew the options and processes for entering into a good school became increasingly more complicated and more competitive than what I experienced in 1994. Upon entering the research community—as a Chinese citizen and researcher in the field of China's education development—I told myself that I should stop taking things for granted. And I felt a desire to explain about the unique urban education phenomenon regarding admission to public junior high schools that exists in urban China.

The specific subject of the book is the competition in urban China for student admission to public junior high schools from grade 6 to grade 7 (G6 to G7) called *Zexiao* (a straightforward English translation is "school choice"). In the international context, school choice is considered a government tool for promoting free choice in parents' decisions about their children's education, the improvement of school accountability, efficiency and educational quality, or the prevention of social problems. Conversely, in China's context, *Zexiao* is not supported by the government at the compulsory education level (G1 to G9) since it violates the essential principle of admission to public schools. Rather, *Zexiao*, which usually takes place around entry to G1 or G7, the beginning of primary school or lower secondary school, creates competition among students, parents, public schools, local education authorities, and private tutoring institutes. Moreover, in the recent past, competition caused stratification in admission to public junior high schools and led to educational inequality in public education in urban China.

In the midst of millions of words that been written and the countless academic papers or news reports that have been published, there are few which interpreted how the positional competition in admission to public junior high schools developed in the midst of rapid social change in Chinese society. Moreover, it was still difficult to figure out how people engaged and interacted in such competition and what are the reasons behind people's engagement and interaction. We are hard pressed to find accounts of why there is a rise of *Zexiao* despite the government continuously saying no to such practices for decades. In addition, little is available to inform us about the current solutions to deal with the competition and social stratification in admission to public junior high schools in urban China.

This book addresses these omissions. It distinguishes *Zexiao* in the context of urban China from school choice in the global debate. Then, it interprets the development of *Zexiao* by analyzing public discourses on such practices between the 1990s and the 2000s. It also reveals interaction among stakeholders in *Zexiao* to further indicate how people engage and interact in *Zexiao* and why they do so through a case study of Community A in Beijing. In addition, it provides a review of current new solutions made by the government to deal with the ongoing competition which has caused social exclusion and educational inequality. More importantly, by adopting the theory of social closure, this book provides a new framework for deepening analysis of the dynamic interactions involved in social exclusion to further construct knowledge of the interrelationship among people in the context of today's urban China.

I am not sure to what extent I have successfully investigated the omissions above. This book is a highly relevant source of information about policy making and policy implementation in balancing efficiency and equity for public education policy makers and planners. It provides scholars with comprehensive data and a detailed interpretation of the diverse issues relevant to educational inequality in Chinese public education in the context of a country in rapid transition from a profit-driven society to a more balanced society post 2015. Moreover, it adds the different interpretations and dynamic practices of *Zexiao* as competition for student placement to the broader field of school choice research. These can be taken as sources for expanding a comparative study about parental choice between countries in non-Western contexts.

Tokyo, Japan   Jing Liu

Acknowledgments

This book is based on a revision of my Ph.D. dissertation submitted to the Graduate School of International Development, Nagoya University, Japan, in 2013. To acknowledge properly the generosity of the people with me on this journey, I started to recall people I met, places I visited, and stories I experienced in the past years.

Breaking with tradition, I express my grateful thanks to my parents who gave me life in the 1980s and allowed me to experience being a special talented student for a successful admission to public junior high school in 1994. Their engagement in making efforts to send me to "good schools" definitely left me with a vivid memory to understand why and how parents actively engage in children's schooling in China. Also, I acknowledge their unconditional support throughout my student life. Their understanding of my dream and patience for the time-consuming process for my Ph.D. study always encouraged me to move forward.

My sincere and warmest appreciation goes to Dr. Shoko Yamada, my former academic advisor and the chairperson of my dissertation committee, for her continuous guidance, critical but constructive comments, and patient instruction intellectually and mentally in the past years. Her kind offers of involving me in her research projects and paper writing gave me precious experiences and training for becoming an independent researcher in the academic world.

My greatest gratitude to the people involved in the fieldwork conducted in Beijing. My appreciations go to all the respondents who generously shared their personal experiences of *Zexiao* with me for this study. Their concern, dedication, and commitment to equality in high-quality public education in China deeply touched me and pushed me to move forward to explore why inequality exists and how to deal with it.

Finally, I heartily express my appreciation to Dr. James Jacob and Dr. Francis Peddie, who generously proofread the book draft and kindly helped me to polish the language used in the book. A special thanks to the anonymous peer reviewers of the book for their comments to improve the shape and the content of my work. I also owe grateful thanks to the team at Springer for their thoughtful suggestions and boundless support for publishing the first book of a young scholar like me.

Tokyo, Japan   Jing Liu

Series Editors' Introduction

This volume by Jing Liu on *Inequality in Public School Admission in Urban China: Discourses, Practices and New Solutions* is the latest book to be published in the long-standing Springer Book Series "Education in the Asia Pacific Region: Issues, Concerns and Prospects." The first volume in this Springer series was published in 2002, with this book by Jing Liu being the 43rd volume to be published to date.

This is an important book on an important subject, since although this volume refers specifically to competition and school choice in urban China for student admission to public junior high schools (which is called *Zexiao*), the topic is also of great interest internationally. The reason is that school choice is regarded as being a tool for promoting free choice in parents' decisions about their children's education. As such the book addresses key matters at the core of promoting access and equity in schools such as strengthening the accountability of schools to their local communities, and society as a whole, and ways of improving efficiency and quality in schooling. The research reported on here explains in a clear evidence-based way, at a time of unprecedented rapid social change in China, how competition for admission to public junior high schools has developed.

Jing Liu explores and interprets the various discussions and practices occurring concerning the development of competition for school admission to public lower secondary education in urban China. He identifies trends and changes in discussions that are shaped by varying forces which exist in public secondary school admission policies and practices, in the move from a profit-driven society to a more equitable society. The research identifies and explains the power relationships among and between various stakeholders involved with decision making and practices concerning public school admissions. In so doing, the research reported on here "exposes how current socio-economic, institutional and educational systems are shaping the engagement of stakeholders in the public school admission process to lower secondary schools in urban China; and presents some ongoing reforms as new solutions for a more equitable public secondary education with balance and quality in China since 2015."

In terms of the Springer Book Series, in which this volume is published, the various topics dealt with in the series are wide ranging and varied in coverage, with an emphasis on cutting-edge developments, best practices, and education innovations for development. Topics examined include: environmental education and education for sustainable development; the interaction between technology and education; the reform of primary, secondary, and teacher education; innovative approaches to education assessment; alternative education; most effective ways to achieve quality and highly relevant education for all; active aging through active learning; case studies of education and schooling systems in various countries in the region; cross-country and cross-cultural studies of education and schooling; and the sociology of teachers as an occupational group, to mention just a few. More information about this series is available at http://www.springer.com/series/6969

All volumes in this series aim to meet the interests and priorities of a diverse education audience including researchers, policymakers, and practitioners; tertiary students; teachers at all levels within education systems; and members of the public who are interested in better understanding cutting-edge developments in education and schooling in Asia-Pacific.

The reason why this book series has been devoted exclusively to examining various aspects of education and schooling in the Asia-pacific region is that this is a particularly challenging region which is renowned for its size, diversity, and complexity, whether it be geographical, socioeconomic, cultural, political, or developmental. Education and schooling in countries throughout the region impact on every aspect of people's lives, including employment, labor force considerations, education and training, cultural orientation, and attitudes and values. Asia and the Pacific are home to some 63% of the world's population of 7 billion. Countries with the largest populations (China 1.4 billion; India 1.3 billion) and the most rapidly growing mega-cities are to be found in the region, as are countries with relatively small populations (Bhutan 755,000; the island of Niue 1600).

Levels of economic and sociopolitical development vary widely, with some of the richest countries (such as Japan) and some of the poorest countries on earth (such as Bangladesh). Asia contains the largest number of poor of any region in the world, the incidence of those living below the poverty line remaining as high as 40% in some countries in Asia. At the same time, many countries in Asia are experiencing a period of great economic growth and social development. However, inclusive growth remains elusive, as does growth that is sustainable and does not destroy the quality of the environment. The growing prominence of Asian economies and corporations, together with globalization and technological innovation, are leading to long-term changes in trade, business, and labor markets, to the sociology of populations within (and between) countries. There is a rebalancing of power, centered on Asia and the Pacific region, with the Asian Development Bank in Manila declaring that the twenty-first century will be "the Century of Asia Pacific."

We believe this book series makes a useful contribution to knowledge sharing about education and schooling in Asia Pacific. Any readers of this or other volumes in the series who have an idea for writing their own book (or editing a book) on any aspect of education and/or schooling, that is relevant to the region, are enthusiastically encouraged to approach the series editors either direct or through Springer to publish their own volume in the series, since we are always willing to assist perspective authors shape their manuscripts in ways that make them suitable for publication in this series.

Office of Applied Research and Innovation   Rupert Maclean
College of the North Atlantic-Qatar
Doha, Qatar
Zhejiang University   Lorraine Symaco
Hangzhou, China
December 2017

Contents

1	Introduction	1
	1.1 Background	2
	1.2 Social Inequality in Education	4
	1.3 Education Stratification in China	8
	1.4 The Imbalanced Distribution of Education Resources	9
	1.5 A Social Closure Framework	10
	1.6 A Social Constructionist Perspective	11
	1.7 Analysis of Discourses on *Zexiao*	12
	1.8 Case Study: Community A	17
	1.9 The Book Chapters	21
	References	23
2	A Critical Definition of *Zexiao*	29
	2.1 Global Trends of Educational Reform	30
	2.1.1 Equity and the Right to Choose	30
	2.1.2 Neo-liberal Market Approach	31
	2.1.3 New Public Management	32
	2.1.4 Global Culture and Policy Borrowing	32
	2.2 Educational Selection and Educational Ideology Change	34
	2.2.1 Mao's Education Ideology	35
	2.2.2 Deng's Ideology in Education	38
	2.2.3 Education and Construction of Harmonious Society	41
	2.2.4 The Chinese Dream in "New Normal"	43
	2.3 The Development of *Zexiao*	44
	2.3.1 The Expansion of *Zexiao*	46
	2.3.2 The Diversity and Complexity of *Zexiao*	48
	2.4 Channels for *Zexiao*	51
	2.4.1 Money-Based *Zexiao* (*Yiqian Zexiao*)	52
	2.4.2 Power (*guanxi*)-based *Zexiao* (*Yiquan(guanxi) Zexiao*)	54
	2.4.3 "Achievement"-based *Zexiao* (*Yifen Zexiao*)	57
	2.5 Summary: *Zexiao* ≠ School Choice	62
	References	63

3	**Public Discourses on *Zexiao***		71
	3.1 The 1990s: The Unauthorized Charge of School Fees		72
		3.1.1 The Limited Education Investment	72
		3.1.2 Imbalance Between Public Schools	74
		3.1.3 Parents' Aspiration	75
	3.2 After 2000: The Imbalanced Educational Development		77
		3.2.1 The Distribution of Limited Education Resources	78
		3.2.2 The Imbalance Between Public Schools	78
		3.2.3 Parents' Aspirations	79
		3.2.4 Newly Emerging Discussions	80
	References		92
4	**Where There Is a Policy, There Is a Countermeasure**		97
	4.1 A Non-choice Public School Admission in China		98
	4.2 School Admission Policy: The 1990s		99
		4.2.1 Government Documents	100
		4.2.2 Beijing's Policy	101
		4.2.3 Public Discussion	101
	4.3 School Admission Policy: After 2000		102
		4.3.1 Government Documents	103
		4.3.2 Beijing's Policy	103
		4.3.3 Public Discussion	104
	References		113
5	**The Key Schools and *Zexiao***		117
	5.1 The Key School System		118
	5.2 The Gap Between Public Schools		123
		5.2.1 The Discussion in the 1990s	123
		5.2.2 The Discussion After the 2000s	128
	5.3 Collusion for Student Selection		134
	References		137
6	**Competition of Family Background with Local Characteristics**		141
	6.1 Public School Admission Policy in Community A		142
	6.2 "Parentocracy"-based School Admission		145
		6.2.1 Admission by School Recommendation	146
		6.2.2 Admission by Special Talents	147
		6.2.3 School Admission for Migrant Children	152
	6.3 "Legalization" of *Zexiaofei*		153
	6.4 The Local Context and Beyond		156
		6.4.1 The Gap Between Public Schools	156
		6.4.2 Parents' Aspirations	160
		6.4.3 Systematic Power Exchange	161
	6.5 Mapping *Zexiao* in Community A		162
	References		164

7	**Admission to Public Lower Secondary Schools as Social Closures**		**165**
	7.1	*Zexiao* as Social Closures	166
		7.1.1 Policy Level	166
		7.1.2 School Level	166
		7.1.3 Parent Level	167
	7.2	*Zexiao*: As Educational Inequality and Social Reproduction	168
	References		170
8	**New Solutions for *Zexiao***		**171**
	8.1	Policy Flow for Balancing Development of Public Education	172
	8.2	Policy Integration in Beijing Municipal Government	174
		8.2.1 Construction of Balanced Development of Public Education	174
		8.2.2 Reform in Admission to Public Junior High Schools	175
	8.3	Emerging Challenges	178
		8.3.1 Influence on the Well-Performing Schools	178
		8.3.2 Persisting Privileges in School Admission	179
		8.3.3 Education Exclusion in Admission for Migrant Children	179
		8.3.4 Barriers for Construction of Balanced Development of Public Education	180
	8.4	Discussion	180
	References		182
9	**Conclusion**		**185**
	9.1	Summary of the Findings	185
		9.1.1 *Zexiao* ≠ School Choice	186
		9.1.2 Trajectory of Public Discourses on *Zexiao*	186
		9.1.3 Multilayered Inequalities in *Zexiao*	188
		9.1.4 New Solutions and Challenges	190
	9.2	Reconsidering *Zexiao*	191
		9.2.1 *Zexiao*: As a Result of the Imbalanced Distribution of Education Resources	191
		9.2.2 *Zexiao*: As a Loophole Left by the Policy Gap Between Central and Local Levels	192
		9.2.3 *Zexiao*: As Educational Inequality and Social Reproduction	193
	9.3	Implication for Theoretical Discussion	195
	9.4	Implication for Practice	196
		9.4.1 Balanced Education Development	196
		9.4.2 Does Balanced Education Development Work?	197
	9.5	Implication for Future Research	199
	References		200
Appendices			**201**
Index			**217**

List of Figures

Fig. 1.1	Map of Community A	17
Fig. 1.2	Enrolment of School A (2000–2011)	19
Fig. 2.1	Interdistricts *Zexiao* in Beijing (2008)	49
Fig. 2.2	School admission options (Nationwide & Beijing)	51
Fig. 2.3	Special talent-based entrance exam (Dongcheng District, Beijing)	59
Fig. 2.4	Olympic math textbook corner	60
Fig. 5.1	Demonstration schools within the 5th Ring Road of Beijing, 2011	121
Fig. 5.2	Diversification of educational fund (1992–2008)	125
Fig. 6.1	Student mobility in Community A	157
Fig. 6.2	Mapping *Zexiao* in Community A	163
Fig. 8.1	Goals of reform for school admission in compulsory education in major cities	173

List of Tables

Table 1.1	Disparity of public education expenditure by region, 2008	9
Table 1.2	List of reviewed newspapers.	13
Table 1.3	List of school principals interviewed	15
Table 2.1	School admission options in Beijing in 2010.	50
Table 2.2	List of co-founding school with FESCO of Beijing (2011)	56
Table 2.3	Comparison of nature between *Zexiao* and school choice	62
Table 5.1	Distribution of demonstration schools and distribution of registered population in Beijing (2008)	122
Table 6.1	School admission options in Community A in 2011	143
Table 6.2	School admission schedule in School B, 2011	145

Chapter 1
Introduction

Abstract The introduction briefly examines the context of Zexiao in public junior high school admission in China. Then it explains data collection and data analysis in the book project. It introduces a conceptual framework to explain why and how the author interprets *Zexiao* as a social closure phenomenon by a discourse analysis approach. Also, it comprehensively introduces how the author utilizes a case study of practices in admission to public junior high schools in Community A to further visualize multilayered social closures among stakeholders in the same process. This section concludes with an outline of the chapters of the book.

> Article 9
> Local people's governments at various levels shall establish primary schools and junior middle schools at such locations that children and adolescents can attend schools near their homes.
> Article 10
> The state shall not charge tuition for students receiving compulsory education.
>
> –*Compulsory Education Law of the People's Republic of China, 1986*
> Article 2
> No tuition or miscellaneous fee may be charged in the implementation of compulsory education.
> Article 12
> The school-age children and adolescents shall go to schools without taking any examination. The local people's governments at all levels shall ensure that the school-age children and adolescents are enrolled in the schools near the permanent residences of the school-age children and adolescents.
>
> –*Compulsory Education Law of the People's Republic of China, 2006 Amendment*

The legal quotes shown at the beginning of the chapter portray that since the 1980s, the government has officially provided a legal guarantee for a "free, non-exam-based, and proximity-based" compulsory education (from Grades 1 to 9 [G1–G9]). Over the past few decades, China has made significant progress in achieving Education for All (EFA) goals and the universalization of basic education. Nevertheless, this basic principle for compulsory education has continuously been challenged by a developing competition for admission to public schools in China. In

Chinese, this phenomenon is called *Zexiao*. In general, it refers to activities in which parents compete for enrolling their children in the limited number of popular schools they prefer instead of the public schools based on the public school admission policies, particularly at the compulsory education level (Liu, 2013, 2015; Xiaoxin Wu, 2008, 2012, 2014). In recent years, despite the government's opposition toward *Zexiao* through releasing a series of regulations, activities of *Zexiao* have not abated. Rather, diverse channels for *Zexiao* were innovated in response to the government's action of mitigating *Zexiao*. *Zexiao* interactions involved not only parents and students but also public schools, private tutoring institutes, and local education authorities.

This book explores and interprets discourses and practices in the development of competition for school admission to public lower secondary education in urban China. It uncovers continuities and changes in discourses shaped by diverse forces in public lower secondary school admission within the social transformation landscape from a profit-driven society to a more equitable society. It elucidates power relationships among and between stakeholders in public school admissions by analyzing their interplay in the process. More importantly, it exposes how current socioeconomic, institutional, and educational systems are shaping the engagement of stakeholders in the public school admission process to lower secondary education in urban China. It also presents some ongoing reforms as new solutions for a more equitable public secondary education with balance and quality in China since 2015.

The introduction chapter presents the background of the study, describes an overall framework used to help guide the study, introduces research methods and research sites, and concludes with an outline of the rest of the book.

1.1 Background

There are increasing global discourses on parental school choice for children's schooling. Internationally, school choice has been an important issue in basic education. For years, governments worldwide have been attempting to find ways to provide more options for parents, such as open enrollments, public subsidies to private schools, and education vouchers. In addition, governments in various countries have also aimed to improve accountability, efficiency, and educational quality of the public school system by offering various options of "school choice," such as charter schools in the USA and grant-maintained schools in the UK. In some countries "school choice" was promoted for the purpose of desegregation, such as magnet schools in the USA and City Technology Colleges in the UK. Some countries introduced school choice policies for preventing social issues, such as bullying and school violence in Japan (Forsey, Davies, & Walford, 2008; Hirsch, 2002; OECD, 1994; Plank & Sykes, 2003). Ironically, school choice-based educational reforms at the global level did not change the "persistent educational inequality" as stratification order in many societies. For the most part, the effect of family background on children's education attainment persisted. School choice became a tool for the

1.1 Background

privileged groups to keep advantages for their children in the competition for education. Meanwhile, it excluded the disadvantaged from such competition (Andre-Bechely, 2005a; Ball, 1993; Forsey et al., 2008; Gewirtz, Ball, & Bowe, 1995; OECD, 2012; Plank & Sykes, 2003).

It is not uncommon that people tend to interpret *Zexiao* in the concept of school choice, regardless of the differences between the two. This book distinguishes *Zexiao* in China from the concept of "school choice" used in the international discourse. In the Chinese context, *Zexiao* is not supported by the government at the compulsory education level since it is felt that it violates the essential principle of admission to compulsory education in public schools. At the same time, it is not considered a tool by the government for promoting free choice for parent's decision on children's education; the improvement of schools' accountability, efficiency, and educational quality; or the prevention of negative social issues in China's education system. In general, *Zexiao* is considered creating competitions among students, parents, public schools, local education authorities, and private tutoring institutes. In addition, *Zexiao* has been used as a means to make profits due to factors such as limited access to popular schools and insufficient government funding in education. In contrast to proximity-based public school admissions, there are diverse channels for *Zexiao*. In recent years, in addition to *hukou* (residential registration) and students' academic achievements as criteria, school admissions also involved other "unofficial" criteria, such as additional payments for school admissions, special talents, donations from powerful work units, memos from the rich and powerful, as well as pre-admission training classes. Qualifications of students for admission depended on various factors, such as local public school admission policies, students' capacities, and parents' socioeconomic status, including parents' incomes, occupations, and social network (21st Century Education Research Institute, 2011; Liu, 2013, 2015; Xiaoxin Wu, 2008, 2009). In other words, whether students are admitted to their "dream" schools depends on a multitude of factors. These factors shape and stratify the participation of various stakeholders and often cause educational inequality and social reproduction in public school admission at the compulsory education level in urban China.

With the abolishment of the entrance exam to public junior high schools in the late 1980s, admission to junior high schools in China was expected to follow the principle of "free, no exam and proximity-based school admission" as stipulated in the *Compulsory Education Law* in China (National People's Congress, 2006). Both central and local governments continually released regulations and policies to protect the right of school-aged children to have equal opportunities to enter public schools at the compulsory education level. However, the educational and social development in China, especially in urban China, was unable to fully accommodate the demands of both the government and the public. On the one hand, due to the limited governmental funding for public education and the imbalanced educational development, the inequality among public schools prevented equal opportunities for children to enter public schools with the same education experience. On the other hand, the proximity-based school admission to junior high schools could not guarantee parents and students access to the schools they preferred. Therefore, there are increasing demands for access to a limited number of well-known public junior high schools. The mismatch between the supply and the demand stimulated a competition among parents for the limited access to popular schools. At the same time, various channels for public school admission to junior high schools were instigated by local education authorities, public school administrators, and parents. Those approaches depended upon not only students' special talents and students' participation in extracurricular activities but also parent's socioeconomic status and social networks. The diversification of channels for *Zexiao* in public school admission provided parents with more options for sending their children to junior high schools they prefer. Consequently, increasing numbers of parents took actions for *Zexiao*. Since these channels for *Zexiao* were closely connected with parents' socioeconomic status, it further deepened the inequality in public school admissions in urban China. As a result, *Zexiao* is provoking various concerns and debates from the government and the public.

Prior to this study, I found that most existing research mainly described policies and channels regarding *Zexiao*. The theoretical framework utilized in most research was on a global understanding of "school choice," which is not fully appropriate to be used in discussion on *Zexiao* in the context of urban China. *Zexiao* is unique and different from the general concept of "school choice" as it reflects China's social, educational, cultural, and historical development. Moreover, only a few studies systematically visualize the historical development of *Zexiao* in urban China and interpret its practical interactions among stakeholders. To further understand this educational phenomenon, it is necessary to conduct an in-depth analysis of *Zexiao* and its interactions among stakeholders in the public school admissions context. The questions to ask are why and how did *Zexiao* occur? What did people think of *Zexiao* and how did they interact in *Zexiao*? How were people positioned in *Zexiao* and what was the meaning behind that? How did stakeholders deal with *Zexiao*? It is worthwhile to find answers to these questions and gain a more comprehensive understanding of *Zexiao* in the historical development of urban China.

1.2 Social Inequality in Education

The review of social reproduction theories and practices provides a hint to investigate the inequality reproduction in public school admissions in urban China. This is done through analyzing how various capitals of families influence practices in *Zexiao* and how people from different social strata take part in such practices.

Since the 1960s, there has been an increasing amount of research which shows that schools were not institutions of equal opportunity but mechanisms which perpetuate social inequalities (Bourdieu & Passeron, 1977; Bowles & Gintis, 1976; Collins, 2009; Lareau, 1989; Willis, 1977). Social inequality has become one of the hottest issues in sociological research. It refers to the inequality in the distribution of social rewards, resources, and benefits, honor and esteem, rights and privileges, and power and influence which is associated with differences in social position. In

1.2 Social Inequality in Education

other words, this concept conveys an idea of the unequal distribution of benefits and privileges related to various social positions (Matras, 1975; Neelsen, 1975). People who occupy the same relative resources in the stratified society form a social class. It means that within a stratification system, there are numbers of social classes categorized by resources held by people in each class. Carnoy and Levin (1985) emphasized education is a site of class conflict and social contradiction. And they argued that schooling can be considered as an instrument of class domination but that it is also a site of struggles for equality. Scholars have analyzed social reproduction in education from various perspectives, including but not limited to economic, cultural, linguistic, and social networks. The review in this section mainly discusses the social reproduction in education from a neoliberalism perspective.

With the rapid globalization and education reform, neoliberals who promoted education reform emphasizing competition driven and freedom of consumers' choice around the world did not fully fulfill their objectives. The neoliberalism perspective holds that competition will enhance the efficiency and responsiveness of schools as well as give disadvantaged children opportunities that they currently do not have. For instance, Coleman (1992) and Coleman and his colleagues (1993) argued that the result of school choice would be to replace the stratification by income and race by a stratification based on students' performance and behavior. Furthermore, the performance-based stratification by school choice would introduce appropriate incentives to improve education outcomes of students.

Nevertheless, the neoliberals' belief above did not always hold true when put into practice. The market approach may serve to reproduce the traditional hierarchies of class and race (Apple, 2001, 2004, 2006). Neoliberalism often results in redistributive rather than generative outcomes through the ways which transfer assets and channel wealth and income either from the mass of population toward the upper classes or from vulnerable to the richer countries (Harvey, 2007). In terms of education, as Bourdieu and Passeron (1977) articulated, modern societies provide the educational system with increased opportunities to exercise its power of changing the social advantages into academic advantages. In other words, different social groups can utilize the capital they hold to convert them into their academic advantages in the society. The more social advantage they have, the more academic advantage they receive. Meanwhile, critics of the neoliberal approach argue that the role of schools often exacerbate or intensify social inequalities. Schooling was considered as the mechanism to reproduce rather than transform existing structural inequalities (Bourdieu, 1984; Bourdieu & Passeron, 1977; Bowles & Gintis, 1976; Johnson & Howard, 2008; Levinson & Holland, 1996; Nash, 1990). As Collins (1979) demonstrated, not all social groups came to an educational market as equals since the various types of capital are not equally distributed among classes and groups. According to Bourdieu (1986), "capital" represents "resources" and "power" can be represented by three forms, including economic capital, which is immediately and directly convertible into money and may be institutionalized in the form of property rights; cultural capital, which is convertible, on certain conditions, into economic capital and may be institutionalized in the form of educational qualifications; and social capital, which is made up of social obligations (connections) and is also convertible, in certain conditions, into economic capital and may be institutionalized in the form of a title of nobility. Students from affluent families generally attend schools with higher qualified teachers, smaller class sizes, and additional curriculum options. At the same time, they gain the access from these schools to professional networks and gain access to human and cultural capital which ultimately contribute to their educational and professional success. Moreover, such educational, social, and economic advantages are often reproduced for the following generations (Bourdieu, 1973).

The inequalities in state socialist societies are basically created and structured by redistributive mechanisms (Szelenyi, 1978). These mechanisms often maintain and increase the advantages of the already privileged and powerful (Nee, 1989). In contrast to social stratification studies of industrialized market societies, the importance of political processes and state policies in socialist states should be considered as stratification dynamics[1]. In contrast to market-based social stratification in capitalist societies, redistribution under state socialism is governed by a political logic that the central authority (e.g., the Communist Party in power) plays a vital role in resource allocation (Zhou, 2004). Therefore, the reward system favors those with political status and loyalty, such as Communist Party membership or those who are closer to the distributive power. With the establishment of the socialist country, a privileged group including communist party members and cadres gradually emerged. They gradually changed policies which were beneficial to themselves (Mateju, 1993). Studies on the effect of social origin on educational attainment in many socialist countries (such as Czechoslovakia, Hungary, and Poland) remained despite the educational expansion through government policy intervention (Heyns & Bialecki, 1993; Mateju; Szelenyi & Aschaffenburg, 1993). Contrasting to these Eastern European countries, education stratification in China showed a special history which was influenced by the periodic shifts in state policies (Bian, 2002; Bian & Logan, 1996; Deng & Treiman, 1997; C. Li, 2006; Wong, 2004; Zhou, 2004; Zhou, Moen, & Tuma, 1998; Zhou, Tuma, & Moen, 1996).

Moreover, from the late 1980s, a theoretical discussion on inequality in state socialist countries in transition to market economy emerged. The theory of market transition claims that, in reforming socialist economies, the transition from redistributive to market coordination shifts sources of power and privilege to favor direct producers, stimulates the growth of private markets, and provides to entrepreneurs an alternative path for socioeconomic mobility (Nee, 1989, 1991, 1996; Nee & Cao, 2002). Researchers identified the "declining significance of redistributive power" (Nee & Cao, 1999; Wu, Goetz, Hartmann, & Wang, 2012). In contrast, studies also showed that there was persistence of power of the political elites (bureaucrats) in the transition to a market economy of socialist states (Bian & Logan, 1996; Nee, 1991; Nee & Cao, 2002; Parish & Michelson, 1996; Walder, 1996; Zhou, 2004). Moreover, the marketization and dismantling of central planning may even exacerbate social

---

[1] According to Zhou (2004, p. 16), stratification dynamics refers to a distinctive pattern of changes in stratification structures and processes. In China's case, it often imposes from the top down and that often has noncumulative and disruptive impacts on individuals' life chances.

1.2 Social Inequality in Education

inequalities. With the expansion of the market, bureaucrats in the socialist state could monetize their political capital. And by utilizing the dismantling central planning on public resources redistribution, they also can wrest the resources into private hands through network ties with the political elite (Nee & Cao, 2002). Through the analysis of the development of inequality in public school admissions to junior high schools in urban China, this study highlights the persistence of power of the political elites in the distribution of public resources.

Parental choice actions are not only the matter of individual choice but are indicative of long-standing cultural and institutional practices that give some people access to school resources while leaving others outside (Andre-Bechely, 2005b; Graue, Kroeger, & Prager, 2001, p. 471). The rise of "parentocracy" indicates that children's education is increasingly dependent upon the wealth and wishes of parents rather than the ability and efforts of pupils (Brown, 1990, p. 65). Comparatively, the middle class has more cultural capital to make educational choices which best advantages their children (Ball, 1993, 2003; Brown, 1990; Gewirtz et al., 1995). Brown and Lauder (1997, p. 177) argued that the introduction of choice and competition provides a mechanism by which the middle class can more securely gain an advantage in the competition for credentials. The emergence of parental choice and school autonomy has further disadvantaged those least able to compete in the market. For most disadvantaged groups, the choice seems to reproduce distinctions between schools and people (Whitty, Power, & Halpin, 1998). Gewirtz, Ball, and Bowe (1995, pp. 40–41) identified that the practice of school choice is strongly class related. They categorized parents as "privileged chooser," "semiskilled chooser," and the "disconnected chooser" based on three different social classes the choosers belong to. The skilled and privileged choosers can keep and reproduce their existing cultural, social, and economic advantages in the complex and hierarchical education system (Ball, Bowe, & Gewirtz, 1996).

The social inequality in education, particularly in terms of school choice within the current global education reform movement, can cause two types of "cream skimming" at both the family and school levels. On the one hand, "cream skimming" may occur with students from families with high socioeconomic status. Their parents have adequate social, economic, and cultural resources to send them to better performing schools. On the other hand, the "cream skimming" effect also occurs at the school level. School administrators are often inclined to select students with higher social status or with better academic achievement backgrounds. The popular schools generally attract and select more students with better academic credentials, while the rest of the schools are left to enroll the remaining students. Consequently, segregation between public schools intensifies in this context (Levin, 1998; West, Ingram, & Hind, 2006; Whitty et al., 1998). Kozol's (1992) observation of America's public schools showed that the segregation of public schools through the disproportionate funding distribution deeply influenced school quality and overall effectiveness. More seriously, it intensified the inequalities between public schools and families.

1.3 Education Stratification in China

A review of the trends of effects of family background and institutional factors on equality in education in Chinese society reminds me to consider the social context and history of Chinese society in the analysis and discussion on the development of inequality in public school admissions in urban China.

Generally, with the education expansion, we cannot deny that more opportunities of education have been distributed to children who were traditionally excluded from education participation. However, I argue that the current inequality issue in China's education sector is not the matter that whether students have the opportunities for the access to school or not. Rather, it is the distribution of these opportunities that is over dependent on family backgrounds or the related government policies, especially at the compulsory education level. As Hannum (1998, p. 6) argued, the distribution across groups is assessed in cross-group differences in educational supply and participation during the 9-year cycle of compulsory education. Given that a stated policy goal of the government is to provide 9 years of education to all children, a standard of meritocratic conditions translates to access for all children in the appropriate age groups. Evidence of differential allocation across groups thus indicates a lack of the preconditions of meritocracy.[2] Studies show that family origins have a strong effect on educational attainment and occupational attainment. The increasing educational inequality is caused by the rapid economic growth and transformation which favored the most advantaged groups in the population—the children of high-rank cadres and professionals, residents of large cities, and men more than women (C. Li, 2006, 2012; Whyte & Parish, 1984; Zhou et al., 1998).

Studies identify various types of inequalities in China's education, such as educational inequalities caused by regional disparities, unequal educational resources distribution, languages, ethnicity, gender, and so forth (Hannum, 1998, 1999; Hawkins, 1983; Hawkins, Jacob, & Li, 2008; Lin, 2006; Mok, Wong, & Zhang, 2009; Postiglione, 2006; Xiaogang Wu & Zhang, 2010; Zhou et al., 1998). Simultaneously, additional studies also give serious concerns on education inequality caused by rural-urban migration (Chan, Liu, & Yang, 1999; Chan, 1995; Han, 2001, 2005; Kwong, 2006; Li, 2004; Liang, Guo, & Duan, 2008; Liu, 2012; Wu, 2005, 2006; Zhang, 2003).

Research shows that there are two diametrically opposite stages of equalization of education opportunities (C. Li, 2006, 2012). The first stage, from 1950 to 1970, featured a sharp increase in educational opportunities and a rapid advancement in the equalization of educational opportunities. The influence of a family's social, economic, and cultural capital on children's educational opportunities declined rapidly. The second stage, from the 1980s and the 1990s, had an increase either in the provision of educational opportunities or the inequality of educational opportunities.

---

[2] In Hannum's research, the preconditions of meritocracy refer to an equitable distribution of basic education across social groups (Hannum, 1998).

During this time period, the effects of a family's social and cultural capital have significantly increased on children's education opportunities.

Moreover, there are effects of institutional factors on the distribution of educational opportunities in China. The effect of the household registration system (*hukou* system) on educational opportunity is an example. Until the 1970s, this system, as an institutional factor for restricting people's mobility, did not have a significant effect on the inequality of educational opportunity. In contrast, from the 1980s to the 1990s, there was an increasing effect of the household registration system on the individual's acquisition of education with the expansion of disparities between urban and rural areas and the imbalance in the urban-rural distribution of educational resources (C. Li, 2006, 2012; Y. Li, 2006; Wu & Treiman, 2004). Since 2000, the government has made strides to relax of the *hukou* system. Nevertheless, the progress of the reform still cannot keep pace with the demand of the rapid social change in the context of urban China. *Hukou* still keeps its dominant role in one's access to public education.

1.4 The Imbalanced Distribution of Education Resources

With the limited educational investment and the implementation of the fiscal decentralization in education sector, education development becomes highly dependent on capability of fund generating at local levels. It is not surprising to see the greater disparities among local governments (Li, Park, & Wang, 2007). Due to the financial resource gap between different regions, richer regions generally have more alternative financing options than poorer regions (Jacob, 2006). As a result, the diversification of financial resources in the education sector may exacerbate greater regional disparities in terms of education (Bray & Borevskaya, 2001; Hannum, 1999; Kusuyama, 2010; Mok et al., 2009; Tsang, 2002). As shown in Table 1.1, comparatively speaking, the coastal regions and eastern part of China

Table 1.1 Disparity of public education expenditure by region, 2008

Region	Public education expenditure (10,000 yuan)
East China	29,235,652
Central South China	22,568,787
North China	14,251,771
Southwest China	12,310,231
Northeast China	8,436,071
Northwest China	7,877,715

Source: China Education Yearbook 2009

have more public education expenditure in 2008. According to Mok and his associates (2009), the marketization and privatization of education have undoubtedly intensified educational inequalities and widened regional disparities between economically developed areas and the less developed regions. As analyzed in the same study, one of the reasons for the rural-urban and regional inequalities is due to the highly uneven government expenditure on education. There are more education resources allocated in the coastal regions compared with the poorer regions.

Moreover, the result of the research also shows that the type of higher education and the promotion to the level of education depend on the income level of the individual family.

1.5 A Social Closure Framework

As this book project aims at interpreting how stakeholders interact with *Zexiao*, I want to adopt a two-direction model of social closure as a conceptual framework to explore and present both positive and negative interactions among stakeholders in the process of admission to junior high schools. Accordingly, education becomes a mechanism that leads to social reproduction and social inequality in our daily lives. Privileged groups generally keep scarce resources within the groups in order to keep advantages of their siblings and themselves in society and exclude disadvantaged groups from already limited educational resources. Scholars introduced the concept of social closure to reveal further how people maximize their own profits by monopolizing limited resources and opportunities. Weber (1968, pp. 341–342) explained the concept of "closure" as follows:

> When the number of competitors increases in relation to the profit span, the participants become interested in curbing competition. Usually, one group of competitors takes some externally identifiable characteristic of another group of competitors-race, language, religion, local or social origin, descent, residence, etc.-as a pretext for attempting their exclusion. It does not matter which characteristic is chosen in the individual case: whatever suggests itself most easily is seized upon. Such group action may provoke a corresponding reaction on the part of those against whom it is directed....The jointly acting competitors now form an "interest group" towards outsiders; there is a growing tendency to set up some kind of association with rational regulations; if the monopolistic interests persist, the time comes when the competitors establish a legal order that limits competition through formal monopolies... Such closure, as we want to call it, is an ever-recurring process; it is the source of property in land as well as all guild and other group monopolies.

In other words, social closure refers to the process that collective groups seek to maximize profits by monopolizing specific resources and opportunities while excluding competitors from access to resources and opportunities (Murphy, 1984; Parkin, 1979). Meanwhile, being different from Weber's exclusionary closure, Parkin (1979) and Murphy (1984) further expand the notion of "closure" by introducing interactive social closure, including both exclusion and usurpation. According to Parkin (1979, p. 45), exclusionary closure represents the use of power in a "downward" direction because it necessarily entails the creation of a group, class, or stratum of legally defined inferiors. In contrast, the usurpation refers to the use of power in an upward direction in the sense of the collective attempts by the excluded to win a greater share of resources. It always threatens to bite into the privileges of legally defined superiors. As two main types of social closure, the latter is always a consequence of and collective response to the former. Similarly, Murphy (1984, p. 548) distinguishes that the main difference between these two modes is that exclusionary closure involves the exercise of power in a downward direction through a process of subordination in which one group secures its advantages by closing off the opportunities of another group beneath it that it defines as inferior and ineligible. Usurpationary closure involves the exercise of power in an upward direction in order to reduce the advantages of higher groups.

1.6 A Social Constructionist Perspective

As mentioned in the sections above, it is necessary to investigate further how stakeholders practice in the process of *Zexiao* instead of simply describing policies or channels of *Zexiao*. Therefore, in this book, I intend to analyze the phenomenon of *Zexiao* from a social constructionist perspective to construct an understanding of *Zexiao* through analyzing interactions among stakeholders in different historical periods.

In contrast to determinism that believes the reality or the society is fixed by nature, social constructionists look at the construction of reality as an ongoing, dynamic process. Social constructionists aim to uncover ways in which individuals and groups participate in the construction of social reality they share. They take a critical stance toward knowledge that people take for granted. And the idea invites people to challenge the objective basis of conventional knowledge (Burr, 1995; Gergen, 1985; Miller & Holstein, 2007). Social constructionists believe that there is nothing fixed or inevitable in the world since people in the society can choose to change the old conventions, theories, ideologies, practices, and knowledge with new ones (Hibberd, 2005).

In general, most of social constructionists hold the stance that the descriptions and explanations of the world can be understood as various forms of social construction of the world. Each social construction involves different types of social actions. And the formation of the understanding of the world is constituted by the support of some patterns of social actions and the exclusion of others. And the support and exclusion can be taken as the result of the interactions or negotiations between people in their daily lives (Burr, 1995; Gergen, 1985).

The formulation of social problems elaborated by Spector and Kitsuse (1973) helps us further understand the negotiation or interaction in the understanding of the world. According to Spector and Kitsuse, the formulation of social problems includes four stages. Firstly, some groups identify and define a specific issue that is offensive, harmful, and undesirable. Secondly, the emergence of the claimed issue is recognized by some official organizations, and it leads to official investigation, proposals for reform, and other responses to relevant claims and demands. Thirdly, there will have reemergence of claims and demands that are not satisfied with established procedures for tackling the recognized issues. And lastly, there may exist rejections or further responses from disgruntled groups toward the responses from relevant governmental institutions. For instance, according to China's education policy, admission to public junior high schools should follow the principle of "free, no entrance exam and proximity-based." However, the government recognized that many public schools still held entrance exams to select well-performing students in early 2000. It violated the government's principle and received substantial public criticism. The government issued regulations to alleviate such activities. However, although public schools stopped their entrance exams by themselves, they collaborated with private tutoring institutes to select students through training classes held inside of private tutoring institutes. Such approaches intensified the burdens on both parents and students. Gradually, it was reported in the media and criticized by the public again. Therefore, the government had to take action to close such training classes held by public schools and private tutoring institutes. However, this problem continues to develop today. The interactions between the government, the public, public schools, parents, and private tutoring institutes keep moving forward. Such interactions can be understood as the process of formulation of a compounding social problem. These interactions continue along with the socioeconomic changes in different historical periods.

Moreover, for constructionists, language is considered as a form of action for people to exchange and construct thoughts and emotions. The concepts and categories have been constituted by the language people use, produce, and reproduce in daily life. The exchange of language between people can be considered a process of "social construction" (Berger & Luckmann, 1966; Burr, 1995). Furthermore, language is structured, maintained, and transformed in a discursive practice occurred in specific contexts (Jorgensen & Phillips, 2002).

Holding a critical stance toward the widely accepted understanding of *Zexiao*, I want to emphasize that the understanding and knowledge of *Zexiao* can be further clarified and strengthened through the analysis of the negotiation and practice. *Zexiao* is an important process of social interaction in the social, economic, cultural, and historical development of urban China. Moreover, the language on *Zexiao* is the core focus of analysis in this study. With the stance of social constructionists, people's understanding and experiences with *Zexiao* would be constructed through the exchange of the languages about *Zexiao* among stakeholders. The diverse languages on *Zexiao* determine the alternative construction of views on *Zexiao*.

1.7 Analysis of Discourses on *Zexiao*

This book adopts discourse analysis as a guiding research method examining stakeholders' interactions through the exchange of languages on *Zexiao*. As mentioned above, discourse refers to forms of languages used in spoken languages,

1.7 Analysis of Discourses on *Zexiao*

written languages, communications, and interactions (Burr, 1995; Dijk, 1997). To be more specific, it refers to a set of meanings that particularly represent an object, event, or the understanding of the world. Discourse analysis as a research method examines people's speech, writing, actions, and products to identify and analyze ways of understanding of the world. Since the meaning of the world is constructed by discourses, discourse analysis is considered an appropriate method to separate both spoken and written texts and identify how they are constructed in a specific way which represents particular people and society. It aims to indicate how current "truths" have come to be constituted, how they were maintained, and what power relations are carried by them through tracing the development of present ways of understanding and the development of current discourses (Burr, 1995; Foucault, 1972). Discourse analysis is utilized in this book to show how the "truth" of *Zexiao* became constituted, maintained, and changed through exploring the ways of understanding of *Zexiao* and the development of discourses on *Zexiao* in order to understand the process of public junior school admissions in urban China.

To analyze discourse on *Zexiao*, I coded newspaper articles, journal articles, books, and interviews that had been transcribed.

Table 1.2 shows the newspaper sources used in this study. In order to identify mainstream discussions on *Zexiao* at the central government level, I selected two major government papers, that is, *China Education Daily*, released by the Ministry of Education, and *People's Daily*, the voice of the Central Committee of the Communist Party of China. Then, in order to involve diverse public discussions on *Zexiao* at the municipal level, I selected major newspapers in five municipal cities of China, including Beijing, Tianjin, Shanghai, Guangzhou, and Chongqing. To reflect criticism of government policies, I collected data from *Wenhui Bao*, *Southern*

Table 1.2 List of reviewed newspapers

Title	Publisher	Period
中国教育报 (China Education Daily)	Ministry of Education	1983–2010
人民日报 (People's Daily)	Central Committee of Communist Party of China	1980–2010
北京日报 (Beijing Daily)	Beijing Municipal Committee	2000–2010
天津日报 (Tianjin Daily)	Tianjin Municipal Committee	2000–2010
解放日报 (Jiefang Daily)	Shanghai Municipal Committee	2000–2010
文汇报 (Wenhui Bao)	Wenhui-xinmin United Press Group	2000–2010
广州日报 (Guangzhou Daily)	Guangzhou Municipal Committee	2000–2010
南方周末 (Southern Weekly)	Nanfang Media Group	2000–2010
重庆日报 (Chongqing Daily)	Chongqing Municipal Committee	2000–2010
重庆商报 (Chongqing Economic Times)	Chongqing Daily Group	2000–2010

Source: Created by author

Weekly,[3] and *Chongqing Economic Times* which were jointly owned by the state and private publishers.

To ensure consistency in the data collection process, documentation was selected and reviewed focusing on public school admission to junior high schools. This included a review of government policies, public options, admission procedures and processes, and fee charges.

Government websites were used as a major source to collect data related to government policies on public school admissions and compulsory education in China. For example, government documents released after 2000 were mainly downloaded from the Beijing Municipal Government website. Government policies promulgated before 2000 were collected from the Government Documents Center at the Capital Library of Beijing.

In addition to government documents and newspapers, I also made extensive use of journals and books on Chinese education. Journal articles were collected based on the Chinese Social Sciences Citation Index. One hundred thirty-seven articles (published after 2000) related to public school admissions in China's compulsory education were selected from 52 major journals on Chinese education. In order to reflect diverse voices on *Zexiao*, books by some distinguished Chinese scholars were also reviewed and utilized as references.

Interviews were conducted with three groups of participants, namely, (1) the principals of eight sample schools (two primary school principals and six junior high school principals) in Beijing, (2) 25 parents, and (3) multi-stakeholder group with small samples, including two city (or municipal) district educational administrators, three scholars, two managers of private tutoring institutes, and a journalist. Interview questions were designed to solicit participants' attitudes and opinions on government policies on public admission to public junior high schools and *Zexiao*, such as their reasons for participating in *Zexiao* in urban China and various approaches they took or experienced in *Zexiao*. During the interviews, I also asked some specific questions based on each interviewee's status and experiences in the admission process of public junior high schools in urban China (see Appendices 1, 2, 3, 4, 5, and 6 for interview questions). The interviews were conducted in Beijing between April and November 2011.

The first group of interviewees consisted of public school principals in major districts of Beijing. As shown in Table 1.3, principals or vice principals from three types of public schools were interviewed. They included principals from key schools, converted schools, and regular schools. Their stances as principals from different types of schools provided diverse attitudes and opinions on *Zexiao*. The questions for principals were mainly about their experiences in public school admissions, their opinions on *Zexiao*, and government policies as well as the development of compulsory education in key schools and converted schools.

The second group I talked with was parents. Twenty-five parents were interviewed and divided into two groups for different purposes (see Appendix 7 for details of

---

[3] According to Elisabeth Rosenthal (2002), *Southern Weekly* was described by *The New York Times* as China's most influential liberal newspaper.

1.7 Analysis of Discourses on *Zexiao* 15

Table 1.3 List of school principals interviewed

School	District	Category	Level	Interviewee
School A	*Fengtai*	Regular school	Secondary	Principal, retired principals, retired vice principal
School B	*Fengtai*	Regular school	Primary	Vice principal
School D	*Xicheng*	Key school	Secondary	Vice principal
School E	*Chongwen*	Converted school	Secondary	Principal/retired principal
School F	*Dongcheng*	Regular school	Secondary	Vice principal
School G	*Chaoyang*	Key school	Secondary	Vice principal
School H	*Haidian*	Regular school	Secondary	Vice principal
School I	*Xuanwu*	Regular school	Primary	Principal

Source: Created by author

parents' socioeconomic status). The first group included parents who participated in *Zexiao* and successfully enrolled their children in popular schools. The purpose of interviews was to provide additional supplement information to further reflect the public discussion on *Zexiao* in general. Due to limited access to this type of parent, I interviewed only three parents who successfully enrolled their children to popular junior high schools in two different districts. Also, as the second group, I conducted 16 interviews with parents from a primary school and a junior high school in the same community in Beijing as a case study to find how *Zexiao* was practiced in contrast to how it was discussed by the public. In order to involve various practices and experiences in *Zexiao* from parents, I interviewed parents of Grade 6 (G6) students in School B and parents of Grade 7 (G7) in School A. Parents of G6 students shared their experiences and feelings of the ongoing practices in *Zexiao*; parents of G7 students shared their experiences and feelings of practices in 2009. Moreover, considering the growing diverse needs for education from migrant families in urban China, I selected both parents who were permanent residents of Beijing and migrant parents in Beijing. With collaboration from the school selected for this study, I randomly selected parents of Beijing permanent residents and migrant parents among parents who attended the parent-teacher meeting.[4] Interviews with those parents were arranged based on their schedules. In total, I interviewed ten parents of Beijing permanent residents and six migrant parents in School A and two parents of Beijing permanent residents and four migrant parents in School B. Interviews with parents were conducted after work or on the weekend in café or places where parents felt comfortable meeting. Questions for parents focused on their options and experiences with *Zexiao*, their access to information on public school admission and

---

[4] In China, parent-teacher meetings are among the most important mechanisms for parents to get to know their children's performance at school. Once or twice a semester, parents are invited to attend these meetings at school. The parent-teacher meeting in School A was held on April 26, 2011. And the meeting in School B was held on April 27, 2011.

Zexiao, and their opinions on public school admissions policies in Beijing and their district. I recorded interviews with parents and principals with their agreements. The recorded interviews were later transcribed and coded for analysis purposes.

In the third interviewee group, I visited managers of local education authorities, scholars, managers of private tutoring institutes, and journalists with small samples. The purpose of these interviews was to utilize these interviewees' insights on *Zexiao* and attempt to involve diverse opinions on *Zexiao*. Firstly, due to the sensitivity of the topic, I could get access to only two educational administrators at the municipal district level. Despite this, their experiences and insights toward *Zexiao* might be representative within local educational administrations. The questions for educational administrators were about the implementation of government policies on public school admission, their opinions on *Zexiao*, and the school development in their districts. Secondly, I interviewed three scholars from the National Institute of Education Science, Peking University, and 21st Century Education Research Institute. They have common research interests in the development of compulsory education and educational inequality in China. I asked them about their opinions on *Zexiao* and their understanding of the reasons for the development of *Zexiao*. Thirdly, the recent research and surveys showed private tutoring institutes have a close relationship with the development of *Zexiao* (21st Century Education Research Institute, 2011; Fang, 2011). In order to involve the voice of private tutoring institutes that became an emerging power in *Zexiao* but were seldom heard in public discussions, I visited two private tutoring institutes in Beijing and interviewed their managers. They were asked to describe their experiences in *Zexiao* and their relationships with key schools in terms of public school admission. Their answers provided unique insights on *Zexiao* and a description of their roles in the negotiation process. In addition, I conducted an interview with a journalist who kept reporting news on *Zexiao* for over 5 years from the Education Section of Sina.com. The purpose of interviewing a journalist was to reflect her opinions on *Zexiao* since she collected from the public firsthand information on the negotiation on *Zexiao* in urban China. Though I was not able to have a face-to-face interview with the journalist, I received her answers to my questions via emails. The interview questions were specifically about her opinions on *Zexiao* and her observations of the diverse approaches that parents chose for *Zexiao*. For the first five groups of interviews, I recorded interviews with interviewees' agreements and transcribed them.

Then, I categorized the coding and divided encoded items into groups that included discourse on the legalization of unauthorized school fees, the gap between schools, public school admission policies, parents' aspiration, and issues beyond the imbalanced educational development. Each group was divided into various subgroups representing opinions from various stakeholders. Next, I linked and mapped the groups to visualize issues involved in public discussions on *Zexiao*. Then, based on the theme of public discourse on *Zexiao*, I divided the development of *Zexiao* into two stages: the 1990s and after 2000. In order to investigate interactions of stakeholders in *Zexiao*, each stage was examined utilizing discourse on *Zexiao* from the perspectives of government documents, newspapers, journals, books, and interviews. While analyzing discourses, I paid close attention to the commonalities and

1.8 Case Study: Community A

differences that formed the public's opinions on *Zexiao*. I also took into consideration of people's social status, historical context (political and institutional change), and reasons as well as attitudes toward *Zexiao*.

1.8 Case Study: Community A

The case study of *Zexiao* in admissions to public junior high schools in Community A of Beijing was conducted for the purpose of exploring how stakeholders practiced in *Zexiao* to contrast with how *Zexiao* was discussed. I conducted the fieldwork in Community A of Beijing from April to June 2011.

With the city reconstructed in late the 1980s, Community A, the newest and largest residential area in Beijing, was founded in *Fengtai* District in the southern part of Beijing. The community covers 5.53 km², with a population of 93,430 residents who held Beijing *hukou* in 2010 and an additional 30,300 residents registered as internal migrants.[5] There were more than 15 ethnic minority groups living in this community. As Fig. 1.1 shows, Community A has four residential areas, Zone A, Zone B, Zone C, and Zone D. People living in Zone A and Zone B are relatively rich and well educated; they work as employers in foreign companies and government offices. In comparison, people living in Zone C and Zone D have lower socioeconomic status. Residents of Zones C and D are primarily factory

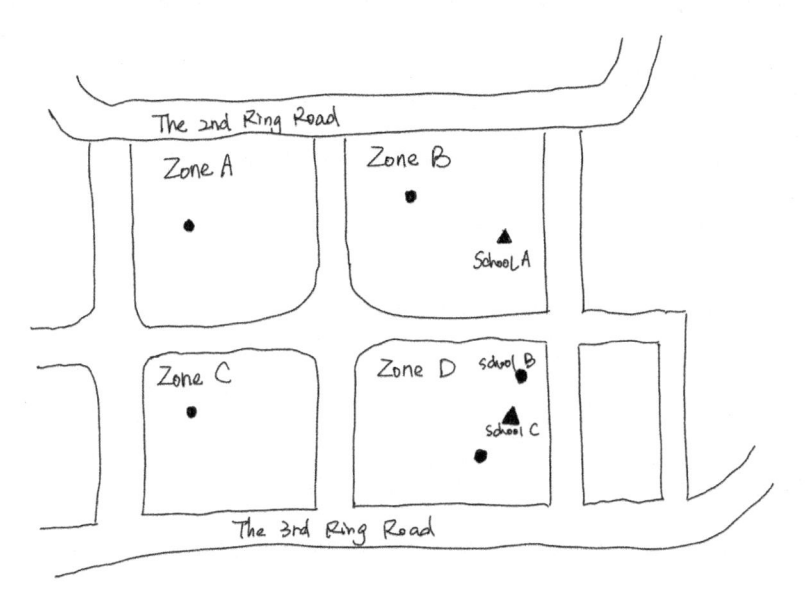

Fig. 1.1 Map of Community A (Source: Compiled by author based on the geographic situation)

---

[5] Information from *Fengtai Yearbook 2010*, Retrieved from http://dfz.bjft.gov.cn/page/ftnj/2010/view-167.html, accessed on March 9, 2012.

workers, migrant workers, or self-employed businessmen.[6] There were two reasons for choosing Community A. Firstly, located in the southern part of Beijing, the suburban community consisted of both affluent and low-income families. Particularly, with a rapid rural-urban migration, the population in that community had become diverse. Community A would be a perfect location for my case study because I could include people with diverse social status. Diverse social groups also indicated diverse demands for education in Community A. Secondly, since *Fengtai* District was a developing area in Beijing, educational resources were relatively limited, compared with districts in the central part of Beijing.[7] When I conducted this research study in 2011, there were five primary schools and two junior high schools in Community A. According to my interview with the principal of one junior high school in Community A for another research project in 2010, parents living in Community A choose schools outside of this community because they were dissatisfied with the quality of education the schools offered (Liu, 2012). As Fig. 1.1 shows, within Community A, there are two junior high schools and five primary schools. School A (a public junior high school), School B (a public primary school), and School C (a demonstration school) are the main focus schools in this study.

In 1989, with the construction of Community A, School A, a public junior high school, with brand new facilities was established to meet the education needs of residents in Community A. School-aged children for lower secondary education in Community A mainly attended School A. According to the principal of School A, since a large number of residents were working in government offices (e.g., Ministry of Foreign Affairs, Ministry of Commerce, Ministry of Justice), student quality[8] in Community A was relatively high. It was until 1995 that School A was considered famous for its high-quality education in *Fengtai* District.[9] However, with aging facilities and rapid urbanization, from the late 1990s, the general makeup of the residential social class in Community A dramatically changed. A large number of longtime local residents moved out of this area. Consequently, there were many apartments for people to rent.

---

[6] Information on residents in Community A collected from interviews with principals from School A and School B involved in this study.

[7] According to the Beijing Municipal Commission of Education, 16.2% of demonstration schools in Beijing are located in *Handian* District. This number in *Fengtai* District is only 5.9%. (see Homepage of Beijing Municipal Commission of Education, retrieved from http://english.bjedu.gov.cn/, accessed on September 21, 2010).

[8] According to the principal of School A, student quality refers to academic achievement and ethics. The interview with the principal of School A was conducted on April 18, 2011.

[9] According to the interview with the principal of School A, "good quality education" mainly refers to the promotion rate from School A to demonstration schools at the upper secondary school level. Until mid-1990s, School A was ranked in one of the Top 10 Junior High Schools in *Fengtai* District since the school had a high promotion rate to key senior high schools. Many students of other school districts came and applied to School A at that time (based on an interview that was conducted on April 18, 2011).

1.8 Case Study: Community A

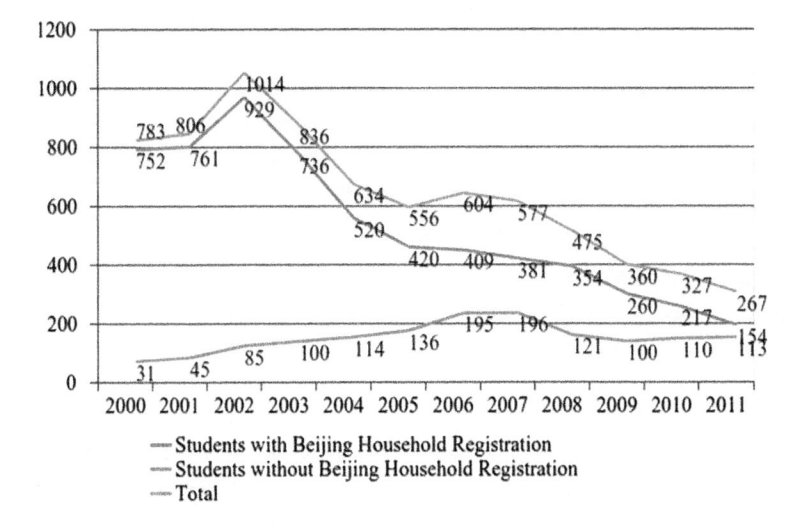

Fig. 1.2 Enrolment of School A (2000–2011) (Source: Collected from School A, compiled by author)

The demographic shift in Community A directly influenced the student structure in School A and its reputation in *Fengtai* District.[10] In addition, due to the limited reform and facility upgrading, School A became less attractive for residents in Community A and had difficulties enrolling good quality students from this area. As the retired principal of School A introduced, School A used to be able to enroll from 30% to 40% of well-achieved primary school students[11] in Community A. However, in recent years, good quality students went to key schools or took part in *Zexiao* and went to schools in neighboring districts. In order to stay in business, School A had to enroll migrant children.[12] Figure 1.2 shows a gradual increase of migrant children enrollment in School A. Although students of the five primary schools in Community

---

[10] According to the interview with the principal of School A, in 2005, the Beijing Municipal Education Committee initiated the "Beijing Junior High Schools Construction Project." There was a saying that described the education system in Beijing: "Browne Head; Iron Feet; Tofu Waist." The head refers to higher education, the feet refer to primary education, and the waist refers to secondary education. Secondary education in Beijing has been considered underdeveloped. The Project aimed to reconstruct secondary education, particularly junior high schools in Beijing with collaboration with some universities in Beijing. In 2005, School A was selected as one of the 32 public junior high schools involved in this project (based on an interview conducted on April 18, 2011).

[11] According to a retired principal of School A, school recommendation students (about 5% of the total number of G6 students) are sent to key schools directly by primary school. Besides them, based on the studying achievement, there are still about 30–40% of the students who have relatively good learning achievements. Most of the time, these students will be enrolled by School A in the past.

[12] The interview with a retired principal of School A was conducted on April 27, 2011.

A had a direct access to School A, most students of the primary schools in Zones A and B participated in *Zexiao* for better schools instead of going to School A.[13] In addition, since the High School Affiliated Central Musical Institute (HSACMI)[14] is located in Zone C, 50% of the primary school graduates in Zone C went to HSACMI.

School B is a public primary school established in 1955. In principle, school-aged children for primary education in Zone D should go to School B and then continue their education in School A. According to the interview with the principal of School B, with the One-Child Policy and the increase of migrants in Community A, the number of local students decreased in recent years (see Fig. 1.2).[15] In contrast, the number of migrant children attending School B had increased from one-tenth of total student enrollment in the late 1990s to about 50% of the total student enrollment.[16]

School C, a public secondary school established in 1951, is well-known in *Fengtai* District. In 1978, the school was given the "Key Secondary School" title by the education authority of *Fengtai* District. In 2005, the school was designated as a "Demonstration Senior High School" by the Beijing Municipal Education Committee. From 2008, School C was reauthorized to enroll junior high school students with the establishment of two new campuses as a junior high school department. Since School C as a key secondary school, is located in Community A, it had the privilege to select the best developed students from the five primary schools since 2009.

Through an analysis of the transcribed interviews with school principals and parents from School A and School B, I investigated parents' practice in *Zexiao* and to explore the themes that emerged from the negotiations on *Zexiao* through discourse analysis. In the analysis, I focused on the themes that are closely related to school admission policies, parents' access to available options for *Zexiao*, and how parents with different socioeconomic status reacted and responded to *Zexiao*.

---

[13] Annually, school leaders go to primary schools in Community A to introduce and promote their schools for school admissions. In 2007, she visited a primary school in Zone B and made a presentation to introduce School A. However, she was interrupted by some parents who said they had already found schools for children in other districts (Interview with retired principal of School A was conducted on April 27, 2011).

[14] Although the High School Affiliated with the Central Musical Institute is located in Community A, the school is administered by the Central Musical Institute and independent from the local education authority that oversees Community A.

[15] The interview with a vice principal of School B was conducted on May 12, 2011.

[16] The data was collected from the interview with a vice principal of School B, which was conducted on May 12, 2011.

1.9 The Book Chapters

To provide a clear picture of the progress of *Zexiao* in admission to public junior high schools in urban China, Chap. 2 starts with a review of the global public education reforms, which emphasized choice, efficiency, equity, excellence, and international competence, to summarize the meaning of school choice in a global context. It also links the meaning of school choice with theories of the educational system and school systems to further explain the nature of the school choice phenomenon. Then, it reviews the development of *Zexiao* in China through social development and the changes in public school admission policy between the 1980s and the 2000s to introduce the diversity and complexity of public junior high school admissions and the channels of student placements in this process. I also define the nature of *Zexiao* by discussing the similarities and differences between *Zexiao* and school choice in general.

Chapter 3 elucidates power relationships in public school admission by analyzing continuities and changes in stakeholders' interactions in public school admissions. It also illustrates a framework of multilayered inequality/stratified engagement of stakeholders in *Zexiao*. The discourse analysis is based on data collected from written and spoken records about public school admission, including newspaper articles, policy documents from the 1980s to the 2000s, and interviews conducted in fieldworks between April and June 2011.

With the rapid social change in Chinese society, the Chinese government launched a series of educational policies for supporting national development. Policies on public school admissions in compulsory education (Grades 1–9) have been amended at both central and local levels to accommodate national needs. Meanwhile, local governments (at the city and district levels) also released their regulations on public school admission in compulsory education to meet requests from the central government and demands from local interests groups. Chapter 4 interprets how gaps of policies on public school admissions to junior high schools at the central and local levels came out and shaped inequalities in admission to public lower secondary education at the school level. It reviews policy changes from the 1980s to 2015 in public school admissions to uncover the diversity of the public school admission policy at different administration levels. Moreover, it analyzes the interactions between the central government and local governments to visualize how the power relationship between governments at different levels shaped the implementation of public school admission policy at the lower secondary education level. Analysis of interviews with stakeholders, such as school principals, local education officials, scholars, and managers of private tutoring institutes, is used to explain further how policy making and implementation affect the practice of student placement to public junior high schools in Beijing.

A key school system, which started in the 1950s, stratified the public school system in China into key schools and regular schools. This system covers the public school system from primary education to higher education. On the other hand, the commercialization of key schools generated more financial resources for local educational administrations to develop the local education sector. In Chap. 5, I explain how stratification of public schools and commercialization of public education affected public junior high school admission. I also untangle collusion among "good schools" and cram schools for student selection in admissions to public lower secondary education in urban China by analyzing interviews with school principals and managers of cram schools in Beijing.

In Chap. 6, I investigate how family background influences the engagement of families in admission to public junior high schools in Community A of Beijing as a case study. I analyze experiences in admission to junior high schools based on interviews with school principals and parents of Community A to visualize how families engaged in junior high school admissions by utilizing their various resources. The analysis follows the stages of admission to public junior high schools in Community A to visualize a full process of competition among parents for public school admissions in urban China which are often based on advantage, privileges, and local characteristics.

As a summary of the analysis of previous chapters, in Chap. 7, I interpret admission to public lower secondary education as social closures by elucidating the power relationship behind the interaction among government, schools, families, and other related stakeholders in public school admission to junior high schools in Community A of Beijing as a case study. I examine how rent-seeking, privileges, and social disparities formulated stakeholders' participation in public school admission to junior high schools. Moreover, I illustrate an interactive social closure constituted by interactions between the advantaged and the disadvantaged to interpret further and discuss the diverse and stratified powers in urban China.

From 2014, China has entered a new stage of economic development with moderate economic growth and social and political reform for establishing a harmonious society. The government at different levels has already recognized that it is necessary to promote appropriate reforms in social development to match the changing economic development demands. In the public education sector, both the central and local governments in China have already been taking actions to terminate privileges and balance resource distribution for public secondary education. Chapter 8 investigates policy construction and ongoing practices of Beijing as new solutions in establishing equitable and quality public secondary education at the local level to uncover opportunities and challenges for stakeholders in this process. It also maps out a policy framework at the local level for reconstructing an equal and balanced development of public lower secondary education while maintaining high quality in urban China to best meet the needs of Chinese society.

The book ends up with summary of definition of *Zexiao* and discussion on how privileges and imbalance broke educational equality in urban China. Moreover, it addresses social interaction/relations among stakeholders in *Zexiao* by discussing the theory of social closure in Chinese context. And it concludes by demonstrating implications to practices and future research.

References

21st Century Education Research Institute. (2011). *Beijingshi "xiaoshengchu" Zexiaore de zhili: luzaihefang?* (Where is the way for alleviation of *Zexiao* fever in transition to junior high schools?). Beijing: 21st Century Education Research Institute.

Andre-Bechely, L. (2005a). *Could it be otherwise? Parents and the inequities of public school choice.* New York: Routledge.

Andre-Bechely, L. (2005b). Public school choice at the intersection of voluntary integration and not-so-good neighborhood schools: Lessons from parents' experiences. *Educational Administration Quarterly, 41*(2), 267–305.

Apple, M. W. (2001). Comparing neo-liberal projects and inequality in education. *Comparative Education, 37*(4), 409–423.

Apple, M. W. (2004). Creating difference: Neo-liberalism, neo-conservatism and the politics of educational reform. *Educational Policy, 18*(12), 12–44.

Apple, M. W. (2006). *Educating the "Right" way.* New York: Routledge Taylor & Francis Group.

Ball, S. J. (1993). Education markets, choice and social class: The market as a class strategy in the UK and the USA. *British Journal of Sociology of Education, 14*(1), 3–19.

Ball, S. J. (2003). The risks of social reproduction: The middle class and education markets. *London Review of Education, 1*(3), 163–175.

Ball, S. J., Bowe, R., & Gewirtz, S. (1996). School choice, social class and distinction: The realization of social advantage in education. *Journal of Education Policy, 11*(1), 89–112.

Berger, P. L., & Luckmann, T. (1966). *The social construction of reality.* London: Allen Lane.

Bian, Y. (2002). Chinese social stratification and social mobility. *Annual Review of Sociology, 28*, 91–116.

Bian, Y., & Logan, J. R. (1996). Market transition and the persistence of power: The changing stratification system in urban China. *American Sociological Review, 61*(5), 739–758.

Bourdieu, P. (1973). Cultural reproduction and social reproduction. In R. Brown (Ed.), *Knowledge, education, and cultural change* (pp. 71–112). London: Tavistock Publications.

Bourdieu, P. (1984). *Distinction* (R. Nice, Trans.). Cambridge, MA: Harvard University Press.

Bourdieu, P. (1986). The forms of capital. In J. G. Richardson (Ed.), *Handbook of theory and research for the sociology of education* (pp. 241–258). New York: Greenwood Press.

Bourdieu, P., & Passeron, J.-C. (1977). *Reproduction in education, society and culture* (2nd ed.). London: Sage Publications.

Bowles, S., & Gintis, H. (1976). *Schooling in capitalist America: Educational reform and the contradictions of economic life.* London: Routledge & Kegan Paul Ltd.

Bray, M., & Borevskaya, N. (2001). Financing education in transitional societies: Lessons from Russia and China. *Comparative Education, 37*(3), 345–365.

Brown, P. (1990). The 'Third Wave': Education and the ideology of parentocracy. *British Journal of Sociology of Education, 11*(1), 65–85.

Brown, P., & Lauder, H. (1997). Education, globalization, and economic development. In A. H. Halsey, H. Lauder, P. Brown, & A. S. Wells (Eds.), *Education: Culture, Economy, Society* (pp. 172–192). Oxford, UK: Oxford University Press.

Burr, V. (1995). *An introduction to social constructionism.* London: Routledge.

Carnoy, M., & Levin, H. M. (1985). *Schooling and work in the democratic state.* Stanford, CA: Stanford University Press.

Chan, K. W., Liu, T., & Yang, Y. (1999). Hukou and non-hukou migrations in China: Comparisons and contrasts. *International Journal of Population Geography, 5*, 425–448.

Chan, R. C. K. (1995). The urban migrants-the challenge to public policy. In L. Wong & S. MacPherson (Eds.), *Social change and social policy in contemporary China* (pp. 166–187). Aldershot, UK: Averbury.

Coleman, J. S. (1992). Some points on choice in education. *Sociology of Education, 65*(4), 260–262.

Coleman, J. S., Schiller, K. S., & Schneider, B. (1993). Parent choice and inequality. In B. Schneider & J. S. Coleman (Eds.), *Parents, their children, and schools* (pp. 147–182). Boulder, CO: Westview Press.

Collins, J. (2009). Social reproduction in classrooms and schools. *Annual Review of Anthropology, 38*, 33–48.

Collins, R. (1979). *The credential society*. London: Academic Press.

Deng, Z., & Treiman, D. J. (1997). The impact of the cultural revolution on trends in educational attainment in the People's Republic of China. *American Journal of Sociology, 103*(2), 391–428.

Dijk, T. A. V. (1997). The study of discourse. In T. A. V. Dijk (Ed.), *Discourse as structure and process* (pp. 1–34). London: Sage Publications.

Fang, X. (Ed.). (2011). *Zhongguo jiaoyu shida redian wenti (Ten hot topics of China's education)*. Fuzhou, China: The Straits Publishing & Distributing Group.

Forsey, M., Davies, S., & Walford, G. (2008). *The globalisation of school choice? An introduction to key issues and concerns*. Oxford, UK: Symposium Books.

Foucault, M. (1972). *The archaeology of knowledge* (A. Sheridan-Smith, Trans.). Oxford, UK: Harper & Row.

Gergen, K. J. (1985). The social constructionist movement in modern psychology. *American Psychologist, 40*(3), 266–275.

Gewirtz, S., Ball, S. J., & Bowe, R. (1995). *Markets, choice and equity in education*. Buckingham, UK: Open University Press.

Graue, M. E., Kroeger, J., & Prager, D. (2001). A Bakhtinian analysis of particular home-school relations. *American Educational Research Journal, 38*(3), 467–498.

Han, J. (2001). Beijingshi liudong ertong yiwu jiaoyu zhuangkuang diaocha baogao (Report of Surveys on the State of Compulsory Education for Children of Migrants' Families in Beijing). *Qingnian wenzhuai (Youth Studies), 8*, 1–7.

Han, J. (2005). Beijing gongli xuexiao zhong liudong ertong de yiwu jiaoyu (Compulsory education for migrant children in Beijing public schools). In T. Jing (Ed.), 2005nian zhongguo shoudu fazhan baogao *(2005 China capital development report)* (pp. 313–324). Beijing, China: Social Science Academic Press (China).

Hannum, E. (1998). *Educational inequality: Hidden consequences of the reform era in rural China. (Degree of Doctor of Philosophy)*. Chicago: The University of Michigan.

Hannum, E. (1999). Political change and the urban-rural gap in basic education in China, 1949–1990. *Comparative Education Review, 43*(2), 193–211.

Harvey, D. (2007). Neoliberalism as creative destruction. *Annals of the American Academy of Political and Social Science, 610*, 22–44.

Hawkins, J. N. (1983). *Education and social change in the People's Republic of China*. New York: Praeger Publisher.

Hawkins, J. N., Jacob, W. J., & Li, W. (2008). Higher education in China: Access, equity and equality. In D. B. Holsinger & W. J. Jacob (Eds.), *Inequality in education: Comparative and international perspectives*, CERC Studies in Comparative Education (pp. 215–239). Hong Kong, Hong Kong: Springer.

Heyns, B., & Bialecki, I. (1993). Educational inequalities in Postwar Poland. In Y. Shavit & H.-P. Blossfeld (Eds.), *Persistent inequality: Changing educational attainment in thirteen countries* (pp. 303–336). Boulder, CO: Westview Press.

Hibberd, F. J. (2005). *Unfolding social constructionism*. New York: Springer.

Hirsch, D. (2002). *What works in innovation in education: School: A choice of directions*. Paris: OECD.

Jacob, W. (2006). Social justice in Chinese higher education: Issues of equity and access. *International Review of Education, 52*(1), 149–169.

Johnson, E., & Howard, T. C. (2008). Issues of difference contributing to US education inequality. In D. B. Holsinger & W. J. Jacob (Eds.), *Inequality in education* (pp. 444–460). Hong Kong, Hong Kong: Springer.

Jorgensen, M., & Phillips, L. (2002). *Discourse analysis as theory and method*. London: Sage Publications.

References

Kozol, J. (1992). *Savage inequalities: Children in America's schools*. New York: Harper Perennial.

Kusuyama, K. (2010). Tyugoku ni okeru gimugyoiku kyoiku seido no tanryokuka to situ hosyo (The Flexibility and Quality Assurance of Compulsory Education System in China). *Hikaku kyoiku kenkyu (Comparative Education), 41*, 49–62.

Kwong, J. (2006). The integration of migrant children in Beijing schools. In G. A. Postiglione (Ed.), *Education and social change in China: Inequality in a market economy* (pp. 163–178). Armonk, NY: M.E.Sharpe.

Lareau, A. (1989). *Home advantage: Social class and parental intervention in elementary education*. Philadelphia: Falmer Press.

Levin, B. (1998). An epidemic of education policy: (What) can we learn from each other? *Comparative Education, 34*(2), 131–141.

Levinson, B. A., & Holland, D. C. (1996). The cultural production of the educated person: An introduction. In B. A. Levinson, D. E. Foley, & D. C. Holland (Eds.), *The cultural production of the educated person: Critical ethnographies of schooling and local practice* (pp. 1–54). Albany, NY: State University of New York Press.

Li, B. (2004). *Urban social exclusion in transitional China*. London: Centre for Analysis of Social Exclusion, London School of Economics.

Li, C. (2006). Sociopolitical change and inequality in educational opportunity: Impact of family background and institutional factors on educational attainment (1940–2001). *Chinese Sociology and Anthropology, 38*(4), 6–36.

Li, C. (2012). Sociopolitical change and inequality of educational opportunities. *Chinese Education & Society, 45*(1), 7–12.

Li, W., Park, A., & Wang, S. (2007). School equity in rural China. In E. Hannum & A. Park (Eds.), *Education and reform in China* (pp. 27–43). Oxon, UK: Routledge.

Li, Y. (2006). Institutional change and educational inequality: Mechanism in educational stratification in urban China (1996–2003). *Zhongguo Shehui Kexue (China Social Science), 4*, 97–207.

Liang, Z., Guo, L., & Duan, C. (2008). *Migration and the well-being of children in China*. Paper presented at the Annual meetings of Population Association of America, New Orleans.

Lin, J. (2006). Educational stratification and the new middle class. In G. A. Postiglione (Ed.), *Education and social change in China* (pp. 179–198). Armonk, NY: M.E.Sharpe.

Liu, J. (2012). Light and shadow of public education for migrant children in urban China. In C. C. Yeakey (Ed.), *Living on the boundaries: Urban marginality in national and international contexts* (Vol. 8, pp. 79–115). Bingley, UK: Emerald Group Publishing Limited.

Liu, J. (2013). The development of inequality in public school admission: Public discourses on Zexiao and practices in urban China. (Ph.D.). Nagoya, Japan: Nagoya University. Retrieved May 24, 2014, from http://ir.nul.nagoya-u.ac.jp/jspui/bitstream/2237/18153/1/k10080.pdf

Liu, J. (2015). Understanding inequality in public school admission in urban China: Analysis of public discourses on *Zexiao*. *Asian Education and Development Studies, 4*(4), 434–447.

Mateju, P. (1993). Who won and who lost in a socialist redistribution in Czechoslovakia? In Y. Shavit & H.-P. Blossfeld (Eds.), *Persistent inequality: Changing educational attainment in thirteen countries* (pp. 251–272). Boulder, CO: Westview Press.

Matras, J. (1975). *Social inequality, stratification, and mobility*. Englewood Cliffs, NJ: Prentice-Hall.

Miller, G., & Holstein, J. A. (2007). Reconsidering social constructionism. In J. A. Holstein & G. Miller (Eds.), *Reconsidering social constructionism: Debates in social problem theory* (pp. 5–23). New Brunswick, Canada: Aldine Transaction.

Mok, K. H., Wong, Y. C., & Zhang, X. (2009). When marketisation and privatization clash with socialist ideals: Educational inequality in urban China. *International Journal of Educational Development, 29*, 505–512.

Murphy, R. (1984). The structure of closure: A critique and development of the theories of Weber, Collins, and Parkin. *The British Journal of Sociology, 35*(4), 547–567.

Nash, R. (1990). Bourdieu on education and social and cultural reproduction. *British Journal of Sociology of Education, 11*(4), 431–447.

National People's Congress. (2006). *Compulsory education law of the People's Republic of China*. Beijing, China.
Nee, V. (1989). A theory of market transition: From redistribution to markets in state socialism. *American Sociological Review, 54*(5), 663–681.
Nee, V. (1991). Social inequalities in reforming state socialism: Between redistribution and markets in China. *American Sociological Review, 56*(3), 267–282.
Nee, V. (1996). The emergence of a market society: Changing mechanisms of stratification in China. *American Journal of Sociology, 101*(4), 908–949.
Nee, V., & Cao, Y. (1999). Path dependent societal transformation: Stratification in hybrid mixed economies. *Theory and Society, 28*(6), 799–834.
Nee, V., & Cao, Y. (2002). Postsocialist inequalities: The causes of continuity and discontinuity. *Research in Social Stratification and Mobility, 19*, 3–39.
Neelsen, J. P. (1975). Education and social mobility. *Comparative Education Review, 19*(1 Politics/Education), 129–143.
OECD. (1994). *School: A matter of choice*. Paris: OECD.
OECD. (2012). *Equity and quality in education: Supporting disadvantaged students and schools*. Paris: OECD.
Parish, W. L., & Michelson, E. (1996). Politics and markets: Dual transformations. *American Journal of Sociology, 101*(4), 1042–1059.
Parkin, F. (1979). *Marxism and class theory: A bourgeois critique*. London: Tavistock Publictions.
Plank, D. N., & Sykes, G. (2003). Why school choice? In D. N. Plank & G. Sykes (Eds.), *Choosing choice: School choice in international perspective* (pp. vii–xxi). New York: Teachers College Press.
Postiglione, G. A. (Ed.). (2006). *Education and social change in China-inequality in a market economy*. New York: M.E.Sharpe.
Rosenthal, E. (2002). Under pressure, Chinese newspaper pulls expose on a charity. *The New York Times*. Retrieved June 5, 2010, from http://www.nytimes.com/2002/03/24/world/under-pressure-chinese-newspaper-pulls-expose-on-a-charity.html
Spector, M., & Kitsuse, J. I. (1973). Social problems: A re-formulation. *Social Problems, 21*(2), 145–159.
Szelenyi, I. (1978). Social inequalities in state socialist redistributive economies -dilemmas for social policy in contemporary socialist societies of Eastern Europe. *International Journal of Comparative Sociology, 19*, 63–87.
Szelenyi, S., & Aschaffenburg, K. (1993). Inequalities in educational opportunities in Hungary. In Y. Shavit & H.-P. Blossfeld (Eds.), *Persistent inequality: Changing educational attainment in thirteen countries* (pp. 273–302). Boulder, CO: Westview Press.
Tsang, M. C. (2002). Intergovernmental grants and the financing of compulsory education in China. *Harvard China Review, 3*(2), 15–20.
Walder, A. G. (1996). Markets and inequality in transitional economies: Toward testable theories. *American Journal of Sociology, 101*(4), 1060–1073.
Weber, M. (1968). In G. Roth & C. Wittich (Eds.), *Economy and society* (Vol. 3). New York: Bedminster Press.
West, A., Ingram, D., & Hind, A. (2006). "Skimming the Cream"? Admissions to charter schools in the United States and to autonomous schools in English. *Educational Policy, 20*(4), 615–639.
Whitty, G., Power, S., & Halpin, D. (1998). *Devolution and choice in education: The school, the state and the market*. Melbourne, Australia: ACER.
Whyte, M. K., & Parish, W. L. (1984). *Urban life in contemporary China*. Chicago: University of Chicago Press.
Willis, P. (1977). *Learning to labor*. New York: Columbia University Press.
Wong, R. S.-K. (2004). Egalitarianism versus social reproduction: Stratification in Eastern Europe. In D. Baker, B. Fuller, E. Hannum, & R. Werum (Eds.), *Inequality across societies: Families, schools and persisting stratification* (Vol. 14, pp. 139–170). Amsterdam: Elsevier.

References

Wu, K. (2005). *Migrants in Nanjing: Personal experiences and social process*. Degree of doctoral of sociology, Syracuse University.

Wu, Q., Goetz, B., Hartmann, D., & Wang, Y.-K. (2012). Income inequality in transitional urban China: The effect of market versus state. *Sociology Mind, 2*(4), 373–381.

Wu, W. (2006). Migrant intra-urban residential mobility. *Housing Studies, 21*(5), 745–765.

Wu, X. (2008). The power of positional competition and market mechanism: A case study of recent parental choice development in China. *Journal of Education Policy, 23*(6), 595–614.

Wu, X. (2009). *The power of market mechanism in the school choice in China: An empirical study*. Retrieved April 13, 2012, from http://www.unige.ch/fapse/ggape/seminaire/programme/progjeudi12/Wu.pdf

Wu, X. (2012). School choice with Chinese characteristics. *Comparative Education, 48*(3), 347–366.

Wu, X. (2014). *School choice in China: A different tale?* Oxon, UK: Routledge.

Wu, X., & Treiman, D. J. (2004). The household registration system and social stratification in China: 1955–1996. *Demography, 41*(2), 363–384.

Wu, X., & Zhang, Z. (2010). Changes in educational inequality in China, 1990–2005: Evidence from the population census data. In E. Hannum, H. Park, & Y. G. Butler (Eds.), *Globalization, changing demographics, and educational challenges in East Asia* (pp. 123–152). Bingley, UK: Emerald.

Zhang, M. (2003). *China's poor regions rural-urban migration, poverty, economic reform and urbanization*. London: Routledge.

Zhou, X. (2004). *The state and life chances in urban China: Redistribution and stratification, 1949–1994*. Cambridge, UK: Cambridge University Press.

Zhou, X., Moen, P., & Tuma, N. B. (1998). Educational stratification in urban China: 1949–94. *Sociology of Education, 71*(3), 199–222.

Zhou, X., Tuma, N. B., & Moen, P. (1996). Stratification dynamics under state socialism: The case of urban China, 1949–1993. *Social Forces, 74*(3), 759–796.

Chapter 2
A Critical Definition of *Zexiao*

Abstract This chapter starts with a review of global public education reforms, emphasizing choice, efficiency, equity, excellence, and international competence, to summarize the meaning of school choice in a global context. By introducing theories and ideologies of educational selection, this chapter summarizes the shift of educational ideology with social change in China as background knowledge to further understand the development of *Zexiao*. Then, it reviews the development of *Zexiao* in China through social development and the changes in public school admission policies between the 1980s and the 2000s. It introduces the diversity and complexity of public junior high school admission and the channels of student placement in this process. The chapter concludes by summarizing the nature of *Zexiao* by examining the similarities and differences between *Zexiao* and school choice in general.

As introduced in the beginning of this book, since *Zexiao* and school choice share similar meanings, people tend to discuss *Zexiao* as a matter of "school choice" which has been taken as one of the pillars in the global education reforms. There are many Chinese scholars who also mixed the two terms in the discussion without distinguishing the differences between them in different social contexts. I argue that it is necessary to distinguish *Zexiao* with school choice by comparing their basic concepts, purposes, approaches, and effects. To further investigate the similarities and differences between *Zexiao* and school choice, firstly, I give a review of neoliberal-oriented global education reform which emphasizes basic human rights for quality education, choice, efficiency, excellence, and international competence. Then, I summarize the theory of education systems and the ideology of educational selection to address it as necessary to understand context and the ideology of an education system to further explore who can make school choice and why they can choose. I also review the history of social change and educational ideology in four stages of China's development. By reviewing the results of previous studies on *Zexiao*, I describe the development of *Zexiao* from its expansion and its diversification. Also, I show the complexity of *Zexiao* through introducing diverse channels for stakeholders to take part in the positional competition for children's admission to junior secondary schools in urban China. I conclude this chapter by distinguishing *Zexiao* and school choice in general.

2.1 Global Trends of Educational Reform

2.1.1 Equity and the Right to Choose

Parental choice has become a vital set of reforms in the education sector of countries around the world. The choice reforms mainly aim at improving schooling efficiency through matching students to schools that reflect their family preferences as well as to increase competition among public schools (Carl, 1994; Levin, 1992). The term "parental choice" in children's education can be understood from two perspectives, including the choice for basic human needs and for educational consumers.

In the late 1940s, parents' choosing the type of education for their children became seen as a universal right. In Article 26 of the Universal Declaration of Human Rights, it is stipulated that parents have a prior right to choose the kind of education that shall be given to their children (UN, 1948). According to Levin and Belfield (2006, p. 627), a common educational experience is a precondition for a citizen to fairly participate in a free and democratic society. The common education experience should not be differentiated according to a family's political, religious, and philosophical preferences. The choice for parents can be considered as the means for accommodating the diverse needs for common education in a pluralistic society (Dewey, 1916; Reich, 2007). Comparing with school choice policies in the USA and UK which intended to improve students' overall academic attainments, Japanese reforms focused on the diversification of the education system (Dierkes, 2008).

Recently, due to the unequal distribution of educational resources and the opportunities in the public education system, there has been an emerging argument that parents must be allowed to have freedom to choose schools they prefer. The argument emphasizes that both the prosperous families and the poor families should have the same range of opportunities for their children's education (Forsey, Davies, & Walford, 2008). With the US Civil Rights Movement in the 1960s, proposals for expanding choices for the disadvantaged to go to private schools were implemented in some poor communities. At the same time, choices are provided to the marginalized groups to pursue desegregation, such as the magnet schools in the USA, school voucher programs for the poor in Milwaukee, WI, and the socially balanced intakes to the City Technology Colleges (CTCs) in the UK (Carl, 1994; Lubienski, Gulosino, & Weitzel, 2009; OECD, 1994; Plank & Sykes, 2003; Whitty, 1997).

2.1.2 Neo-liberal Market Approach

Another type of parental choice is considered as the choice for educational consumers. It is promoted by the neoliberals who believed that the market-based education sector could stimulate competition among public schools to improve their efficiency, quality, and accountability. At the same time, the parental choice which was given by the market can protect freedom of parents to choose schools for their children.

From the late 1970s to the early 1980s, an educational reform movement based on the adoption of neoliberalism and free-market ideology in the education sector swept across the Western world. Such reforms were seen in the Thatcher and Reagan administrations, for example. According to Harvey (2005, p. 2), neoliberalism proposes that human well-being can best be advanced by liberating individual entrepreneurial freedoms and skills within an institutional framework characterized by strong private property rights, free markets, and free trade. Competition among stakeholders presents the virtue of neoliberalism. The advocates of this doctrine believe that competition can improve efficiency and productivity.

According to Friedman (1962), competitive enterprises are likely to be far more efficient in meeting consumer demand than nationalized enterprises. Similarly, denationalizing schooling would widen the range of choice available to parents. At the same time, the competition among schools could stimulate the development of schools, introduce flexibility into the school system, and improve the overall quality of schools. In 1980, Friedman furthered the idea of giving more freedom and choice to parents for children's schooling in public or private education through promoting the use of voucher plan. The introduction of a voucher system for elementary and secondary education would give parents at all income levels freedom to choose the schools their children attended (Friedman & Friedman, 1980). Educational choice involves expanding the freedom of families to send their children to schools other than the public schools in their assigned attendance zones. Thus, educational choice will force schools to compete among themselves for students, and the resulting market pressures will stimulate innovation, responsiveness, and improvements in school performance (Henig, 1994).

Regarding the efficiency and quality of public schools in the USA, Chubb and Moe (1990, 1997) found that private schools outperform public schools and are more effective than public ones. Also, they argued this gap was caused by the limitation in autonomy, weak leadership, unclear goals, and conflict between teachers and local education authorities in the public education sector. Thus, they argued the limitations of the public education system made public education inefficient. It is necessary to decentralize the power of local education authorities to public schools and consumers of educational services through alternative approaches, such as voucher and school choice systems under democratic control.

2.1.3 New Public Management

With the reform for "the minimal state" initiated in the mid-1980s by the Thatcher and Reagan administrations in the UK and USA, the privatization of the public sector, individual interests, and self-discipline were promoted by scholars and politicians under the umbrella of neoliberalism. The "big government" of the welfare state became the enemy of the efficient and free market. Moreover, citizens were sometimes considered as consumers of government products. The expansion of consumers' choice became a goal for the developed world (Forsey et al., 2008). Extreme perspectives on the public-choice theory further argue that governments can do nothing right. The stakeholders in the society, individually or in groups, act mainly on self-interests. In some cases, it caused the misallocation of resources and reduced individual freedoms. This new political economy approach argued that "small government" is the best (Todaro & Smith, 2006).

The promotion of "small government" can be seen in the emergence of the New Public Management (NPM) advocated by the emergence of the plural state in the UK from the late 1970s. The aim of NPM is to determine how best to organize for the provision of goods and services from the government (O'Toole & Meier, 2004). Since the welfare state always focused on the provision of a minimum standard of services to all citizens, public service users increasingly demanded higher quality services with greater choice. Meanwhile, Thatcherism supported the privatization and marketization of public services to improve its efficiency and effectiveness (Hood, 1991; Minogue, 1998; Osborne & McLaughlin, 2002). Moreover, the new managerialism which stressed constant attention to the quality of public services, being close to the customer and the value of innovation, also deeply influenced the marketization of the public education sector (Ball, 1998).

In some countries, such as the UK and the USA, the governments took actions to respond to critiques by reducing taxes, increasing deregulation, decentralizing administrative authorities, and accelerating the privatization of public sectors. In terms of the public education sector, in order to reduce cost, increase efficiency and competitiveness, and improve educational quality, choice and competition were encouraged (Brown, Halsey, Lauder, & Wells, 1997; Chubb & Moe, 1990; Plank & Sykes, 2003). The charter schools in the USA are a widely recognized and accepted approach representing a public-private hybrid approach for educational provision (Lubienski, 2008).

2.1.4 Global Culture and Policy Borrowing

With rapid globalization, the world has never been connected as closely as today. At the same time, countries have never been as interdependent as today. The dissemination of universal understanding and policies, such as universal human rights, neoliberalism, marketization and privatization of public services, self-management of

2.1 Global Trends of Educational Reform

public sectors and efficiency, quality, pluralism, choice of public services, flew through networks, the rise of international student mobility and the sponsorship and enforcement of policy by multilateral agencies (Ball, 1998; Brown & Lauder, 1997; Forsey et al., 2008; Halpin & Troyna, 1995; Plank & Sykes, 2003; Taylor, Rizvi, Lingard, & Henry, 1997).

With the boundary-eroding imperatives of the new technologies as well as the imperatives of economic globalization, globalization is deeply affecting the educational culture around the world. Education systems became a market platform in the microeconomic reform driven by the promotion of national efficiency (Taylor et al., 1997). The globalization and the emergence of marketization of the education sector in some developed countries deeply influenced education reforms through marketization internationally (Plank & Sykes, 2003; Whitty & Edwards, 1998). With the trend of neoliberalism, the global education policy reached a consensus on advocating decentralization, a greater focus on excellence rather than equity and the shift of the emphasis on national governance from citizenship and service to clientship and consumerism (Adnett & Davies, 1999; Forsey et al., 2008). For instance, in the developed world, with policy borrowing from Britain, market-based education reforms, such as privatization of the public education sector and school-based management, became dominant thinking by many scholars and politicians in the USA (Chubb & Moe, 1990). For example, the school choice reform in the UK provided references for relevant reforms in the public education sector of the USA. The charter schools in the USA shared a similar characteristic with grant-maintained schools in the UK (Ball, 1993; Whitty & Edwards, 1998). While in the developing world, with the reduction of public investment in education through structural adjustment reforms, the cost sharing with the private sector for public education became a growing concern (Carnoy, 1995). Furthermore, although equity and quality of education for the low-performing students and disadvantaged groups were continuously given concerns, the neoliberal thinking shaped such policies to embed within choice and accountability frameworks (Forsey, et al., 2008). In other words, education policies became increasingly more market-oriented and competition driven.

In addition, when it comes to discussing the trend of global education policy borrowing, we should not forget the rise of international assessments as a powerful force shaping education policy making and reform at the national level. The international comparison evaluations, such as the Programme for International Student Assessment (PISA), provided countries involved in a benchmark to monitor how well students in their countries learned knowledge and skills and to what extent they applied these into diverse settings by region, types of school, and student groups with diverse socioeconomic status backgrounds. These international exams also shed light on the difference in the achievement of students among participating countries. In other words, it is a platform for participating countries to present their educational excellence at the international level. While not without faults, the higher ranking presents the better performing education system in the countries/territories (OECD, 2016; Takayama, 2008). Moreover, the top performing countries in such international comparison assessments are often considered a global model of education reform. Moreover, their practices will be learned by other countries globally

(Breakspear, 2012). Nevertheless, scholars showed concern on the "unconditioned policy borrowing" from these "best practices." It is necessary to nationalize and localize a globalized education policy to meet specific national and local context needs of a specific country context (Ball, 1998; Bonal & Tarabini, 2013; Sellar & Lingard, 2013; Takayama, 2008; Waldow, Takayama, & Sung, 2014). Based on PISA 2009 results, OECD launched reports on policy options to delay selection, defer tracking, and avoid segregation to increase equity in education (OECD, 2012).

School choice as a global policy has been widely introduced and implemented around the world. Although school choice policies are influenced by the market-based educational reform, cases in different countries showed differences and similarities in the reform. On the one hand, these cases shared the general characteristics of the neoliberal thinking in public education reform. On the other hand, beyond the general market-based thinking, the term "choice" with diverse focuses that include desegregation is often better able to accommodate the demands for pluralism in education and adapt to local cultural-political landscapes (see Appendix 8). Meanwhile, a review of global education reforms for school choice that showed a general concern about inequality in the era of educational reform at the global level is increasing (Andre-Bechely, 2005; Forsey et al., 2008; Gewirtz, Ball, & Bowe, 1995; Plank & Sykes, 2003).

2.2 Educational Selection and Educational Ideology Change

The last section gives a review of a global trend of educational policy reform in the past few decades. It also indicates that there is an emerging focus on school choice as a means of achieving efficiency, equity, and excellence in various education systems at the international level. In addition to this, in the following section, I borrow the discussion on educational selection and the theory of school systems to extend consideration of school choice as a global trend. In other words, I think it is necessary to understand the school choice phenomenon by considering features of the education system and educational ideology in specific society. The educational system is considered a selection machine for upward social mobility of people in a society. However, how, when, who, and why the selection is determined by the ideology of the education system, the ideology of legitimization, and the social norms of a specific society and its historical development stage (Hopper, 1971). Ralph H. Turner (1971) argues that the modes of upward social mobility depend on organizing folk norms of specific societies. He distinguishes a "sponsor-based school system" with a "contest-based school system." In the former system, elites are selected through an established criterion which is decided by elite groups. The criterion is based on merit and cannot be met by self-effort. In contrast, in the latter system, elites are selected by an open and fair contest through the participants' own efforts. The established elites have no right to make a decision in the selection. As Turner (1971, pp. 74–75) addressed, "the objective of contest mobility is to give elite status to those who earn it, while the goal of sponsored mobility is to make the best use of the talents in society by sorting persons into their proper niches." Moreover, it is also important to understand the educational selection from the degree of early differentiation and specialization in the selection progress and the ideologies of the implementation of the selection. Based on an elitist ideology, the "educability" of each citizen determined by genetic factors is the benchmark for an early separation of citizenship and distinguishes a number of their education possibilities. The other approach is based on an egalitarian ideology which specifies the maximum amount of education as the basic right of each citizen. The "educability" depends on the environment which can provide proper instructions to its citizens (Hopper, 1971). In addition, when it comes to understanding an education system, we also need to pay attention to "ideologies of legitimization" of the educational selection process. Who should be selected and why they should be selected illustrate a power distribution of a specific society with a conflict in the competition and exchange for powers among the stakeholders. More importantly, it also reminds us to further understand school choice by considering who can make school choice and why they can choose. Furthermore, it is necessary to understand the above by taking the social change and social context of the specific country into consideration. The next section gives a review of the ideology of education in different stages of China's social development.

There is a constant shift of selection policies between merit-based and political-based criteria in China which have different effects on shaping linkages between social origins and educational attainment across historical periods of China since 1949 (Zhou, 2004). The role of education in Chinese society changed dramatically with the rapid social change. Moreover, the change is deeply influenced by the educational ideologies of its leadership and the social context. With the change of leadership, the role of education in China shifted from a tool for class struggle to a means for economic development. More recently, it became an approach for the fulfillment of the construction of harmonious society and the realization of the Chinese Dream for the nation and its people. In the following section, I review Mao's and Deng's ideologies in education and their effects on Chinese society, respectively. Then, I introduce the education ideology under the construction of a harmonious society and the one presenting the Chinese Dream in China's current context.

2.2.1 Mao's Education Ideology

Mao's era has two historical time periods, including the Pre-Cultural Revolution (1949–1965) and the Cultural Revolution. The Pre-Cultural Revolution period is recognized as the period of nation building and economic development for China (Zhou, Tuma, & Moen, 1996). The primary goal of the state was to promote economic development, culminating in the rushed-growth policy of the Great Leap Forward (*dayuejin*) from 1958 to 1959. The Communist government centralized resources and its power through collectivization and nationalization, especially in urban China (Whyte & Parish, 1984). Workers as the ruling class were united with peasants and soldiers. The capitalists in the urban areas and the landowners and rich farmers were perceived negatively; even intellectuals were kept at a distance. During this period, educational opportunities were expanded dramatically because of the increasing demand for an educated workforce (Zhou, Moen, & Tuma, 1998). Furthermore, as one of the procedures for solidifying administrative control, the household registration system (*hukou*) was established by the Chinese government in 1955. By this system, most Chinese people were assigned a registration status as either "agricultural" or "nonagricultural" population (Cheng & Selden, 1994; Wu & Treiman, 2004; Zhang, 2003). Any transfer of *hukou* registration status from agricultural to nonagricultural had to go through official channels, as either a regular or a special transfer. This system separated China into two worlds, including rural and urban China. In addition, in the early 1960s, due to natural and economic disasters, the government carried out political interventions that increased with the initiation of state de-stratification policies, which aimed at reducing or eliminating social inequalities among social groups (Zhou et al., 1998).

The Cultural Revolution was one of the major political movements in China since 1949. It was considered a mass political struggle for the seizure of power (Bridgham, 1968; Goldman, 2006; Pepper, 1996; Wan, 1998). According to Pepper (1991, p. 26), the Cultural Revolution can be divided into two stages. At the beginning was the destructive Red Guard phase. Young people throughout the country were mobilized to attack old ideas and customs. People in authority positions were generally considered as the ones going the capitalist road; they became targets of the revolution. Accusing the party had capitalist tendencies, bureaucratism, elitism, inefficiency, and the loss of revolutionary favor, Mao Zedong launched the Cultural Revolution by encouraging youth in China to regain their revolutionary spirit (Wan). Another significant historical issue is the "send-down policy" (*shangshanxiaxiang*) and the dispatch of 17 million[1] urban youth to live and work in rural areas (Giles, Park, & Wang, 2008; Zhou & Hou, 1999). Urban youth from either working class or educated bourgeois families were sent to rural areas. In "the lost decade" for China, the Cultural Revolution and its immediate aftermath were not only large-scale political purges and repression but also labor force participation and other opportunities that were highly politicized and severely affected by sharp shifts in state policies (Zhou et al., 1996). During the Cultural Revolution, following Mao's faith that the countryside must be the chief beneficiary of China's revolution, a radical egalitarian agenda dominated the society. As a result, those well-educated and upper-class individuals lost their former priority focus and status. In contrast, the working class (workers and farmers) became the dominant class. It is said that the Chinese society reached an equal level in its history during the Cultural Revolution. As Deng and Treiman (1997) argued, the Cultural Revolution was probably the most drastic attempt the world has yet seen to reduce the intergenerational transmission of advantage. In order to change the tough situation for students from working class to

---

[1] According to Goldman (2006, p. 405), the number of urban youth in "sending down" movement was 14 million.

2.2 Educational Selection and Educational Ideology Change

compete with students from educated bourgeois families in school admission examinations, school admission examinations at each level of education were abolished during the Cultural Revolution (Wan, 1998). As Goldman (2006) concluded on the result of the Cultural Revolution, although China made achievements in public health construction, the Green Revolution in agriculture, and helped eliminate illiteracy, the Cultural Revolution tarnished Mao's image for his people. And the nation as a whole was further isolated and impoverished.

As the leader of the radicals, Mao believed that the achievement of political consciousness, ideological devotion to communism, and human liberation were the primary goals for China's development. Education has a key role to play in the political and ideological development of China. As a Marxist, Mao's ideology in education was deeply influenced by Marx and Engels. He strongly supported the idea to combine work and instruction in society. Mao's writings give focus on the role of education in the building of socialism. Like Lenin, he also wanted schooling free from religious control, factory-run schools, and priority given for vocational and science work at the senior level (Tsang, 2000, pp. 39–47; Cleverley, 1985, pp. 85–87; Lofstedt, 1980). Mao's famous statement on education known as the *May Seventh Statement* indicates that:

> While the students' main task is to study, they should also learn other things, that is to say, they should not only learn knowledge from books, they should also learn industrial production, agricultural production, and military affairs. They should also criticize and repudiate the bourgeoisie. The length of schooling should be shortened, education should be revolutionalized, and the domination of our schools and colleges by bourgeois intellectuals should not be tolerated any longer. (Mao, 1969, pp. 56–57, translated by the author)

The work-study program was established in this historical context to have students participate in productive labor in school farmlands and factories. In order to protect the core status of the working class and peasants in China to achieve equality in education, Mao also criticized the education system which excluded peasants and people from the working class. There were needs to change the exam-based enrollment and the cramming method of teaching.[2] With the start of the Cultural Revolution in 1966, Mao's ideology in education was fully presented in the series of movements regarding education. The universal primary schooling and even secondary schooling were given great efforts to expand for peasant and the working class. By shortening schooling years, practical learning was emphasized. The hierarchical key school system was abolished. Schools for elite education and cadres' children were also terminated. Even the unified entrance examinations at the junior high and senior high levels were put to an end. Moreover, educated youth in urban areas were sent to rural areas for reeducation by the poor and lower-middle peasants (Lofstedt, 1980; Pepper, 1980).

---

[2] Enrollment by examination had the effect of excluding children from worker, peasant, and revolutionary ranks. The exam system was argued that it had been justified and supported by leading cadres in the ministry, those "handfuls of renegades, secret agents, and capitalist roaders" scraped together by Liu Shaoqi (Cleverley, 1985, p. 168).

2.2.2 Deng's Ideology in Education

After the Cultural Revolution, especially with the implementation of the economic reform and the Open Door Policy in China since 1978, the series of positive change have mushroomed within China. With the introduction of the market economy and capitalism, the focus of the entire society shifted toward rapid modernization[3] of the country through the achievement of a conflict-free social order. The "class struggle" was replaced by a series of reforms to speed up the nation's development (Chen, 2002). Furthermore, Hawkins (1983) pointed out that a particular kind of person, such as the new socialist man, is not especially important. The Chinese leaders believed that the color of the cat does not matter—what matters is whether or not he catches mice (*buguanheimaobaimao, zhuodaolaoshujiushihaomao*). Social and political status will no longer be the standard for judging the success of people in Chinese society. By adapting the strategy known as "crossing the river by feeling stones" (*mozheshitouguohe*), the leadership launched a series of reforms to promote the economic development, market economies, consumer goods industries, and establishment of special economic zones along the coast by taking dynamic economies as neighboring countries in East Asia as references (Goldman, 2006; Whyte, 2010; Wong & Mok, 1995). Meanwhile, the de-collectivization of agriculture and the loosening of migrant restrictions also stimulated the rural economy. New opportunities for rural people engaged them into diverse activities to generate higher incomes. Simultaneously, it also unleashed waves of rural-urban migration in China (Logan & Fainstein, 2008; Solinger, 1999; Whyte, 2010). However, due to the limitation of household registration and other relevant social system, rural migrants were excluded from the mainstream urban society in China. And it was difficult for them to enjoy the same social welfare as their urban counterparts. Meanwhile, the increasing "floating population" from rural area to urban area generated great pressure on urban facilities, such as schools and hospitals (Goldman, 2006; Li, 2005). Moreover, with the reform of state-owned enterprises from the mid-1990s, there were a large number of laid-off workers caused by the bankrupt of state-owned

---

[3] According to Henze (1992, pp. 103–104), it has always been used as a verbal weapon among competing political factions and intellectual circles in China. This term has been used in conjunction with calls for advancement or with programs of immediate action, which would subsequently receive support from particular groups in the leadership for some level of implementation. The term has been used to refer to the PRC's backwardness in comparison with developed nations, that is to say, with "modern" societies—predominately those in the West. Not surprisingly, the indigenous term "four modernizations" stood first and foremost for a conception of economic reform that was to increase production and improve distribution and was guided by more rational modes of planning than had previously been relied on. Whether it was later called "socialist modernization" (*shehui zhuyi de xiandaihua*) or "modernization with Chinese characteristics" (*Zhongguo tese de xiandanhua*), to quote Deng Xiaoping, "the four modernizations mean economic construction." Henze pointed out that modernization with development was equalized by Deng Xiaoping and other political elite in China even though it is not the case in the established view in Western sociology. From the very beginning, the assumption has been accepted that "modernization" will lead to material wealth, to a happier life for most of the population, and thus to a "strong socialist China."

enterprises in urban areas. Consequently, it caused emerging urban poverty and urban unemployment (Appleton & Song, 2008; Goldman, 2006; Whyte, 2010).

In contrast to Mao's ideology in education and its influence on China's development, Deng strongly holds the standpoint that national development is mainly economic and technical and less political and ideological. In his speech at the 1978 National Conference on Education, Deng showed his different point of view toward ideology in education during the Cultural Revolution. He emphasized the main task of students is to study and to learn book knowledge, but not devoting a big proportion of schooling time in political education. Education has the key role in improving the productivity of human beings and supporting the development of science and technology. Comparing with the emphasis on education equality by Mao, Deng gave more focus on quality education and efficiency (Encyclopedia of China Publishing House, 1984).[4] His famous statement "Education should be oriented to modernization, the world and the future" (*jiaoyu yao mianxiang xiandaihua, mianxiang shijie, mianxiang weilai*) showed his attitude toward the important role of education in modernization. In order to achieve education with high-quality and efficient education for economic development in China, Deng stressed the strict exam-based school admission and stratified school system would prepare a diversified workforce for China's development. Furthermore, the support for the selection of students through the key school system presents Deng's ideology for the elites in education (Hannum, 1999; Lewin & Hui, 1989; Rosen, 1985; Sautman, 1991; Tsang, 2000). As Rosen (1985) pointed out, with the shift of leadership from Mao to Deng after the Cultural Revolution, the Chinese education system was restructured into

---

[4] A historical review of policies shows that the concept of quality education is not totally new in China's education development. The similar concept has already existed in Mao's era. In 1957, Mao (1969) pointed out that: "Our education doctrine should let students develop through moral education, intellectual education and physical education. They should become laborers with socialist consciousness and knowledge." In the following years, Mao repeatedly expressed his opinion to require students to take part in productive labor and necessary social activities instead of studying all days. Besides advocating that the exam system should be reformed, Mao also pointed out that students should do something else while studying. They should study not only knowledge but also learn from workers, farmers, and soldiers. Also they should criticize capitalism. Furthermore, school hours should be reduced (Mao, 1969). Mao's statements had already showed his focus on the development of individual students, balance between study and productive labor, and reform of the examination system. In fact, these opinions on education of Mao were put into action in the Cultural Revolution. The exam system was terminated. And the young people in urban areas were sent to rural areas to work and study from farmers. Similar to Mao's education policy, during the National Education Conference in 1978, Deng reemphasized the need for the well-rounded development of individuals. He pointed out that the school admission should also give focus on this perspective. Nevertheless, in terms of the attitude toward exams, Deng held a different opinion from Mao. In the same conference, Deng explained that, "The exam is an important method to check study and teaching effect. It just looks like the quality control which is a necessary system for keeping a productive level in the factory. Of course, we cannot over depend on exams as viewing them as the only approach to evaluate education performance. Rather, we need to do serious research and experiment to improve content and types of exams to improve performance. Regarding those who do not perform well on the exam, we should encourage and help them instead of giving them unnecessary mental pressure" (Encyclopedia of China Publishing House, 1984).

"bifurcated educational system" on the eve of Deng's economic revolution. The system includes a small pro-"elite" sector which trains and accumulates human resources for modernization and a large pro-"mass" sector which provides basic educational skills and training for the majority.

Furthermore, the education reform in 1985 shows the purpose of the education reform is to improve the quality of people and to cultivate more human resources and human resources with good quality. Moreover, the government document indicates the basic standard for evaluating school's achievement. That is not how many profits the school generates but the quantity and quality of human resources the school cultivates (Chinese Communist Party Central Committee, 1985). According to Liu (2007), "efficiency first, give attention to equity" (*xiaolv youxian, jiangu gongping*) can be considered as Deng's principle of education reform in the 1980s and the 1990s. On the one hand, the reform aims at pursuing educational efficiency. They hope to educate as many human resources as possible within a short period to support the country's construction. On the other hand, the reform gives concern on equity of schooling. They emphasize the equal opportunities for individuals. With the introduction of "Efficiency first, give attention to equity" to the economic reform from the 1980s, this concept also became the core ideology for educational reform in China.[5] Schools, areas, and stages of education selected by the government got priorities for development. In other words, in order to generate economic profits for the nation, the government treated members in the society differently. Some members fulfilled their educational interests while others could not.

Simultaneously, since education was widely recognized as a ladder for upward social mobility in Chinese society especially after the start of economic development in the late 1970s, the formula "university degree = good jobs = better income = social prestige" appears to provide a common understanding of why people need to invest in education. As Bai (2010, p. 120) concluded, monetary reward as the main aspiration for education fuels the Chinese enthusiasm for education, and so every year millions of students cram for the university entrance examinations. The idea of education for a monetary reward can be found in a survey on people's perception regarding the role of education in Asian societies conducted by a group of Japanese scholars in 2006. It shows that the income generation was the most (68.7%) selected role of education in Chinese society (Sonoda, 2008, p. 58).[6] In recent years, the close link between education degree and individual socioeconomic status pushed most schools at primary and secondary education level to teach students for exams

---

[5] Originally, "Efficiency first, give attention to equity" is an economic principle in terms of income and distribution. However, this slogan was directly simplified and used as reform criteria in various fields. In fact, such phenomenon is very representative in Chinese society. The focus on economic reform made the discourse on economy a hegemonic power. Due to the left behind reform in education and other fields, these fields had to borrow many concepts and ideologies from economic reform. Consequently, people started to use economic concepts and understanding to deal with issues in education (D. Yang, 2006, p. 103).

[6] In this survey, the choices for respondents also include (1) enriching humanity, (2) getting preferred jobs, (3) living overseas, (4) getting higher social status, (5) contributing to national development, (6) for the society, and (7) becoming internationally active (Sonoda, 2008, p. 58).

and tests for helping students to advance to upper-level education. The "diploma disease" in Chinese education became serious and made education as means for self-fulfillment. Consequently, the pressures on schools, parents, and students for examination were intensified at all education level, even expanding to the preschool education level. On the other hand, there is a rise of "inflation of credential" presented by the increasing number of unemployed graduates in recent years (Sonoda, 2008).

2.2.3 Education and Construction of Harmonious Society

China's economy achieved unprecedented development during this period. According to the World Bank (2012), China overtook Japan to become the second-largest economy in the world in 2010. Moreover, the Bank predicted that the rapid economic growth in emerging markets would give rise to the remarkable expansion of the middle class.

Until the end of the Cultural Revolution in 1976, the middle class was virtually nonexistent in Chinese society (Lin, 2006). With the formulation of the construction of a "well-off society" (*xiaokangshehui*) and the strategy of allowing some to "get rich first" (*rang yibufenren xianfuqilai*), people in the private sector, collective enterprises, urban professionals, and skilled employees in both public and private sectors benefited from these strategies in the 1980s and the 1990s (Tomba, 2004). According to Chinese Scholar Qiang Li (2008), from the 1980s, there were five conditions which accelerated the emergence of the middle class in contemporary Chinese society. They include the adjustment of industry, the adjustment of employment, the adjustment of urbanization, the mass of higher education, and the adjustment of income. The rapid growth of employment in the third industry accelerated the emergence of the middle class in urban China. Meanwhile, the enlargement of higher education and the middle class focused China's income adjustment strategy made by the central government and also contributed to the rise of a middle class in urban China. A current definition of middle class in China generally refers to people who possess property, have major savings in banks, live a life of relative comfort, and have received tertiary or higher education. More importantly, the middle class has increasingly higher-quality education demands for their children. It generated the fierce competition for the limited education resources in urban China (Lin, 2006). Meanwhile, the economic reform in the late 1990s also caused increasing urban unemployment. For example, many workers were laid off from state-owned enterprises during this period (Appleton & Song, 2008; Goldman, 2006; Li, 2005, Lin, 2006).

Accordingly, the economic evolution created a widening gap between the rich and the poor, as well as resulting social and economic instability (Chen, 2002; Farrell, Gersch, & Stephenson, 2006; Sonoda, 2008). From the 1980s, there is a growing *Gini* coefficient in China. In this period, the new leadership under Hu Jintao and Wen Jiabao showed serious concerns about the increasing inequality caused by the imbalanced development. The central government announced some policies aimed at alleviating poverty and inequality for constructing a "harmonious society" (*hexieshehui*) (National Congress of Communist Party of China, 2006; Whyte & Guo, 2009). In order to cut off burdens of peoples in rural areas and close the disparities between rural and urban areas, the fourth generation of leaders reduced agriculture taxes for the farmer and provided an educational subsidy for rural education (Goldman, 2006). Furthermore, the real "free compulsory education" was officially implemented with the launch of the *New Compulsory Education Law* in 2006 (National People's Congress, 2006).

From the 1980s, the unprecedented socioeconomic development generated increasing need for qualified laborers and skilled technicians. As a continuation, quality education was reemphasized in the 1990s, especially after the establishment of a socialist market economic system in 1993. It is said that the notion of a "quality education" (*sushi jiaoyu*) was firstly mentioned in government documents in 1994 (Dello-Iacovo, 2009).[7] In *Opinions on Further Strengthening and Promoting Moral Education in Schools*, the quality education was required to respond to the new demand from the construction of socialist market economic system (Chinese Communist Party Central Committee, 1994). Education of the constitution; cultivation of pioneering spirit, independent spirit, and moral education; and the implementation of music, arts, and PE in compulsory education were given emphasis. In 1998, the *Action Plan for Invigorating Education in the 21st Century* introduced the implementation of the *Cross-Century Quality Education Project* which promoted quality education (Ministry of Education, 1998). As a further step, the 2003–2007 *Action Plan for Invigorating Education* raised a similar project titled as *Project for Quality-Oriented Education in the New Century*. It aims to strengthen and improve moral education in schools; intensify reform of the curriculum and assessment system; promote reform and development of secondary education, preschool education, and special education; strengthen and improve physical and art education in schools; and strengthen standardization of language and characters (Ministry of Education, 2004). In the *Outline of the Eleventh Five-Year Plan for National Education Development* released in 2007, implementation of quality education was given the priority in the education sector (State Council, 2007). As with similar policies mentioned above, moral education, further education and teaching reform, and the collaboration among schools, families, and society were emphasized. Dello-Iacovo (2009) explained the emergence of quality education in China was the reflection of the criticism on the rigorous exam-oriented education. Wu and Shen (2006) also pointed out that quality education was a newly developed education idea in the era of exam-oriented education. In other words, quality education is used to tackle problems caused by the exam-oriented education, such as one-sided pursuing enrollment rate and increasing study workload of students.

China is trying to establish a socialist market economic system which has many challenges for the ideology in a socialist country. Rapid economic development with the underdeveloped social welfare system caused social inequality in China.

---

[7] This information also took reference from http://www.edu.cn/20051018/3156152.shtml, accessed on August 19, 2011.

The Gini coefficient which presents the inequality of a society increased from 0.29 in 1981 to 0.44 in 2005 (Chen, Hou, & Jin, 2008, p. 16). A larger Gini coefficient implies greater income inequality. With the release of the *Decisions on Construction of Harmonious Society* by the Sixth Plenary Session of the 16th National Congress of the CPC in 2006, China's government paid more attention to the emerging social inequality (National Congress of Communist Party of China, 2006).[8] Under such circumstances, China's government made a decision to construct harmonious society. Development of quality education was given priority by the government. The balanced allocation of education resources in different regions has been emphasized to gradually narrow down gaps between rural and urban areas and between regions. The government's investment in education was set up to achieve 4% of GDP gradually (Zhu, 2011). The donation to education from society was continuously encouraged. The charge of illegal school fees was firmly opposed. Moreover, reduction course workload of students was repeatedly given emphasis. Nowadays in China, the imbalanced educational development has been considered as one of the challenges for the construction of harmonious society. In other words, the building of the balanced education is seen as a part of the construction of harmonious society.

2.2.4 The Chinese Dream in "New Normal"

With the power transfer from Hu Jintao to Xi Jinping in 2012, educational equality becomes a major goal for both individuals and the nation to realize the Chinese Dream. The new administration started drawing a picture of the Chinese Dream for national rejuvenation and the well-being of the people in China. The government kept emphasizing the Chinese Dream as a goal for the country. And they also addressed the goal of realizing the dream of individual Chinese citizens, such as securing housing, employment, public health, and education and preserving the environment (Mahoney, 2014; Wang, 2014). The Minister of Education in 2013 also claimed taking education development as a priority and further promoting education equality and protecting education for all as part of the Chinese Dream (Gao, 2013,

---

[8] According to the policy above, the government pointed out that Chinese society as a whole was in harmony. However, there were many problems which were conflicting with the harmony in the society. Mainly, the conflicts include imbalanced socioeconomic development between urban and rural areas and regions with the increasing pressure of demography and environment. The serious problems also include employment, social security, income redistribution, education, medical care, housing, security in production, social safety, and so forth. Related systems and mechanisms were not satisfactory; the democratic legal system has not been accomplished. The social trust and social morality are losing among some members in the society. Some leaders' quality and capability are not suitable for the new trend in China's development. Corruption was relatively serious in some fields. And there were some anti-government activities which were threats to national security and social stability (National Congress of Communist Party of China, 2006).

October 16). With the introduction to the "new normal"[9] to the public by President Xi at the Asia-Pacific Economic Cooperation summit in 2014, education development also should accommodate the needs for the economic slowdown and economic transformation and upgrade. Gu (2016) elaborated the "new normal" of education in China is to "enhance morality, foster talents" as the key principles, to run education by law, promote equal education and quality education, and make connotative development to accommodate people's need for education. Moreover, with the launch of a political campaign against corruption and discipline in the party and with government officials in 2012, the education administration has continued to pay much more attention to equality issues in public education (Ministry of Education, 2014).

2.3 The Development of *Zexiao*

In this section, I review the development of *Zexiao* based on the published information and the existing literature, mainly including newspaper articles, government documents, journal papers, published survey results, and the published books on *Zexiao*. Firstly, I introduce the residence-based public school admission policy. Secondly, I describe the development of *Zexiao* from its expansion and its diversification by reviewing the results existing based on existing surveys and researches on *Zexiao*. Thirdly, I show the complexity of *Zexiao* through introducing the diverse channels for stakeholders to take part in the positional competition for children's admission to junior secondary schools in urban China. I conclude by distinguishing *Zexiao* and school choice in general. The reviews indicated that the mismatch between residence-based public school admission to junior high schools and people's demand for sending children to better schools was the original reason for people to take part in *Zexiao*. Review of the development of *Zexiao* indicated that *Zexiao* was widely practiced in urban China from the late 1980s. With the rapid development of *Zexiao*, the diversification of channels for *Zexiao* intensified complexity of the admission process to public junior high schools. *Zexiao* was linked with parents' socioeconomic status and children's achievement in the study.

Traditionally, with the consensus of "He who excels in the study can follow an official career (*xueeryouzeshi*),"[10] education is considered as one of the most important tools for climbing the social ladder in Chinese society. Hundreds of years ago, individuals spent years to become government official through government's civil examination. Moreover, in order to change children's lives and fortune of the family,

---

[9] President Xi Jinping elaborated the "new normal" as the following features. First, the economy has shifted gears from the previous high-speed to a medium-to-high-speed growth. Second, the economic structure is constantly improved and upgraded. Third, the economy is increasingly driven by innovation instead of input and investment (Zhang & Yao, 2014).

[10] This is a widely known Confucian slogan for education. It means a good scholar can become an official.

2.3 The Development of *Zexiao*

parents were willing to sacrifice everything they had to create any opportunity for children's education. A well-known story of "Mencius' mother, three moves (*mengmusanqian*)" tells parent's aspiration for children's education by selecting a satisfied education environment.

As a culture, selecting good education environment for children does not change even though there are shifts of political atmosphere and administrations in China. Even in the early stage after the establishment of the People's Republic of China, under the exam-based school admission system, there were a small number of people who utilized their power and *guanxi*[11] to send children to well-known schools (Fang, 2011; Li, 2009; Yang, 2006). After the Cultural Revolution, with the rapid economic development, living standard in China, especially in urban areas, improved dramatically. The increasing family income stimulated parents' aspiration for enrolling children in popular schools in order to send them to universities. The sponsor fee-based school admission became a widely accepted approach for people to send children to well-known schools which did not belong to the school catchment area they registered.

With the implementation of *Compulsory Education Law 1986*, the government abolished the standard entrance exam to junior high school in 1993. Without standard evaluation of students for admission to public junior high schools, parents started to spend money and use power to have access to send children to better school. As a result, *Zexiao* started sweeping over urban China. The government repeatedly emphasized the importance of equity in school admission at compulsory education level based on the principle of proximity. Nevertheless, due to the big gap between public schools, the "school lottery system"[12] adopted from Hong Kong did not receive a warm welcome from parents and public schools. On the one hand, parents worried that their children would be randomly assigned to "bad schools." On the other hand, key schools had the privilege to skip the "school lottery system" and organize their own student selection (21st Century Education Research Institute, 2011). Therefore, the majority of schools involved in the system are regular schools. As a result, *Zexiao*, which presents a positional competition for popular schools among parents and students, expanded and became popular in urban China. According to Yang (2006), there are diverse features of *Zexiao*. Firstly, the areas have expanded from big and middle-sized cities to counties and rural areas.

---

[11] The term *guanxi* is understood as "connections" between people in order to exchange favors (Bian, 1994; Hwang, 1987). *Guanxi* represents a relational Chinese culture or interpersonal connections of sentiments and obligations that dictate social interaction and facilitate favor exchanges in Chinese society, past and present (Bian, 2002).

[12] According to Fang (2011), originally, this system aims to distribute G6 students within a region equally and randomly to junior high schools by computer. However, due to the different school facilities and human resources between schools within one region, there is a gap between public schools in the same region. Since the established school lottery system was not reliable to guarantee the access to better schools for children, parents were not interested in this system. Comparing with school lottery system, *Zexiao* provided possibility for parents to send their children to better public school through paying additional school fees. Consequently, *Zexiao* became more and more popular in urban China.

Secondly, participants in *Zexiao* have shifted into young age groups. Moreover, it has shifted from senior high school to junior high school and continuously shifted to primary schools and kindergartens. Thirdly, "Olympic math fever" (*aoshure*) and "certificate fever" (*kaozhengre*) became more closely connected with *Zexiao* in the public school admission to junior high schools. Fourthly, the cost of *Zexiao* is becoming more expensive. Yang (2006, p. 126) demonstrated that "*Zexiao* Fever is badly against the rule of free and residence-based public school admission. It terribly caused study burden of students at compulsory education level, badly influenced children's health and significantly intensified gaps between schools and classes."

According to my review of the literature on *Zexiao*, in the past years, there are two features of the development of *Zexiao* in urban China. Firstly, *Zexiao* becomes popular by involving more participants, such as parents, students, schools, and other new stakeholders. Secondly, *Zexiao* becomes complex by involving diverse issues inside and outside of education sector including but not limited to the cost of *Zexiao*, Olympic math training in private tutoring institute, special talent training, memo student, and co-founding student. In the following two sections, I elaborate the two features of the development of *Zexiao* by reviewing the collected surveys and reports on education published in China since the 1980s to the present.

2.3.1 The Expansion of Zexiao

In general, these surveys show that *Zexiao* is rapidly expanding in recent years. Since there is no officially published survey at the national level regarding *Zexiao* so far, most of the data shown in this research are based on surveys conducted by media and academic institutes. In 2003, a questionnaire survey on *Zexiao*, which involved 94 leaders from different local education authorities by *China Education Daily*, showed that *Zexiao* became a common practice in public school admission in many places of China. The result of the survey showed that 59.57% of participants admitted that they had *Zexiao* issue in their places. *Zexiao* at senior high school level was widely practiced in 85.11% of places involved. There were 69.15% of places where *Zexiao* at junior high school level was popular. This number at primary school level was 41.49% (Zhang et al., 2003, October 26). According to a survey conducted in 2005 by National Survey Research Center, 46% of parents would choose better quality schools without following the principle of proximity (He, Xu, & Wang, 2005, May 24). A survey conducted by Beijing Normal University in 2009 showed that around 40.5% of students in ten cities of China were *Zexiao* students (Zheng, 2011). The same survey also showed that *Zexiao* in the capital city at province level was more widely practiced than other areas. Moreover, a survey conducted by *Guangming Ribao* indicated the socioeconomic status of the family strongly influenced participation in *Zexiao*. Fathers working in private sector, fathers who were cadres, and fathers who owned private business were the main players in *Zexiao* (Zeng & Ma, 2009, December 28). In 2011, according to a survey conducted by 21st Century Education Research Institute, about 46% of parents prepared for

2.3 The Development of *Zexiao*

children's *Zexiao* from G6 to G7. In the same year, the survey showed that *Zexiao* ratio at compulsory education level (including primary education to lower secondary education) was 40.5% (Che, 2011, November 24). In a survey conducted by *China Youth Daily* in 2009, 98.5% of the participants believed that *Zexiao* phenomenon became a common issue in the entire education sector from preschool education to upper secondary education (Wang, 2009, November 12).[13] According to Li (2011, pp. 145–160), in a survey involving 400 parents, 96.5% of parents had the plans to take part in *Zexiao* in order to select better quality junior high schools for their children.

There are also surveys on *Zexiao* conducted in big municipals, such as Beijing and Shanghai. An investigation report published by Beijing government in 1996 showed that within seven urban areas, 3.99% of newly enrolled G7 students were students who entered junior secondary schools using *Zexiao* (hereafter, they are called *Zexiao* students). Among all *Zexiao* students involved in visited districts totaling 7,042, *Dongcheng* District[14] had the largest number of *Zexiao* students which shared 10.75% of the total new G7 students. *Haidian* District[15] had the second largest number of *Zexiao* students which shared 3.75% of the total new G7 students (Qiao, Zhou, & Zheng, 1996, p. 46). In contrast, a survey conducted one decade later (2006) showed that about 45% of parents involved in the survey admitted that they took part in one or another form of *Zexiao* in the process of their children's promotion from primary school to junior high school. The same survey showed that *Zexiao* mainly occurred at compulsory education level in Beijing, especially in the transition from G6 to G7. Mainly, it happened in the urban areas. It also indicated that most popular schools for parents who commit *Zexiao* practices were so-called "key schools." 70% of students who had experience in committing *Zexiao* were promoted to key junior high schools. It also showed that only about 30% of parents did not commit *Zexiao* (He, Lu, & Xue, 2008, p. 75). According to *Renmin Ribao*, an Internet-based survey on *Zexiao* held by Shanghai Municipal Education Committee showed that about 36% of parents took part in *Zexiao* (He et al., 2005, May 24) (see more information regarding *Zexiao* in other urban areas of China in Appendix 9).

In recent years, various surveys showed there were an increasing number of families involved in *Zexiao*. According to Wu (2008, p. 599), in a survey conducted in Beijing, 66% of the respondents selected schools for their children. Moreover, a study conducted in Beijing indicated that not only parents in key schools but also parents in regular schools had the experience in committing *Zexiao* for children's education transition to junior high schools (Li, 2008). A TV program made by China Central Television (CCTV) also predicted that over 50% of G6 students at Beijing

---

[13] This survey involved 14,081 participants from 31 provinces of China.

[14] Dongcheng District is one of the core areas of Beijing. Traditionally, there are many old and popular primary schools and junior high schools in this district.

[15] Haidian District is located in IT industry area of Beijing. There are many nation class universities in this district. And it has rich public education resource, including countrywide known primary schools and junior high schools.

primary schools in 2011 would take part in *Zexiao* instead of following the school assignment by the local education authority (CCTV, 2011, June 3). The result of computer lottery-based school assignment in the northern part of Dongcheng District in Beijing in 2011 showed that only 51% of G6 student in this area participated in this type of admission.[16] It means that almost 50% of G6 students in this area found their places in junior high schools through other channels than by the computer lottery, namely, *Zexiao*. Data above showed that *Zexiao* became a widespread practice in education transition from G6 to G7 in Beijing. In most major cities of China, *Zexiao* was widely practiced. According to the 21st Century Education Research Institute (2011, p. 261), over 74% of respondents from 35 major cities in China agreed that *Zexiao* was a serious education issue in their cities.

As Fig. 2.1 shows, *Haidian* District, *Dongcheng* District, and *Chongwen* District became the major receiving areas which enroll interdistrict students in public school admission to junior high schools. Considering the imbalanced distribution of good quality public schools within Beijing, it is clear to identify that the major receiving areas have more good education resources which are attractive for parents and students.

2.3.2 The Diversity and Complexity of Zexiao

With the rapid expansion of *Zexiao*, there are increasing numbers of issues reflecting public attitudes and practices toward the rise of the social phenomenon. *Zexiao* starts to involve wider varieties of practices and became more complicated. Although students are supposed to follow the principle of "no exam, no cost, and proximity" in their transition from G6 to G7, a survey report[17] in 2011 showed that besides the lottery-based school assignment system, there were diverse channels used by parents to enroll children in junior high schools. As Table 2.1 shows, regarding school admission channels in eight major districts of Beijing in 2010, besides the lottery system and the counterpart school-based admission which follow the principle of proximity, there were 13 recognized channels for parents and students to choose in order to enter junior high schools depending on the districts in Beijing (21st Century Education Research Institute, 2011). An Internet-based survey[18] showed the principle of proximity-based school admission repeatedly emphasized by the government

---

[16] This information comes from homepage of Educational Examinations Center of *Dongcheng* District of Beijing. Retrieved from http://www.dcks.org.cn/news/show.php?id=505, accessed on August 7, 2011.

[17] The survey was conducted by 21st Century Education Research Institute from April 2011 to August 2011. The author was one of the members of the project.

[18] This survey was conducted from July 11 to August 12, 2011, by 21st Century Education Research Institute in cooperation with Education Channel of Sina.com. There were 525 participants from 35 cities involved in this survey.

2.3 The Development of *Zexiao*

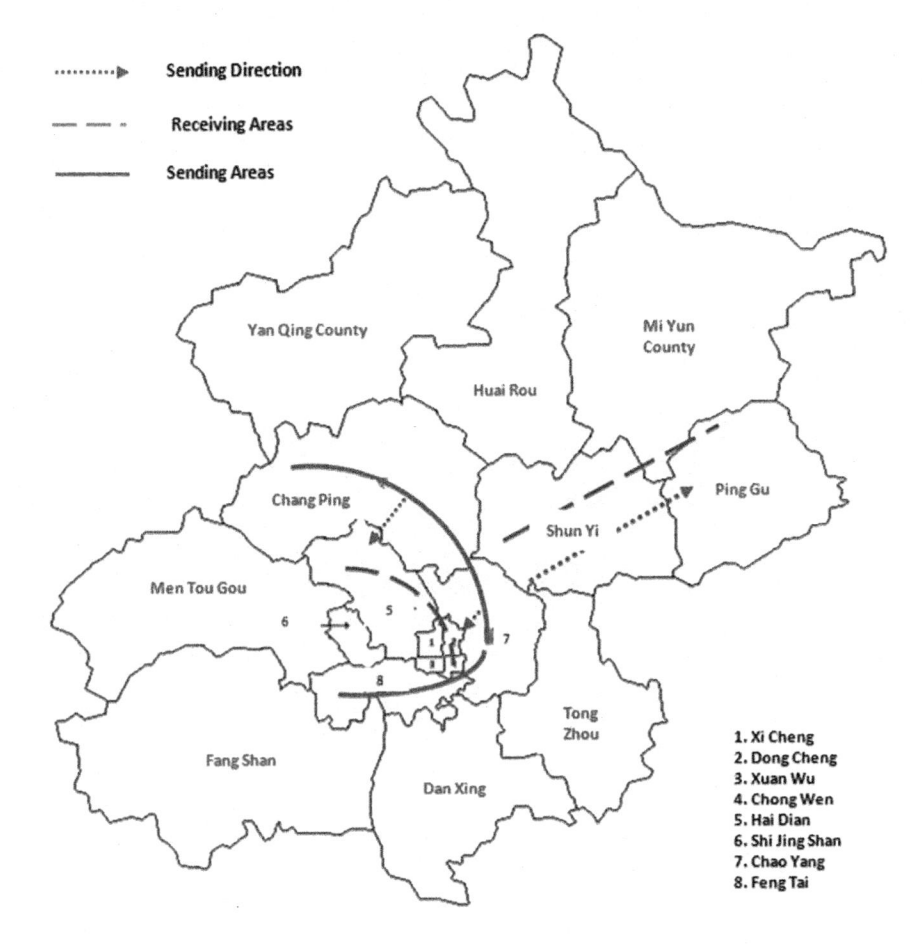

Fig. 2.1 Interdistricts *Zexiao* in Beijing (2008) (Source: Unpublished paper. Collected by author from 21st Century Educational Research Institute)

was not much supported by the public. According to the result of the survey, the most popular approach parents selected for children's education transition from G6 to G7 at the national level was the school recommendation approach. In contrast, only 9.8% of parents took part in the school lottery system. In Beijing, the most popular school admission approach was the pre-admission training class-based approach. And only 9.1% of parents followed the lottery-based school assignment system (see Fig. 2.2).[19] Interestingly, 28.9% of parents chose other school admission channels at the national level. And this number in Beijing was 22.7%. These numbers also showed the diverse school admission options in the transition from G6 to G7.

---

[19] The diverse of *Zexiao* was also identified by Li (2008).

Table 2.1 School admission options in Beijing in 2010

Admission options	Dongcheng District	Xicheng District	Haidian District	Chongwen District	Xuanwu District	Chaoyang District	Fengtai District (2011)	Shijingshan District
1. Lottery-based school assignment system	●	●	●			●	●	
2. Counterpart school	●			●	●		●	●
3. Special talents	●	●	●	●	●	●	●	●
4. Recommendation	●	●	●	●		●	●	●
5. Boarding school	●	●	●	●	●	●	●	●
6. Minban school	●	●						
7. Characteristic school	●	●		●	●		●	●
8. Mutual selection		●			●			
9. Co-founding	●	●	●	●	●	●	●	●
10. Enterprises/university-owned school			●					
11. Nine-year school	●	●	●	●	●	●	●	●
12. Relocation	●	●	●	●	●	●	●	●
13. Non-*Hukou*	●	●			●	●	●	●
14. Special education								●
15. Local education authority dispensation					●			

Source: 21st Century Education Research Institute, 2011, p. 6

2.4 Channels for *Zexiao* 51

Nation Wide

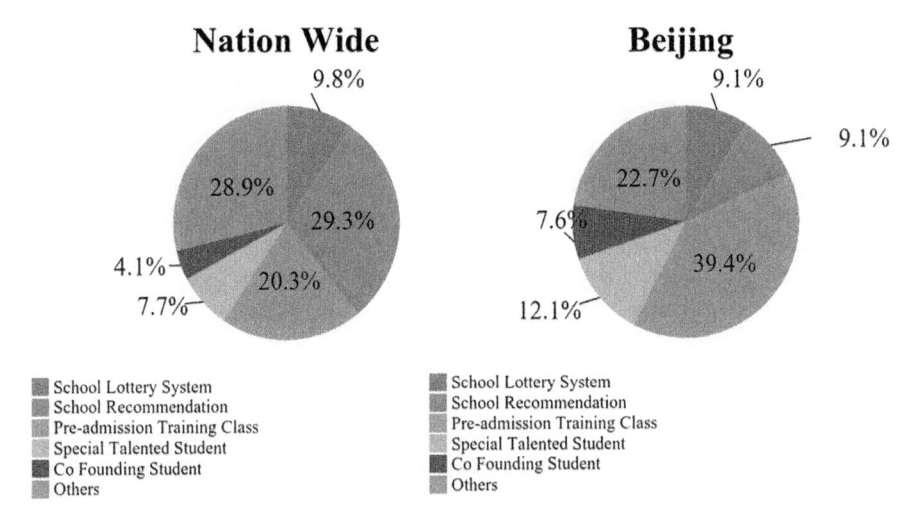

9.8%
28.9%
29.3%
4.1%
20.3%
7.7%

- School Lottery System
- School Recommendation
- Pre-admission Training Class
- Special Talented Student
- Co Founding Student
- Others

Beijing

9.1%
9.1%
22.7%
7.6%
39.4%
12.1%

- School Lottery System
- School Recommendation
- Pre-admission Training Class
- Special Talented Student
- Co Founding Student
- Others

Fig. 2.2 School admission options (Nationwide & Beijing) (Source: 21st Century Education Research Institute, 2011, p. 62)

2.4 Channels for *Zexiao*

The literature review showed that the diverse channels for parents to commit *Zexiao* could be categorized into three types, including money-based *Zexiao*, power-based *Zexiao*, and achievement-based *Zexiao* (China Education Daily, 2003, September 15; Fang, 2011; Li, 2009).[20] According to *China Education Daily*, money-based *Zexiao* badly destroyed the equity in education, power-based *Zexiao* negatively influenced social value and morality, and achievement-based *Zexiao* intensified students' burden in study (China Education Daily, 2003, September 15). In this part, I introduce the three types of *Zexiao* in details, respectively. Then, I explain the complexity of *Zexiao* by elaborating the channels for *Zexiao* introduced in the beginning of this section. The information involved in this section was collected from various sources, such as newspapers, journal papers, and books.

---

[20] Mainly, existing discourses on *Zexiao* was categorized as money-based *Zexiao*, power-based *Zexiao*, and score-based *Zexiao*. With the abolishment of the entrance exam to junior high schools, comparing with exam scores, awards received from various contests, and certificates issued for special talents and other relevant certificates is becoming important in the process of *Zexiao*. Therefore, in this research, I would like to use the term "achievement-based *Zexiao*" to involve both exam-based *Zexiao* and certificate-based *Zexiao*.

2.4.1 Money-Based Zexiao (Yiqian Zexiao)

The first type of *Zexiao* is money-based *Zexiao*. According to Fang (2011, p. 131), money-based *Zexiao* refers to the practice of sending children to well-known schools by paying money. There are two main channels for conducting money-based *Zexiao*, including *Zexiaofei* (fees charged for choosing a school) and tuition for converted schools (*zhuanzhixiaoxuefei*). Money-based *Zexiao* has its history with the change of school admission policy in China. In the early stage, although the school admission to junior high school was still based on the exam scores in the late 1980s and the early 1990s, parents were "willing" to pay money for enrolling children in well-known public schools if children's scores were lower than the enrollment standards of these schools.

Although the charges for this type of school admission were considered as unauthorized school fees by education authority and was strictly banned, money-based *Zexiao* became a common practice from the late 1980s onward. In 1984, the problem of charging *Yijia* student[21] has already been reported in the news related to the charge of unauthorized school fees in Jiangxi Province and Sichuan Province (Cheng, 1984, December 8; Huang, 1984, April 24). In 1993, according to the Shanghai Education Bureau, a survey showed that within 21 schools, 11 schools had "*Yijia* students." In one key school, they enrolled 20 *Yijia* studens and charged 230,000 yuan. More importantly, this amount of money was not recorded (Quan, 1993, July 29). Conversely, in Xiamen, although the local education authority declaimed that the school admission and fee charge should not be linked and the payment should be paid voluntarily. The enrollment of "*Xuanxiao* students" and the charge of these students were allowed by the local education authority. More interestingly, the "education donation" fee was collected and managed by the local government. Fifty percent of the donation is designated by the local government to be spent on teaching facilities to improve teaching conditions; 20% of donations is to be submitted to the upper education authority to assist in the construction of schools in difficulties; and 30% of the donation could be put into fund generation by schools to supplement teachers' salaries (Tan, 1993, September 14). According to a letter to the *China Education Daily* from a junior high school manager in Beijing, *Zexiao-based* fund generation was 140 million yuan in 1994 and 126 million yuan in 1995. In 1995, within 126 million yuan, 40% was used for the improvement of school facilities, 15% was used for teachers' salaries, 15% was used for teachers' welfare, and there was a 40 million yuan surplus. However, 70% of 126 million yuan was used for only less than 100 schools among 3,000 primary schools and 700

---

[21] In Chinese, "*Yijia*" means negotiable price. "*Yijia* students" (*yijiasheng*) refers to students whose school admission can be negotiated by paying a school fee. And the school fee is negotiable. "*Xuanxiao* students" refers to students who choose their preferred schools without going to the school assignment by the local education authority. "*Jiedu*" means borrowing space for schooling. "*Xuanxiao*" means choosing school. "*Jiedu s*tudents" refers to students who do not have local *hukou* in specific school districts enter school through paying money.

2.4 Channels for Zexiao

junior high schools. It is clear to see there was a big imbalance in the distribution of education resources (Liu, 1996, July 11).

Zexiaofei, as one channel for money-based *Zexiao*, has already been widely practiced by the public. And it was considered as the reason for the enlargement of the inequality gap between public schools (Huang, 1996, August 4). News in *China Education Daily* in 1995 reported that it was popular for parents to pay a fee for entering into key schools in Beijing. Parents pointed out that the price charged by the key schools in Beijing was surprising and over their affordability. The minimum was about 20,000 or 30,000 yuan, and the maximum was about 70,000 or 80,000 yuan. It seemed that it did not matter whether the students were qualified or not. The enrollment in key schools was based on how much parents could pay (Pu & Jian, 1995, August 19). In 1996, a survey report conducted in Beijing showed that the part of private educational donation in total education donation increased dramatically from 32% in 1993 to 82% in 1995 (Qiao et al., 1996, p. 46). According to a survey conducted by Beijing Normal University in 2005, within urban areas of Beijing, the average *Zexiaofei* was 19,600 yuan at primary school level and 13,700 yuan at junior high school level. *Zexiaofei* at the primary school level was 36.11% of family income. And *Zexiaofei* at the junior high school level was 35.13% of family income (Li, 2011, p. 146). In 2008, a nationwide survey on family cost in compulsory education showed that, at the national level, *Zexiaofei* shared the largest part of family costs in terms of school education (China Education Daily, 2008, March 6). In other words, it is difficult for low-income families to take part in *Zexiao* through paying education donation fee. According to another nationwide survey conducted by the *China Youth Daily* in 2009, 75.8% of participants considered *Zexiaofei* as the most unequal education phenomenon in China (Xiao, 2009, December 15).

The charge of tuition for converted schools, as another channel for money-based *Zexiao*, started with the privatization of the public education system. Beginning in the mid-1990s, the government positively promoted the development of *minban* (people-run) schools[22] at the compulsory education level in order to supplement the limited government investment in education and to accommodate the growing demand for parental choice for children's schooling (Tsang, 2000, 2003; Wang, 2009; Wu, 2008; Yang, 2006). No doubt, the conversion from public schools into *minban* schools generated school revenue through charging high tuition from parents. It mobilized additional private resources for education development. Simultaneously, to some extent, this reform provided more choices for parents to send children to schools they prefer. However, with the growing interests of schools regarding the conversion reform, this policy was distorted at the implementation level. Some key schools recognized the benefits from school conversion and started to convert from public schools to *minban* schools or establish branch schools affiliated to key schools. As a result, the conversion of these schools stimulated parents'

---

[22] According to Tsang (2003, p. 165), people-run schools are schools sponsored and managed by a community of people or a collective organization and funded by resources from the community or financial assistance from the state, etc.

aspirations for paying tuition fees for children's *Zexiao* (Xiaoxin Wu, p. 601). In 2005, CCTV reported the fee charge for entering into a converted school invested by two key schools in Nantong City. By charging each student 18,000 yuan, this converted school generated 20 million yuan through enrolling 1,200 G7 students (Yang, 2006, pp. 130–131).

2.4.2 Power (guanxi)-based Zexiao (Yiquan(guanxi) Zexiao)

The second type of *Zexiao* is power-based one. In Chinese culture, power refers to the sociomoral situation, or peer-group pressure, that one may use to change the attitudes, motivation, or behavior of another to conform to one's will during the process of social interaction (Hwang, 1987, p. 947). And *guanxi* is understood as "connections" between people in order to exchange favors (Bian, 1994; Hwang, 1987). As Bian (1994) clarified, for two individuals to develop *guanxi*, they must know a good deal about each other and share a good deal with each other. Therefore, in terms of education, people use power to satisfy people's demands for education. As Fang (2011) defined, power (*guanxi*)-based *Zexiao* refers to the practice that some leaders utilize their power to give pressure on school side in order to help their children or children of related people to take part in *Zexiao*. Mainly, there are two channels for power-based *Zexiao*. One is a memo student (*tiaozisheng*). The other is a co-founding student (*gongjiansheng*).

In terms of memo students, generally, memos come from powerful departments in one district administration, such as an industrial and commercial department, tax bureau, planning department and discipline inspection department, and so forth (Fan, 2005, May 9). A popular school principal pointed out that every year he could meet many *Zexiao* students and receive various memos from the provincial to district levels. It was almost 600 pieces on average. These memos could be divided into different categories, including memos from government institutes, memos from education authority or education-related institutes, memos from other administrative departments (e.g., police, fire, finance, sanitation, tax), and memos from other related work units (Li, 2007, June 19). According to a survey conducted in Beijing, *guanxi* students come from work units which control daily school management, such as water, gas, heat, sanitation, community authority, police station, and so forth; children of teaching staffs; students through personal donation-based enrollment; and students through co-founding-based enrollment (Qiao et al., 1996, pp. 46–47). According to a report published in the *China Education Daily*, an official, who is in charge of a Beijing district education authority, clarified that in this district there were 2,000 memo students based on precontact from leaders at the upper level and various *guanxi*. Power-based *Zexiao* includes both leader-based *Zexiao* and powerful institute-based *Zexiao*. Either of both is difficult for education administration or school leaders to refuse (Li, 2007, June 19). According to Qiao and her colleagues (1996, p. 46), there were 10 key primary schools and 14 key junior high schools in Dongcheng District of Beijing. The enrollment ratio of memo

2.4 Channels for *Zexiao*

students was 20.56% of total enrollment. And the enrollment ratio of *guanxi* student was 26.54% of total enrollment in 1996. A recent survey report on *Zexiao* in Beijing explains that a memo student refers to "the backdoor student" (*houmensheng*). Some parents use special *guanxi* to send children to key schools. It shows that most of the memo students are directly managed by leaders at the city or district level. In every district, annually, some key schools have to leave several open positions for memo students. Some memo students come from commerce and industry administrative departments, tax bureau, city planning sections, and so on. And some of them are from high ranking government officials in the central government. The quota of memo student annual enrollment is from 8% to 10% of total enrollment in key Beijing schools (21st Century Education Research Institute, 2011).

As to co-founding students, in recent years, it became a sensitive term in the process of *Zexiao*. Some government institutes and work units signed agreements with well-known schools at the compulsory education level in order to get enrollment quota for their staffs' children through paying a specific amount of money (Fang, 2011). Students enrolled through this way are called co-founding students. As Wu (2008) introduced, it is common in China for schools (especially the key schools) to cooperate with some work units through an exchange education donation (co-founding fee) with an enrollment quota for children from the work units. For instance, according to the *China Education Daily*, one ministry paid an annual 600,000 yuan as sponsor fees to one university-affiliated school in order to enroll their staffs' children to one class in the department of a junior high school and one class in the department of a senior high school. Students enrolled in these two classes generally had lower scores than students enrolled through official ways. The exchange between education donations and school admission was widely criticized by the public. Moreover, there was a "shadow donation" to education through the exchange of money and power. It is reported that one Hong Kong businessman came to a key school in Beijing to show his willingness to donate 100,000 yuan to the school. As an exchange, the school needed to enroll three relatives of the businessman. The school accepted the deal. However, in the beginning of the semester, the school found that the parents of the three children worked in Ministry of Commerce (Pu & Jian, 1995, August 19).

Sometimes, the co-founding fees are collected from parents by co-founding work units and are paid to the school directly. Some units are even granted privileges without paying to schools with cooperation. In Beijing, there are 400 pairs of schools and work units that have established "co-founding" relationships. Table 2.2 shows that FESCO[23] as a state-owned company in Beijing established co-founding agreements with 13 key schools or popular schools in Beijing for their employees' children. Basically, schools with co-founding work units are key schools and rela-

---

[23] FESCO refers to Beijing Foreign Enterprise Human Resources Service Co., Ltd., founded in 1979 and being the first state-owned company in China to provide professional service of human resources to foreign enterprises' representative offices in China foreign financial institutions and economic organizations, has a long history of providing professional HR service, and is highly experienced in the market and fully qualified to provide such service.

Table 2.2 List of co-founding school with FESCO of Beijing (2011)

School	District	Characteristics
Beijing Dongzhimen Junior High School	*Dongcheng*	Key school (district level)
Beijing No.2 Junior High School Branch School	*Dongcheng*	Key school (city level)
Beijing No.5 Junior High School Branch School	*Dongcheng*	Key school (city level)
Beijing No.171 Junior High School	*Dongcheng*	Key school (district level)
Beijing No.166 Junior High School	*Dongcheng*	Demonstration school (city level)
Beijing No.13 Junior High School Branch School	*Xicheng*	Key school (district level)
Beijing Sanfan Junior High School	*Xicheng*	Converted school
Beijing No.8 Junior High School	*Xicheng*	Key school (city level)
Beijing No.80 Junior High School	*Chaoyang*	Key school (district level)
Chenjinglun Junior High School	*Chaoyang*	Demonstration school (city level)
Chenjinglun Junior High School Branch School	*Chaoyang*	Converted school
Haidian Experiment Junior High School	*Haidian*	Popular public school in Haidian district
Beijing Bayi Junior High school	*Haidian*	Key school (district level)

Source: 21st Century Education Research Institute, 2011, p. 17

tively popular schools. And the work units are mainly government institutes or "affluent" administration departments (Wang, 2008). Currently, co-founding-based school admission becomes more complicated since popular schools want to have their own quality control of students they enroll. They provide children of co-founding work units opportunities to take entrance "test" for going to popular schools. The final result of the enrollment depends on each child's capacity. In practice, this type of school admission has a "one stone for two birds" effect on the school side. On the one hand, schools can receive co-founding fees for school development. On the other, the quota for co-founding students enriches the flexibility of enrollment in popular schools. These schools can fully utilize the quota to select students they want. Consequently, co-founding-based school admission has been criticized by the public since it favors the privileged groups while excluding other groups. It is considered as a collective power-based *Zexiao*, and it has led to increased education inequality (Fang, 2011; Yang, 2006). A recent survey showed that in one key school of Beijing, there were 70 seats reserved for co-founding students with a total enrollment of only 400 seats in 2011. Interestingly, more than 400 children took part in the entrance test for the 70 seats (21st Century Education Research Institute, 2011).

2.4.3 "Achievement"-based Zexiao (Yifen Zexiao)

The third type is achievement-based *Zexiao*. Achievement-based school admission mainly depends on students' learning achievement and is the traditional approach for students to transit from G6 to G7. However, with the abolishment of entrance exams to junior high schools, the meaning of the term "achievement" was diversified. According to Fang (2011, p. 132), it refers to the practice of *Zexiao* by achievement in exams. In general, there are two channels for achievement-based *Zexiao*, including school recommendation students (*tuiyousheng*) and special talent students (*techangsheng*). With the abolishment of entrance exams to junior high schools, besides achievement made inside of schools, such as awards or high scores on comprehensive exams, various types of academic certificates, special talent certificates, and even exam scores received from private tutoring institutes have been recognized as "achievement" which can be utilized as important requirements for school admission.

One of the channels for achievement-based *Zexiao* is to become a school recommendation student. School recommendation (also called school recommendation lottery-based admission) is considered as one of the most important school admission options at the compulsory education level. The objective of the option is to provide access for students to popular schools. It is also considered as an approach for key schools and popular schools to select students. According to the number of G6 students and the enrollment plan in popular schools, the quota of school recommendation student is decided by district education authorities on an annual basis (Du & Zhang, 2011, May 10). In Beijing, this approach started in 2008. And the quota increased gradually in different districts. In 2011, this quota was 13% of total G6 students in *Haidian* District, 20% in *Dongcheng* District, 10% in *Shijingshan* District, and 30% in *Xicheng* District (21st Century Education Research Institute, 2011, p. 8). The selection standard of school recommendation students is complicated and diverse in different districts. It includes various criteria, such as good health, overall development (*quanmianfazhan*),[24] three excellence students (*sanhaosheng*),[25] excellent student leaders, good academic achievement, etc. For example, in 2010, *Xicheng* District in Beijing took in three excellence students at the municipal or district level as the first criterion for school recommendation student selection. And the second criterion is the achievement in the comprehensive

---

[24] The overall development, originally defined by Mao Zedong, refers to the holistic moral, intellectual, physical development of individual students. Deng Xiaoping reemphasized this idea in 1977 (Encyclopedia of China Publishing House, 1984).

[25] Regarding three excellence students, Mingyuan Gu, President of Chinese Education Society, showed his opinion to abolish the evaluation activity in 1998. He elaborated the positive role of this evaluation in stipulating that students' motivation increased to study hard. On the other hand, he pointed out that since some places linked it with education transition, it has been involved into the track of exam-oriented education. And thus, "three excellence student" becomes the competition for education transition (Gu & Li, 2007).

exams held in the second semester in G5 and the first semester in G6.[26] In 2011, in *Haidian* District of Beijing, criteria of school recommendation students included not only the exam scores in G5 but also included various awards and recognized special talents (21st Century Education Research Institute, 2011). Since school recommendation students should be well-rounded, it forces students to take after-school classes or private tutoring in order to get as many certificates as possible to meet the stringent selection criteria. This approach intensified competition in education transition (Du & Zhang, 2011, May 10).

The other channel is special talent students. It is one of the options for parents to enroll children in schools with high quality. As Wang (2008, pp. 140–142) illustrated, there is no explanation on special talent students in Chinese dictionaries since this term is created by educators in recent years. This innovation can be considered as a magical "open sesame" spell for students to skip the school lottery system and go to key schools through education transition from G6 to G7. According to Wu (2008), special talents refer to any skills normally learned outside the school curriculum, such as being good at certain kind of sports and having a musical talent and special extracurricular activities in academic subjects like English or math. Mainly, there are three widely used channels for becoming special talent students, including Olympic math (*aoshu*), Public English Test (PETS; *gonggongyingyukaoshi*),[27] and Pre-admission training classes (*zhankengban*).[28]

In Beijing, special talent-based school admission is officially permitted at the municipal and district levels. Annually, the municipal government sets up the schedule for special talent student tests. Each student is allowed to apply for two or three schools within the district they registered. Mainly, special talent students are divided into three categories, including sports talent students, art talent students, and science talent students (Beijing Municipal Education Committee, 2006, 2007, 2008, 2009, 2011). In 2011, in *Haidian* District of Beijing, the quota of special talent students was 11% of the total enrollment of G7 students. The quota was 12% in *Xicheng* District of Beijing and 10% in *Dongcheng* District (21st Century Education

---

[26] From 2003, Beijing Municipal Education Commission established a compulsory education monitoring system through a standard test for students in G5 in some districts. This system was gradually introduced at the city level in recent years. According to this standard, the result of the standard test in G5 shares 60% of the total student quality evaluation. It is considered as the only standard evaluation of students from G1 to G5. Retrieved from http://www.jiajiaxue.com/Course-987.html, http://www.aoshu.com/e/20100712/4c3a888f4d492.shtml, accessed on July 6, 2011.

[27] According to National Education Examination Authority, PETS is a five-level framework of proficiency English examination in China. It is being established to satisfy the requirements of social reform and opening up policies, to assist in meeting the needs of expansion in communications with foreign countries and to reform the current public English examination in China. The five-level framework ranges from the level of English equivalent to that of junior high school level to the level required by graduates studying/working overseas. It is available to all learners of the language, with no restriction on age, profession, or academic background. Starting in 1999, there is an increasing number of participants in PETS. In 2007, the number of participants reached over one million for the first time. Retrieved from http://sk.neea.edu.cn/yydjks/xmjs.jsp?class_id=26_12_01_03, accessed on March 2, 2012.

[28] According to Wu (2012), *Zhankeng* refers to "place-holding."

2.4 Channels for *Zexiao*

Fig. 2.3 Special talent-based entrance exam (Dongcheng District, Beijing) (Source: Taken by author on May 21, 2011, Beijing)

Research Institute, 2011, p. 8). Figure 2.3 shows parents waiting for their children outside two junior high schools in Beijing which held the entrance exams for selecting special talent students in Beijing.

Olympic math[29] is one of the channels for becoming a special talent student. As introduced above, in order to become special talent students, students have to take various contests and competitions to get certificates and awards to prove their talents. Olympic math contests provide opportunities for students to get such an opportunity to fulfill their objectives. Surveys showed Olympic math was the most popular option for children to get access to popular schools. In big cities of China, 80% of students over G3 studied Olympic math, and 90% of students in G5 went to Olympic math classes in a survey conducted in 2004 at the national level (Yang, 2004, February 18). A survey conducted at the national level in 2005 showed that 95% of parents took Olympic math as an approach for children's school admission (Chai, 2005, March 2). A recent survey conducted in Beijing in 2011 showed 62.2% of parents involved sent children to Olympic math classes (21st Century Education Research Institute, 2011). Some key junior high schools started taking Olympic math as a criterion for student selection in school admission. As a result, Olympic math training became popular. Figure 2.4 shows the Olympic math textbook corner in one of the biggest Beijing bookstores. Parents and students can easily buy diverse types of Olympic math textbooks from such stores.

Similar to the role of Olympic math in *Zexiao*, in recent years, the Public English Test System (PETS) is also closely linked with *Zexiao*, especially after the promulgation of the prohibition of linking Olympic math with education transition and school admission by the Ministry of Education in 2000 (Ministry of Education,

---

[29] According to Fang (2011), the International Olympic Math Contest started from 1959 aiming at searching for genius in math among junior high school students. From 1985, China officially sent players to take part in the international contest. In recent years, winners in this contest were enrolled by top-ranking universities.

Fig. 2.4 Olympic math textbook corner (Source: Taken by author in Beijing Wangfujing Bookstore on May 18, 2011, Beijing)

2000). According to Fang (2011), since many schools take PETS as a criterion for school admission, there are many primary school students who take such exams every year. According to *Beijing Wanbao*, annually there were 100,000 students at the basic education level who take PETS. And the majority of them were primary school students. Some students started their preparation for the exam since G3. In a class-based survey held by *Beijing Wanbao*, 27 out of 40 G6 students have experience in taking PETS. Among the 27 students, 19 students took PETS for education transition to junior high schools (Beijing Wanbao, 2007, May 16). Responding to the growing participation of students at the primary education level in PETS, in 2007, Ministry of Education released regulations to prohibit the participation of students at the compulsory education level to take PETS (Ministry of Education, 2007). In the same survey mentioned above, unexpectedly, regarding the order made by the Ministry of Education which originally aimed at reducing study burden of students, 36 students believed that if the junior high school admission policy did not change, other exams would soon arise to replace PETS even though PETS was terminated (Beijing Wanbao, 2007, May 16). The news showed the importance of PETS to parents and children. Responding to the decision made by the Ministry of Education to prohibit students at the compulsory education level to take PETS, 28 parents from Haerbin wrote to the Ministry of Education a letter to request them to amend the released order to free students at the compulsory education level to take part in PETS (Tianfu Zaobao, 2007, July 2).

Pre-admission training class is a new innovation for *Zexiao*. It has become one widely accepted channel for parents to send children to popular schools. A survey conducted in Beijing showed that 37% of parents sent children to such class for

2.4 Channels for *Zexiao*

education transition (21st Century Education Research Institute, 2011). In general, it has several titles, such as *Zhankengban* or *Kengban*. *Kengban* refers to classes held by public schools or classes collaborated between public schools and private tutoring institutes for selecting primary school students from G6 to G7. Students cannot enter into *Kengban* without passing entrance exams for this class. After entering into *Kengban*, students have to take weekly or monthly tests in order to get an advantage for the final student selection (Wu, 2012). Based on past records in sending students to popular schools, parents categorized such *Kengban* into several levels, such as *Golden Keng (jinkeng)*, *Silver Keng (yinkeng)*, *Earth Keng (tukeng)*, and *Trash Keng (fenkeng)*. In order to increase the likelihood of their child being admitted to their top choice, some parents even send children to several such classes at the same time (Fang, 2011).[30] According to the 21st Century Education Research Institute (2011), *Zhankengban* originally started in 1998. With the full implementation of the lottery-based school assignment system from G6 to G7, on the one hand, parents refused to enroll children in regular schools. On the other hand, key schools had a concern on student quality and were unwilling to accept assigned students through a lottery system or even school recommendation students. As a result, Olympic math training-based student selection for key schools started over. Therefore, *Zhankengban* became an important avenue to help students gain access to key schools. Meanwhile, these classes became a platform for key schools to select students they prefer.

In addition to the above, there is another approach for *Zexiao* called *Xuequfang*-based *Zexaio*. *Xuequfang* refers to housings which are located in the school district having good quality public schools. With the elimination of money-based *Zexiao* and power-based *Zexiao*, parents believe *Xuequfang*-based *Zexiao* is the most efficient approach to enrolling their kids in good quality schools (Fan, 2015). Research shows that houses located in school districts with quality education facilities become more expensive than the school districts which do not have quality education resources. The demand for *Xuequfang* stipulates the rise of housing prices in the school districts which have quality schools (Shi & Wang, 2014; Wen, Zhang, & Zhang, 2014; Zheng, Hu, & Wang, 2016). In 2011, the price of housing within the school districts with key primary schools was RMB 2,266 per square meter more than the housing which is outside the school districts (Zheng et al.). A survey conducted by the Shanghai Academy of Social Sciences in 2016 showed that 11.1% of respondents bought *Xuequfang* for their kids' school promotion to quality public schools (Shanghai Academy of Social Sciences, 2016). In another survey conducted

---

[30] A survey conducted by the 21st Century Education Research Institute gives a detailed explanation on these terms. "Golden Class" refers to classes which have close connection with the top-ranking junior high schools. Without taking such a class, it is impossible to be enrolled by the top-ranking schools. "Silver Class" refers to the classes which are closely connected with the popular schools among parents, and the possibility of enrollment through taking these classes is relatively lower than "Golden Class." "Earth Class" refers to classes related to ordinary key schools. "Trash Class" represents classes which have no relation with key school enrollment (21st Century Education Research Institute, 2011).

in 19 major cities of China, 57.27% of the respondents believed the price of *Xuequfang* was seriously expensive (Zhang, 2016).

2.5 Summary: *Zexiao* ≠ School Choice

The literature review illustrates the essential difference between school choice and *Zexiao*. The essential difference reminds us to distinguish *Zexiao* from school choice when it comes to talking about channels for public school admission in China. Table 2.3 further demonstrates the different nature between *Zexiao* and school choice. The most different parts between *Zexiao* and school choice include the government's attitudes, basic ideology, purpose, and approaches. Firstly, in contrast to school choice policies that are promoted by the government, the government in China generally held a negative attitude toward the adoption of *Zexiao* in compulsory education. Meanwhile, due to the limited educational investment by the government, they also depended on tuition fees generated through *Zexiao* to supplement the education finance despite the opinion that it is against the principle of free compulsory education. Secondly, the basic concepts of education reform are different even though both are influenced by neoliberalism. The basic concept of education reform in China is for the modernization of the state which takes education as a tool for cultivating human resources necessary for the country's development. In contrast, school choice as a policy in education reform in most of the developed world is based on the concept of efficiency of public education, freedom for consumers in the education market, and accommodation of needs from consumers. Thirdly, the different basic concepts of education reforms have different purposes for *Zexiao* and school choice. In China, mainly, *Zexiao* can be considered as the approach for generating funds to supplement limited educational investment by the government, while school choice policy aims at improving efficiency, quality, and accountability

Table 2.3 Comparison of nature between *Zexiao* and school choice

	Zexiao	School choice
Government's policy	Official opposition/dilemma	Official support and promotion
Basic concept of education reform	Efficiency as priority (profit-driven)	Neoliberalism/freedom/need-driven
Purpose	Fund generation for supplement of the limited government's investment in education	Competition among public schools/efficiency, quality, and accountability of public education/diverse educational needs
Approach/channel	Money-based/power-based/achievement-based	School autonomy/diverse choices for parents and students
Effects	Increasing inequality in education/polarization of public schools/exam-driven education	Increasing inequality in education/diverse education

Source: Created by author

of public education through competition among public schools and choice of consumers in the education market. Fourthly, in contrast to the government subsidy-based school choice (e.g., education vouchers) in the developed world, the tuition-based *Zexiao* in China is covered entirely by parents. Besides the achievement-based *Zexiao* that is similar as the one in the developed world, power-based *Zexiao* through parents' social capital (*guanxi*) and money became a common practice in public school admission. Finally, the effect of school choice promoted diverse education in the developed world. Meanwhile, it caused the inequality in education caused by the effect of family background on parents' choices for children's education. As to China's case, *Zexiao* intensified inequality in public education. And it also fostered the exam-driven education in China.

To conclude this chapter, the review of the development of *Zexiao* showed that the positional competition in public school admission to junior high schools had been widely practiced in urban China, particularly in major cities. The review further distinguished between *Zexiao* and school choice even though they are lexical equivalents. Choice in public school admission to junior high schools in urban China does not have the same meaning of freedom or shared focus on the quality improvement of the public education system. As Kipins (2008) pointed out, *Zexiao* in urban China does not present the neoliberalism discussion in the context of school choice in another part of the world. Besides its rapid expansion, the review highlighted the diversification and the increasing complexity of *Zexiao*. *Zexiao* has been committed by money, power, and children's achievement. Furthermore, the review asserts that there are various channels for parents to take part in *Zexiao*. Meanwhile, it also showed that the stakeholders involved in *Zexiao* are not limited to parents. The diverse channels for *Zexiao* have closely connected public schools, local education authorities, private tutoring institutes, and parents' work units in the process of public school admission to junior high schools.

References

21st Century Education Research Institute. (2011). *Beijingshi "xiaoshengchu" Zexiaore de zhili: luzaihefang?* (Where is the way for alleviation of *Zexiao* fever in transition to junior high schools?). Beijing: 21st Century Education Research Institute.
Adnett, N., & Davies, P. (1999). Schooling quasi-markets: Reconciling economic and sociological analyses. *British Journal of Educational Studies, 47*(3), 221–234.
Andre-Bechely, L. (2005). *Could it be otherwise? Parents and the inequities of public school choice*. New York: Routledge.
Appleton, S., & Song, L. (2008). The myth of the "new urban poverty"? Trends in urban poverty in China, 1988–2002. In J. R. Logan (Ed.), *Urban China in transition* (pp. 48–65). Oxford, UK: Blackwell Publishing.
Bai, L. (2010). Human capital or humane talent? Rethinking the nature of education in China from a comparative historical perspective. *Frontiers of Education in China, 5*(1), 104–129.
Ball, S. J. (1993). Education markets, choice and social class: The market as a class strategy in the UK and the USA. *British Journal of Sociology of Education, 14*(1), 3–19.

Ball, S. J. (1998). Big policies/small world: An introduction to international perspectives in education policy. *Comparative Education, 34*(2), 119–130.
Beijing Municipal Education Committee. (2006). *Opinions on primary school and junior high school admission*. Beijing, China: Beijing Municipal Education Committee.
Beijing Municipal Education Committee. (2007). *Opinions on primary school and junior high school admission*. Beijing, China: Beijing Municipal Education Committee.
Beijing Municipal Education Committee. (2008). *Opinions on primary school and junior high school admission*. Beijing, China: Beijing Municipal Education Committee.
Beijing Municipal Education Committee. (2009). *Opinions on primary school and junior high school admission*. Beijing, China: Beijing Municipal Education Committee.
Beijing Municipal Education Committee. (2011). *Opinions on school admission at compulsory education level*. Beijing, China: Beijing Municipal Education Committee.
Beijing Wanbao. (2007, May 16). *Jinkao quanguo gonggong yingyu dengji jiefang shiwan haizi* (Permission for 100,000 kids for PETS). Retrieved July 15, 2011, from http://edu.sina.com.cn/yyks/2007-05-16/112482660.html
Bian, Y. (1994). Guanxi and the allocation of urban jobs in China. *The China Quarterly, 140*, 971–999.
Bian, Y. (2002). Chinese social stratification and social mobility. *Annual Review of Sociology, 28*, 91–116.
Bonal, X., & Tarabini, A. (2013). The role of PISA in sharing hegemonic educational discourses, policies and practices: The case of Spain. *Research in Comparative and International Education, 8*, 335–341.
Breakspear, S. (2012). *The policy impact of PISA: An exploration of the normative effects of international benchmarking in school system performance*. Retrieved August 13, 2014, from https://doi.org/10.1787/5k9fdfqffr28-en
Bridgham, P. (1968). Mao's cultural revolution in 1967: The struggle to seize power. *The China Quarterly, 34*, 6–37.
Brown, P., Halsey, A. H., Lauder, H., & Wells, A. S. (1997). The transformation of education and society: An introduction. In A. H. Halsey, H. Lauder, P. Brown, & A. S. Wells (Eds.), *Education: Culture, economy, society* (pp. 1–44). Oxford, UK: Oxford University Press.
Brown, P., & Lauder, H. (1997). Education, globalization, and economic development. In A. H. Halsey, H. Lauder, P. Brown, & A. S. Wells (Eds.), *Education: Culture, economy, society* (pp. 172–192). Oxford, UK: Oxford University Press.
Carl, J. (1994). Parental choice as national policy in England and the United States. *Comparative Education Review, 38*(3), 294–322.
Carnoy, M. (1995). Structural adjustment and the changing face of education. *International Labour Review, 134*(5), 653–673.
CCTV (Producer). (2011). *Morning News*. Retrieved June 10, 2011, from http://news.cntv.cn/china/20110603/101697.shtml
Chai, M. (2005, March 2). Cong 'aoshu' xianxiang shuokaiqu (Starting from 'Olympic Math'). *China Education Daily*, p. 1.
Che, H. (2011, November 24). Diaocha cheng woguo *Zexiao* fasheng gailv yu sicheng (Survey Shows One-Quarter Students Chose *Zexiao*). *Gongren Ribao*, p. 3.
Chen, J., Hou, W., & Jin, S. (2008). *A review of the Chinese Gini coefficient from 1978 to 2005*. Paper presented at the International Symposium on China's Local Government Finance Reforms Peking University. Retrieved September 19, 2012, from http://ssrn.com/abstract=1328998
Chen, S. (2002). Economic reform and social change in China: Past, present, and future of the economic state. *International Journal of Politics, Culture, and Society, 15*(4), 569–589.
Cheng, T., & Selden, M. (1994). The origins and social consequences of China's Hukou system. *The China Quarterly, 139*, 644–668.
Cheng, Y. (1984, December 8). Xuexiao buneng ban 'Yijianban' zhao 'Yijiaxuesheng' (Prohibition on 'Yijiaban' and 'Yijiaxuesheng'). *China Education Daily*, p. 1.

References

China Education Daily. (2003, September 15). Shangxue yao jiao naxie fei? (What fees should be paid for schooling?). *China Education Daily*, p. 2.

China Education Daily. (2008, March 6). *Yiwu jiaoyu jieduan jiating jiaoyu zhichu you duoshao* (Cost of compulsory education for families). *China Education Daily*, p. 9.

Chinese Communist Party Central Committee. (1985). *Reform of China's education structure*. Beijing, China: Chinese Communist Party Central Committee.

Chinese Communist Party Central Committee. (1994). *Opinions on further strengthening and promoting moral education in schools*. Beijing, China: Chinese Communist Party Central Committee.

Chubb, J. E., & Moe, T. M. (1990). *Politics markets & America's schools*. Washington, DC: The Brookings Institution.

Chubb, J. E., & Moe, T. M. (1997). Politics, markets, and the organization of schools. In A. H. Halsey, H. Lauder, P. Brown, & A. S. Wells (Eds.), *Education: Culture, economy, and society* (pp. 363–381). Oxford, UK: Oxford University Press.

Cleverley, J. (1985). *The schooling of China*. North Sydney, Australia: George Allen & Unwin Australia Pty Ltd.

Dello-Iacovo, B. (2009). Curriculum reform and quality Education' in China: An overview. *International Journal of Educational Development, 29*(3), 241–249.

Deng, Z., & Treiman, D. J. (1997). The impact of the cultural revolution on trends in educational attainment in the People's Republic of China. *American Journal of Sociology, 103*(2), 391–428.

Dewey, J. (1916). *Democracy and education*. New York: Macmillan.

Dierkes, J. (2008). Japanese shadow education: The consequences of school choice. In M. Forsey, S. Davies, & G. Walford (Eds.), *The globalisation of school choice?* (pp. 231–248). Oxford, UK: Symposium Books.

Du, G., & Zhang, J. (2011, May 10). Beijing yancha 'juanzizhuxuekuan' yanjin qiaoli mingmu she *Zexiaofei* (Educational donation as *Zexiaofei* is not allowed in Beijing). *Guangmin Ribao*, p. 6.

Encyclopedia of China Publishing House. (1984). *China education yearbook*. Beijing, China: Encyclopedia of China Publishing House.

Fan, W. (2005). Beijing 'diannaopaiwei' quanxian bengkui? (*The failure of computer lottery school assignment in Beijing?*) Retrieved April 13, 2010, from http://zqb.cyol.com/content/2005-05/09/content_1079278.htm

Fan, W. (2015, April 15). Jiaogaixinzhengxia Jiujinggaibugai Maixuequfang (Whether we should buy Xuequfang or not under the newly launched education reform). *China Youth Daily*, p. 1.

Fang, X. (Ed.). (2011). *Zhongguo jiaoyu shida redian wenti* (Ten Hot Topics of China's Education). Fuzhou, China: The Straits Publishing & Distributing Group.

Farrell, D., Gersch, U. A., & Stephenson, E. (2006). The value of China's emerging middle class. *The Mckinsey Quarterly, 2006 Special Edition*, pp. 60–69.

Forsey, M., Davies, S., & Walford, G. (2008). *The globalisation of school choice? An introduction to key issues and concerns*. Oxford, UK: Symposium Books.

Friedman, M. (1962). *Capitalism and freedom*. Chicago: The University of Chicago Press.

Friedman, M., & Friedman, R. D. (1980). *Free to choose: A personal statement*. New York: Harcourt Brace Jovanovich.

Gao, L. (2013, October 16). Nuli Rang Quantirenmin Xiaoyou Genghaogenggongpingde Jiaoyu (To make a more equal and better education for people in China). *China Education Daily*, p. 1.

Gewirtz, S., Ball, S. J., & Bowe, R. (1995). *Markets, choice and equity in education*. Buckingham, UK: Open University Press.

Giles, J., Park, A., & Wang, M. (2008). *The great proletarian cultural revolution, disruptions to education, and returns to schooling in urban China*. Washington, DC: The World Bank.

Goldman, M. (2006). The post-Mao reform era. In J. K. Fairbank & M. Goldman (Eds.), *China: A new history* (2nd ed., pp. 406–456). Cambridge, MA: The Bleknap Press of Harvard University Press.

Gu, M. (2016). The new normal, the new education. *Xinjiaoshi* (Teachers Today), *2016-01*, 5–7.

Gu, M., & Li, M. (2007). *Gumingyuan jioayu koushushi (Oral educational history by Gumingyuan)*. Beijing, China: Beijing Normal University Press.
Halpin, D., & Troyan, B. (1995). The politics of education policy borrowing. *Comparative Education, 31*(3), 303–310.
Hannum, E. (1999). Political change and the urban-rural gap in basic education in China, 1949–1990. *Comparative Education Review, 43*(2), 193–211.
Harvey, D. (2005). *A brief history of neoliberalism*. Oxford, UK: Oxford University Press.
Hawkins, J. N. (1983). *Education and social change in the People's Republic of China*. New York: Praeger Publisher.
He, Y., Xu, Y., & Wang, Y. (2005, May 24). Zexiao beihou de jiaoli (Negotiation at the Back of Zexiao). *Renmin Ribao*, p. 11.
Henig, J. R. (1994). *Rethinking school choice: Limits of the market metaphor*. Princeton, NJ: Princeton University Press.
Henze, J. (1992). The formal education system and modernization: An analysis of development since 1978. In R. Hayhoe (Ed.), *Education and modernization* (pp. 103–140). Oxford, UK: Pergamon Press.
Hood, C. (1991). A public management for all seasons? *Public Administration, 69*(1), 3–19.
Hopper, E. (1971). A typology for the classification of educational systems. In E. Hopper (Ed.), *Readings in the theory of educational systems* (pp. 91–110). London: Hutchinson University Library.
Hu, Y., Lu, K., & Xue, H. (2008). Zhongxiaoxue Zexiao wenti de shizheng yanjiu-jiyu beijingshi zhongxiaoxue de diaocha (The empirical study on school choice-based on the survey of elementary and secondary schools in Beijing). *Jiaoyu Xuebao* (Journal of Education Studies), *4*(2), 74–78.
Huang, C. (1996, August 4). 'Zexiao' xianxiang toushi (Looking through 'Zexiao'). *China Education Daily*, p. 1.
Huang, Q. (1984, April 24). Jiejue shouqu xuezafei 'duo, luan, gao' de wenti (To deal with the charge of unauthorized school fees). *China Education Daily*, p. 2.
Hwang, K.-K. (1987). Face and favor: The Chinese power game. *American Journal of Sociology, 92*(4), 944–974.
Kipins, A. (2008). Competition, audit, scientism and school non-choice in rural China. In M. Forsey, S. Davies, & G. Walford (Eds.), *The globalisation of school choice?* (pp. 165–184). Oxford, UK: Symposium Books.
Levin, H. M. (1992). Market approaches to education: Vouchers and school choice. *Economics of Education Review, 11*(4), 279–285.
Levin, H. M., & Belfield, C. R. (2006). The marketplace in education. In H. Lauder, P. Brown, J.-J. Dillabough, & A. H. Halsey (Eds.), *Education, globalization & social change* (pp. 620–641). Oxford, UK: Oxford University Press.
Lewin, K., & Hui, X. (1989). Rethinking revolution; reflections on China's 1985 educational reforms. *Comparative Education, 25*(1), 7–17.
Li, B. (2005). Urban social change in transitional China: A perspective of social exclusion and vulnerability. *Journal of Contingencies and Crisis Management, 13*(2), 54–65.
Li, F. (2008). Beijingshi yiwu jiaoyu jieduan Zexiao de xianzhuang fenxi (Analysis on current situation of Zexiao in compulsory education in Beijing). *Jiaoyu kexue yanjiu* (Education Science Research) (2), 26–30.
Li, J. (2009). *Yiwu jiaoyu jieduan jiujin ruxue zhengce fenxi (Analysis on proximity-based school admission in compulsory education)*. Shanghai, China: Xue Lin Chu Ban She.
Li, M. (2011). *Yiwu jiaoyu-fei junheng fazhan dongle jizhi yanjiu (Research on imbalanced education development mechanism in compulsory education)*. Beijing, China: Zhongguo Shehui Kexue Chubanshe.
Li, Q. (2008). Gaige 30nianlai Zhongguo Shehui Fenceng Jiegou de Bianqian (The change of social stratification in China in the past 30 years). In Q. Li (Ed.), *Zhongguo shehui bianqian 30nian 1978–2008* (Social Change in China, 1978–2008) (pp. 1–56). Beijing, China: Shehui kexue wenxian chubanshe (Social Sciences Academic Press, China).

References

Li, X. (2007, June 19). Youdao zhaoshengshi, 'tiaozi' miantianfei (School admission comes, memo flies). *China Education Daily*, p. 8.
Lin, J. (2006). Educational stratification and the new middle class. In G. A. Postiglione (Ed.), *Education and social change in China* (pp. 179–198). Armonk, NY: East Gate Book.
Liu, J. (1996). Zhongxiaoxue luanshoufei: hongdengliangle (Stop! The charge of unauthorized school fees). *China Education Daily*, p. 1.
Liu, S. (2007). *Jiaoyu zhengce lunli wenti yanjiu* (On the Ethics of Educational Policy). PhD, East China Normal University, Shanghai.
Lofstedt, J.-I. (1980). *Chinese educational policy*. Stockholm, Sweden: Almqvist & Wiksell International/Humanties Press.
Logan, J. R., & Fainstein, S. S. (2008). Introduction: Urban China in comparative perspective. In J. R. Logan (Ed.), *Urban China in transition* (pp. 1–23). Oxford: Blackwell Publishing.
Lubienski, C. (2008). School choice research in the United States and why it doesn't matter: The evolving economy of knowledge production in a contested policy domain. In M. Forsey, S. Davies, & G. Walford (Eds.), *The globalisation of school choice?* (pp. 27–54). Oxford, UK: Symposium Books.
Lubienski, C., Gulosino, C., & Weitzel, P. (2009). School choice and competitive incentives: Mapping the distribution of educational opportunities across local education markets. *American Journal of Education, 115*(4), 601–647.
Mahoney, J. G. (2014). Interpreting the Chinese dream: An exercise of political hermeneutics. *Journal of Chinese Political Science, 19*(1), 15–34.
Mao, Z. (1969). *Maozhuxi lun jiaoyu geming (Mao Zhuxi's Educational Revolution)*. Beijing.
Ministry of Education. (1998). *Action plan for invigorating education in the 21st century*. Beijing, China: Ministry of Education.
Ministry of Education. (2000). *Urgent notice of reduction of over heavy burden of primary school students*. Beijing, China: Ministry of Education.
Ministry of Education. (2004). *2003–2007 action plan for invigorating education*. Beijing, China: Ministry of Education.
Ministry of Education. (2007). *Notification of the prohibition of participation of students at compulsory education level in PETS*. Beijing, China: Ministry of Education.
Ministry of Education. (2014). *Implementation opinions of further better doing free and proximity-based school admission at primary and junior secondary schools*. Beijing, China: Ministry of Education.
Minogue, M. (1998). Changing the state: Concepts and practice in the reform of the public sector. In M. Minogue, C. Polidano, & D. Hulme (Eds.), *Beyond the new public management: Changing ideas and practices in governance* (pp. 17–37). Cheltenham, UK: Edward Elgar.
National Congress of Communist Party of China. (2006). *Decisions on construction of harmonious society*. Beijing, China: National Congress of Communist Party of China.
O'Toole Jr., L. J., & Meier, K. J. (2004). Parkinson's law and the new public management? Contracting determinants and service-quality consequences in public education. *Public Administration Review, 64*(3), 342–352.
OECD. (1994). *School: A matter of choice*. Paris: OECD.
OECD. (2012). *Equity and quality in education: Supporting disadvantaged students and schools*. Paris: OECD.
OECD. (2016). *PISA 2015: Results in focus*. Paris: OECD.
Osborne, S. P., & McLaughlin, K. (2002). The new public management in context. In K. McLaughlin, S. P. Osborne, & E. Ferlie (Eds.), *New public management* (pp. 7–14). London: Routledge.
Pepper, S. (1980). Chinese education after Mao: Two steps forward, two steps back and begin again? *The China Quarterly, 81*, 1–65.
Pepper, S. (1991). Post-Mao reforms in Chinese education: Can the ghosts of the past be laid to rest? In I. Epstein (Ed.), *Chinese education: Problems, policies, and prospects* (pp. 1–41). New York: Garland Publishing.

Pepper, S. (1996). *Radicalism and education reform in 20th-century China*. Cambridge: Cambridge University Press.
Plank, D. N., & Sykes, G. (2003). Why school choice? In D. N. Plank & G. Sykes (Eds.), *Choosing choice: School choice in international perspective* (pp. vii–xxi). New York: Teachers College Press.
Pu, W., & Jian, P. (1995, August 19). Zhilichuzhonghexiaoxue*Zexiao*shenggaoshoufei (Managing over fee charge of *Zexiao* student in primary and junior high schools). *China Education Daily*, p. 2.
Qiao, L., Zhou, Z., & Zheng, L. (1996). *Guanyu Woshi Zhongxiaoxue Zexiaosheng Shoufei Wenti Diaoyan Baogao*. Beijing, China: Beijing Municipal Education Bureau.
Quan, Z. (1993, July 29). Shanghai zaisha zhongxiaoxue luanshoufeifeng (Blowing wind of the charge of unauthorized fees in Shanghai). *China Education Daily*, p. 1.
Reich, R. O. B. (2007). How and why to support common schooling and educational choice at the same time. *Journal of Philosophy of Education, 41*(4), 709–725.
Rosen, S. (1985). Recentralization, decentralization, and rationalization: Deng Xiaoping's bifurcated educational policy. *Modern China, 11*(3), 301–346.
Sautman, B. (1991). Politicization, hyperpoliticization, and depoliticization of Chinese education. *Comparative Education Review, 35*(4), 669–689.
Sellar, S., & Lingard, B. (2013). Looking East: Shanghai, PISA 2009 and the reconstitution of reference societies in the global education policy field. *Comparative Education, 49*(4), 464–485.
Shanghai Academy of Social Sciences. (2016). *Report of survey of public opinions on education for offsprings*. Retrieved July 28, 2016, from http://www.shanghai.gov.cn/nw2/nw2314/nw2315/nw17239/nw17244/u21aw1149343.html
Shi, Y., & Wang, Y. (2014). The impacting mechanism of housing prices in the school districts in Shanghai City. *China Land Sciences, 28*(12), 47–55.
Solinger, D. J. (1999). *Contesting citizenship in urban China: Peasant migrants, the state, and the logic of the market*. Berkeley, CA/Los Angeles: University of California Press.
Sonoda, S. (2008). *Fubyodokoka tyugoku* (Unequal State: China). Tokyo: Chuokoron-shinsha.
State Council. (2007). *Outline of eleventh five year plan for national education development*. Beijing, China: State Council.
Takayama, K. (2008). The politics of international league tables: PISA in Japan's achievement crisis debate. *Comparative Education, 44*(4), 387–407.
Tan, N. (1993, September 14). Xiamenshi jiaowei guiding zhi 'luan' (Actions taken by Xiamen City Education Committee). *China Education Daily*, p. 2.
Taylor, S., Rizvi, F., Lingard, B., & Henry, M. (1997). *Educational policy and the politics of change*. Oxon, UK: Routledge.
The World Bank. (2012). *China 2030*. Washington, DC: The World Bank.
Tianfu Zaobao. (2007, July 2). 28mingjiazhang lianming shangshu: weishenme burang haizi kao PETS (Why do not allow kids to take PETS: Letter from 28 parents). Retrieved September 28, 2009, from http://edu.qq.com/a/20070702/000023.htm
Tomba, L. (2004). Creating an urban middle class: Social engineering in Beijing. *The China Journal, 51*, 1–26.
Todaro, M. P., & Smith, S. C. (2006). *Economic development* (9th ed.). Essex, UK: Pearson Education Limited.
Tsang, M. C. (2000). Education and national development in China since 1949: Oscillating policies and enduring dilemmas. *The China Review*, 579–614.
Tsang, M. C. (2003). School choice in the People's Republic of China. In D. N. Plank & G. Sykes (Eds.), *Choosing choice* (pp. 164–195). New York: Teachers College Press.
Turner, R. H. (1971). Sponsored and contest mobility and the school system. In E. Hopper (Ed.), *Readings in the theory of educational systems* (pp. 71–90). London: Hutchinson University Library.
UN. (1948). *The universal declaration of human rights*. New York: UN.

References

Waldow, F., Takayama, K., & Sung, Y.-K. (2014). Rethinking the pattern of external policy referencing: Media discourses over the 'Asian tigers' PISA success in Australia, Germany and South Korea. *Comparative Education, 50*(3), 302–321.

Wan, G. (1998). *The educational reforms in the cultural revolution in China: A postmodern critique.* Paper presented at the AERA Annual Meeting San Diego, CA.

Wang, B. (Ed.). (2009). *Zhongguo jiaoyu gaige 30nian* (30 Years Education Reform in China). Beijing, China: Beijing Normal University Publishing Group.

Wang, C. (2009, November 12). *Xiaoji chaju shi Zexiao shouyin 63% de ren renwei jiaoyu gongping bei jiaokong* (Gap between schools is the first reason for Zexiao: 63% of respondents believe educational equality broke). Retrieved June 15, 2012, from http://zqb.cyol.com/content/2009-11/12/content_2931126.htm

Wang, J. (2008). *Jiaoyu: Cong junhen zouxiang gongping (Education: From Balance to Equality).* Beijing, China: Beijing Normal University Publishing Group.

Wang, Z. (2014). The Chinese dream: Concept and context. *Journal of Chinese Political Science, 19*(1), 1–13.

Wen, H., Zhang, Y., & Zhang, L. (2014). Do educational facilities affect housing price? An empirical study in Hangzhou, China. *Habitat International, 42*, 155–163.

Whitty, G. (1997). Creating quasi-markets in Education: A review of recent research on parental choice and school autonomy in three countries. *Review of Research in Education, 22*, 3–47.

Whitty, G., & Edwards, T. (1998). School choice policies in England and the United States: An exploration of their origins and significance. *Comparative Education, 34*(2), 211–227.

Whyte, M. K. (2010). Social change and the urban-rural divide in China. In H. Fan & J.-C. Gottwald (Eds.), *The Irish Asia strategy and its China relations* (pp. 45–60). Amsterdam: Rozenberg Publishers.

Whyte, M. K., & Guo, M. (2009). How angry are Chinese citizens about current inequalities? Evidence from a national survey. In K.-b. Chan, A. S. Ku, & Y.-w. Chu (Eds.), *Social stratification in Chinese societies* (pp. 17–54). Leiden, The Netherlands: Brill.

Whyte, M. K., & Parish, W. L. (1984). *Urban life in contemporary China.* Chicago, IL: University of Chicago Press.

Wong, L., & Mok, K.-H. (1995). The reform and the changing social context. In L. Wong & S. MacPherson (Eds.), *Social change and social policy in contemporary China* (pp. 1–26). Aldershot, UK: Avebury.

Wu, X. (2008). The power of positional competition and market mechanism: A case study of recent parental choice development in China. *Journal of Education Policy, 23*(6), 595–614.

Wu, X. (2012). School choice with Chinese characteristics. *Comparative Education, 48*(3), 347–366.

Wu, X., & Treiman, D. J. (2004). The household registration system and social stratification in China: 1955–1996. *Demography, 41*(2), 363–384.

Wu, Z., & Shen, J. (2006). School choice and education equity-changes in school choice policies and new direction in public school reform in China. *Tsinghua Journal of Education, 27*(6), 111–118.

Xiao, S. (2009, December 15). Zexiao wenti jiushi zhengwei shifou zuowei de wenti (*Zexiao*: A problem of government?). *China Youth Daily,* p. 2.

Yang, D. (2006). *Zhongguo jiaoyu gongping de lixiang yu xianshi* (The Wish and Reality of Educational Equality in China). Beijing, China: Peking University Press.

Yang, Y. (2004, February 18). Aoshu zhengzai chengwei xianjing? (Olympic math: A fall-trap?). *China Education Daily,* p. 3.

Zeng, X., & Ma, S. (2009, December 28). 'Zexiao re' weihe gaowen nanjiang? (Why 'Zexiao Fever' continues?). Retrieved May 18, 2011, from http://edu.ifeng.com/news/200912/1228_6978_1490073.shtml

Zhang, J., Yu, J., Yu, L., Li, C., Zhao, H., & Bao, J. (2003, October 26). Toushi zhongxiaoxuexiao shoufei wenti (Looking through the fee charge in compulsory education). *China Education Daily,* p. 3.

Zhang, M. (2003). *China's poor regions rural-urban migration, poverty, economic reform and urbanization*. London: Routledge Curzon.

Zhang, X. (2016). Monitoring and assessment of balanced development of compulsory education in 19 major cities of China. In D. Yang (Ed.), *Annual report on China's education (2016)* (pp. 207–221). Beijing, China: Social Sciences Academic Press (China).

Zhang, Y., & Yao, C. (2014). *Xi's "new normal" theory*. Retrieved November 15, 2014, from http://en.people.cn/n/2014/1110/c90883-8807112.html

Zheng, J. (Ed.). (2011). *Zhongguo jichu jiaoyu yuqing lanpishu 2009 (Blue Book on Basic Education in China 2009)*. Fuzhou, China: The Straits Publishing & Distributing Group.

Zheng, S., Hu, W., & Wang, R. (2016). How much is a good school worth in Beijing? Identifying price premium with paired resale and rental data. *The Journal of Real Estate Finance and Economics, 53*(2), 184–199.

Zhou, X. (2004). *The state and life chances in urban China: Redistribution and stratification, 1949–1994*. Cambridge, MA: Cambridge University Press.

Zhou, X., & Hou, L. (1999). Children of the cultural revolution: The state and the life course in the People's Republic of China. *American Sociological Review, 64*(1), 12–36.

Zhou, X., Moen, P., & Tuma, N. B. (1998). Educational stratification in urban China: 1949–94. *Sociology of Education, 71*(3), 199–222.

Zhou, X., Tuma, N. B., & Moen, P. (1996). Stratification dynamics under state socialism: The case of urban China, 1949–1993. *Social Forces, 74*(3), 759–796.

Zhu, Y. (2011). *Zhongguo dangdai jiaoyu sixiangshi* (The history of Chinese contemporary educational thoughts). Beijing, China: Zhongguo renmin daxue chubanshe.

Chapter 3
Public Discourses on *Zexiao*

Abstract This chapter documents power relationships in public school admission by analyzing changes in stakeholder interactions with public schools. It also illustrates a framework of multilayered inequality/stratified engagement of stakeholders in *Zexiao*. The discourse analysis is based on data collected from written and spoken records about public school admission, including newspaper articles and policy documents from the 1980s to the 2000s.

As already mentioned in the Introduction, this chapter documents a trajectory of public discussions on *Zexiao* to unveil similarities and changes of stakeholders' interactions regarding *Zexiao* in admission to public junior high schools in China. It also introduces a framework of power relationships among stakeholders in the process of admission to public junior high schools. According to the data I collected from both written texts and interviews on *Zexiao*, two themes emerged regarding the discussion, where *Zexiao* separated into two stages from the 1990s to the present. In the 1990s, discussion on *Zexiao* was mainly focused on the unauthorized charge of school fees. The theme after 2000 was on the imbalanced educational development. The shift of the themes is almost consistent with the third (Economic Revolution) and fourth periods (Building a Harmonious Society) of social change in China introduced in Chap. 1. Chinese society shifted from a profit-oriented model in the 1990s to a more balance-centered development model in the 2000s. The data I used for the analysis of public discussion on *Zexiao* in the 1990s involved written texts, mainly including collected government documents and newspaper articles. And the analysis of the data about the public discussion on *Zexiao* after 2000s included both written texts and in-depth interviews. The written texts include government documents, newspaper articles, journal papers, and books. In order to supplement the analysis of the discussed issues about *Zexiao* in the written texts, particularly the issues which emerged after 2000, I also included interviews with various stakeholders on *Zexiao* to provide more evidence. In order to portray the interactions between stakeholders, I presented the data analysis by following the order of opinions and discussions on one specific topic from the voice of the government followed by the corresponding public responses.

3.1 The 1990s: The Unauthorized Charge of School Fees

During the 1990s, with the further implementation of the open door policy, China experienced unprecedented rapid economic growth. Education was considered a tool for achieving China's modernization. With an efficiency-driven development strategy, the education system includes a small pro-elite sector which fostered human resources for modernization and a large pro-mass sector which provided basic education and training for the majority. Under such social background changes, the government-centered discussion about *Zexiao* consisted of issues about limited education investment, the imbalance between public schools, and parents' aspiration for their children's education.

3.1.1 The Limited Education Investment

Firstly, analysis of government documents showed paradoxical attitudes of the government toward the unauthorized charge of *Zexiaofei* by schools when parents choose public school admissions (State Education Commission, 1993a, 1993b, 1994a, 1994b, 1995a, 1996, 1997a, 1997b). On the one hand, the government repeatedly warned public schools not to charge *Zexiaofei*. In 1993, the State Education Commission[1] issued a *Notice on the Rectification for Charging unauthorized Fees in Primary and Middle Schools*, which stated that "it is not allowed to charge unauthorized fees on new student admissions. And it is not allowed to link education donations with new student enrollments" (State Education Commission, 1993a). In the same year, the State Education Commission released another document—the *Notice on the Strengthening Management for Charging School Fees in Primary and Middle Schools*. The document emphasized the same issue, asserting that "Students in compulsory education are only charged fees for school facility maintenance. It is not allowed to enroll 'high-priced students'." The sponsor fee to schools education should not be linked with school admissions. Practices such as using money to buy a score[2] or school place[3] and using the money to select public schools or key schools must be banned without hesitation. The sponsor fees should be managed by local education authorities [to ensure equity] (State Education Commission, 1993b). Government policies firstly showed firm opposition to the charge of "*Zexiao* students" in 1995. In *opinions regarding the implementation of the rectification for charging unauthorized fees* released by the State Education Commission, the government formulated that:

---

[1] Until the Institutional Reform of the State Council in 1998, the Ministry of Education was called the State Education Commission.
[2] Scores refers to the achievement in tests or exams related to education transition.
[3] School place refers to the student's status or identification at school.

3.1 The 1990s: The Unauthorized Charge of School Fees

> The issue of *Zexiao* students has expanded from the post-compulsory education stage to the compulsory education stage, including in junior high schools and primary schools. It stressed that nine years compulsory education should follow the principle of proximity and should not enroll "*Zexiao* students". The sponsor fees for education should not be linked to enrollments; junior high schools and primary schools should strictly follow the new curriculum and are not allowed to take any fees paid to a remedial class, interest class, improvement class, or an extraordinary class. (State Education Commission, 1995a, translated by the author)

On the one hand, the government authorized popular schools to charge *Zexiaofei* to supplement the limited government education investment. Moreover, due to the limited governmental education investment in compulsory education, education donations from the private sector were encouraged and promoted by the government. On the other hand, with the shift toward a socialist market economy, diverse channels and types of fund generation and school management were positively encouraged (Central Committee of the Chinese Communist Party, 1993). In 1994, the government repeatedly encouraged enterprises and other social forces to participate in providing education funding and management through diverse methods. And "sponsor fees for education" from the private sector were warmly welcomed (State Council, 1994). The government's attitude toward the charge of *Zexiaofei* started to change in 1997. Government documents left certain loopholes for some public schools in some large- and medium-sized cities in terms of *Zexiao*. It illustrated that *Zexiao* students could be accepted for the time being by a few public schools located in the cities which encountered great difficulty in implementing the school placement by the principle of proximity. The funds generated from taking *Zexiao* students went primarily to the state for reconstructing disadvantaged schools (State Education Commission, 1997b). With the inclusion of ambiguous phrases such as "a few public schools" and "for the time being," the privilege of enrolling *Zexiao* students was officially granted to key schools in 1997. The authorized *Zexiaofei* further pushed parents to get involved in *Zexiao*.

In contrast, the analysis of public discussion showed the general public was concerned the "legalization of *Zexiaofei*" stimulated parents' aspirations for sending their children to popular schools by financial means (Pu & Jian, 1995, August 19; Wang, 1997, July 30). The legalization accommodated needs from the local government and schools for additional investments. Meanwhile, it also satisfied the needs for mutual selection among schools and parents. As the *China Education Daily* reported, school principals offered their reasons to defend their actions for charging *Zexiaofei*. They argued that schools were entitled to charge student fees since schools lacked sufficient operational funds. Some principals even believed that it was reasonable to charge exorbitant student fees since they were used in school facilities and not for their own benefits (Du, 1986, August 23). Lanqing Li, the Vice Premier Minister of 1996, identified the critical relationship between the charge of *Zexiaofei* and school income. He pointed out that there would be a barrier to terminate the charge of *Zexiaofei* since it might reduce the income of some schools (Zeng & Yi, 1996, July 30). Bin Liu, former Deputy Director of the National Education Committee, demonstrated that the fees collected from *Zexiao* students could supplement for the limited education fund. However, the government should increase investment in compulsory education rather than charging fees from *Zexiao* students to supplement government investment in education (Ji, 1997, August 16). Moreover, Jie Wen, former Member of the Beijing Education Committee, asserted that a common misunderstanding was that educational resources could be distributed by the market or exchanged by money, which was one of the reasons for the rise of the charge of *Zexiaofei* (Dong, 1997, July 31). With the introduction of the market economy and the promotion of the industrialization of education in the 1990s, education, especially quality education resources, was widely considered as goods for consumers to exchange. However, this ideology ran against the *Compulsory Education Law* and challenged education equality at the compulsory education level. In addition, one interesting phenomenon called the "legalization of educational donations" stimulated parents' aspirations for sending their children to popular schools by paying *Zexiaofei*. Due to limited government investment in education, donation for education from the private sector was warmly welcomed by the government (State Council, 1994). Figure 2.1 shows the increasing proportion of donations and fundraising for operating schools in the diverse educational fund in the 1990s. A legalized fee charge that was dubbed an "education donation" was considered as another type of *Zexiaofei* with an agreement between schools and parents' employers. Since *Zexiaofei* was based on what parents could afford, they had to get help. According to an interview with parents in Beijing, in the early 1990s, the majority of parents could not afford *Zexiaofei*. Therefore, they had to get help from their employers. Consequently, there was a cost sharing model established between parents and their employers (Xi, 1993, October 7).

Accordingly, the government had paradoxical attitudes toward the charge of *Zexiao Fei* in school admissions. On the one hand, the government kept showing opposition to the charge of *Zexiaofei*. On the other, government policies left room for stakeholders to legalize the charge of *Zexiaofei* in order to supplement the limited governmental investment in public education. Moreover, parents' employers took part in the cost sharing of the charge of *Zexiaofei* for their employees' children. Considering the focus of "efficiency as priority" in China's development in the 1990s, the charge of *Zexiaofei* generated additional funds to help provide additional funding toward education. The analysis of the public discussion showed the public had already taken charge of *Zexiaofei* as an approach for achieving efficiency in public education.

3.1.2 Imbalance Between Public Schools

Secondly, the key school system and the school conversion reform broke an imbalance between public schools, where the distinguished status of public schools became largely based on their ability to charge school admission fees. This only intensified *Zexiao*. The analysis of government documents showed the government's paradoxical attitudes toward the abolishment of key schools which led to gaps among public schools. On the one hand, the government understood the existence of the key school system broke the balance between public schools (State Education Commission, 1993c, 1994c, 1995b, 1997c). In the government policies during the 1990s, the government kept emphasizing the importance in reducing the gap between public schools in the aspects of both hard and soft investments. On the other hand, under a pro-elite ideology, they attempted to strengthen the position of key schools through establishing 1000 demonstration senior high schools nationwide (State Council, 1994; State Education Commission, 1995c). The demonstration senior high schools further enhanced the advantages of the former key schools in the public school system, and it further intensified the gaps among public schools.

Moreover, the government launched its school conversion reform for public schools to generate additional investments through charging tuition fees. With the implementation, the central government recognized the reform intensified the unauthorized charge of school fees, further enlarged the gap between public schools and intensified *Zexiao* (State Council, 1998). Nevertheless, interestingly, the State Council addressed the delegation of its educational administration to local authorities and further exacerbated the imbalance of public schools. This only led to the intensification of *Zexiao* (Bi, 1996, March 11; Dong, 1997, July 31).

The analysis of public discussion indicated that people believed that the key school system separated public schools and forced parents to take part in *Zexiao* (Luo & Lai, 1992, December 3; Wang, 1997, July 30). Meanwhile, the privileges of key schools to charge *Zexiaofei* broke the free compulsory education policy and intensified *Zexiao* (Li, 1997, July 18). Moreover, the analysis showed that key schools were given special privileges to select students by their own school admission standard. Certificates or awards in the competition of students became the key criteria for key schools to select students they preferred (Ba, 1994, October 29). In contrast to the central government's concern on the influence of school conversion reform on *Zexiao*, interestingly, there was not much relevant discussion on the school conversion reform and *Zexiao* by the public in the 1990s.

3.1.3 Parents' Aspiration

Thirdly, parents' aspirations toward their children's education intensified *Zexiao* in the 1990s. The review of government documents in the 1990s did not show relevant discussion about the effect of parents' aspirations on the development of *Zexiao*. In contrast, public discussions showed that it could be interpreted by the cultural aspects, the result of the one-child policy, and the increasing social competition in China. Firstly, traditional thinking about education, such as "He who excels in study can follow an official career", shaped many parents' aspirations for sending children to popular schools (Yu, 1996, February 1). According to Songhua Tan, Deputy Director of the National Education Committee Research and Development Center, due to the traditional culture, blue-collar workers had low social status in Chinese society. Therefore, to prevent children from becoming blue-collar workers, parents were willing to exhaust their financial resources on *Zexiao* by sending their children to popular schools (Wang, 1997, July 30). Secondly, the implementation of the one-child policy forced parents to be willing to invest everything toward their children's education (Dong, 1997, July 31). In an interview about *Zexiao* in 1997, Jie Wen, a Member of the Beijing Education Committee, offered a comprehensive analysis on parents' aspirations for *Zexiao*. She pointed out that:

> It [*Zexiao*] is caused by the One Child issue. Parents of the One Child generation are almost those who spent their student period in the Cultural Revolution. Therefore, they have high expectations and expect their children to fulfill their own dreams. Under this old fashioned education value, the value of human resources and employment standard, there is a high demand for education. To some extent, this is a blind pursuit for "high quality" education. (Dong, 1997, July 31, translated by the author)

Lastly, the fierce competition in higher education and the labor market pushed parents to "voluntarily" send their children to good quality schools by paying *Zexiaofei* (Bao, 1996, March 11). In 1997, according to Songhua Tan, Deputy Director of the National Education Committee Research and Development Center, the current employment system in the labor market focused more on educational credentials while ignoring student's capacity. Therefore, to make sure their children entered universities, parents had to send their children into good primary schools and junior high schools (Wang, 1997, July 30).

The *China Education Daily* reported an interview with a parent in 1993, which showed parents' "willingness" and understanding of *Zexiaofei* for children's education. One parent said:

> In fact, schools charge fees, and parents pay the fees. Every parent would like to enroll [his or her] child in a good school. Therefore, parents are willing to pay. However, the price of the fees just went up because of the competition among parents. Schools are not rich. In order to keep good teachers through improving teachers' welfare, they (schools) have no choice instead but to charge fees. (Xi, 1993, October 7, translated by the author)

On the one hand, the quote above shows parents' understanding of the charge of *Zexiaofei* by public schools. On the other hand, it indicates that competition among parents for sending children to schools they prefer generated an environment for schools to raise the price of *Zexiaofei*.

Accordingly, an analysis of government documents and newspaper reports on *Zexiao* in the theme of the unauthorized charge of school fees in the 1990s illustrated, in the government-dominated public discussion on social issues, discussion on *Zexiao* among stakeholders in the 1990s was mainly influenced by the limited government education investment, the imbalance between public schools, and parents' aspiration for their children's education. First, due to limited government education investment in the 1990s, the government legalized the charge of *Zexiaofei* as an educational donation option from the private sector to public education. It can be considered the result of a government policy that encouraged schooling investment by social funding. It stimulated parents' aspirations to pay *Zexiaofei* in order to enroll their children in schools parents preferred. Second, Deng's ideology on the cultivation of human resources for the modernization of China in the short term deeply influenced the development of an elite channel in Chinese public education. The key school system together with the demonstration school system and the policy on conversion of public schools to *minban* schools created gaps between public schools. Those gaps might have forced parents to take any action to send their children to popular schools. Moreover, the privileges to charge *Zexiaofei* and select students in school admission authorized key schools to further push parents to pay *Zexiaofei* or to send their children to after-school classes. Thirdly, the traditional consensus that one's education largely dictated people's fortunes, high expectations for the one-child policy of the family, and the fierce competition in higher education and the labor market forced parents to believe that the only way for their children to climb up the social ladder and have a prosperous life was to send them to universities. Therefore, in order to achieve this objective, parents were willing to devote anything they had toward their children's education through *Zexiao*.

3.2 After 2000: The Imbalanced Educational Development

With an unprecedented economic development from the 1980s, China overtook Japan to become the second-largest economy in the world in 2010 (The World Bank, 2012). Conversely, the country was also divided by the imbalanced distribution of the outcomes of economic development. It caused a widening gap between the rich and the poor, as well as resulting social and economic instability (Appleton & Song, 2008; Li, 2005; Lin, 2006; Sonoda, 2008). The central government announced a number of policies aimed at alleviating poverty and inequality for constructing a more "harmonious society" (National Congress of Communist Party of China, 2006; Whyte & Guo, 2009). The imbalanced educational development has become as one of the challenges for realizing a harmonious society. Equality in education was given priority by the government. The balanced allocation of education resources in different regions has been emphasized to gradually narrow down gaps between rural and urban areas and between regions.

The discussion on *Zexiao*, after 2000, was under the scheme of the imbalanced educational development. On the one hand, issues on the limited education investment, imbalance between public schools, and parents' aspirations were continuously highlighted as major reasons for *Zexiao*. On the other hand, there emerged discussions which focused on the mismatch between economic and education development, the systematic exchange between power and education resources, and government's ambiguous attitude toward *Zexiao*.

3.2.1 The Distribution of Limited Education Resources

After 2000, the limited education investment was continuously considered one of the forces which forced popular schools to charge *Zexiaofei* through school admission in urban China. And the government continuously addressed and firmly prohibited *Zexiaofei* as an unauthorized charge of school fees (Ministry of Education, 2002; Ministry of Education et al., 2003; Ministry of Education & State Council for Rectifying, 2002; State Council, 2001; State Council Office for Rectifying & Ministry of Education, 2001). From 2007, the government kept emphasizing the balanced development of compulsory education to prevent public schools from charging unauthorized fees in school admissions (Ministry of Education, 2007, 2010a; Ministry of Education et al., 2008, 2009, 2010, 2011). Moreover, the government shifted their understanding that *Zexiao* was considered as the result of imbalanced education development. Meanwhile, the public discussion indicated that people shifted their focus on *Zexiao* from the amount of education investment to the balance in the distribution of the limited education resources.

Similar to the public discussions on *Zexiao* in the 1990s, the public discussion after 2000 continuously showed concerns on the limited education investment and relevant issues which caused *Zexiao* and the charge of *Zexiaofei* (Xiao, 2009, December 15; Zhao, 2009).[4] On the other hand, public discussion on *Zexiao* after 2000 gave more focus on the balanced distribution of the limited educational investment. They considered that the inappropriate distribution of the limited education investment among public schools was the underlying reason for *Zexiao* and unauthorized charge of *Zexiaofei* (Fan, 2004, March 15; Jiao, 2003, May 22; Wang, 2005, November 7; Wen, 2003, July 21; Xia, 2004, February 24; Xinxiaoxibao, 2009, August 16).[5]

3.2.2 The Imbalance Between Public Schools

An analysis of government documents and the public discussion on *Zexiao* after 2000 indicated the key school system, and its conversion intensified the gap between public schools in urban China. And the gap ultimately gave rationale for *Zexiao*. The government continuously addressed their firm opposition toward the existence of a key school system (National People's Congress, 2006; State Council, 2010). Also, the government launched policies to terminate the conversion of public key

---

[4] According to the *China Youth Daily* (Xiao, 2009, December 15), the results of a survey conducted by the *China Youth Daily* among 30 cities showed that 75.8% of participants involved in this survey felt the school gap caused schools to charge high *Zexiao* fees and was considered as the more serious educational inequality phenomenon in China.

[5] The left behind construction of poor quality public schools is also considered as one of the main reasons that led to the development of *Zexiao* (Weng, 2003; Xia, 2004, February 24; Zhang et al., 2003, October 26).

schools to *minban* schools (National Development and Reform Commission & Ministry of Education, 2005; State Council, 2004). They also gave emphasis on the enhancement of the existing weak public schools to balance school development (Ministry of Education, 2002, 2009, 2010b; State Council, 2007). Similar to the public discussion on key schools in the 1990s, stakeholders argued that the gap between public schools was the result of the imbalanced educational development which intensified *Zexiao* in urban China. Nevertheless, stakeholders presenting interests of different groups in admission to public junior high schools showed diverse opinions on the reason for this gap (see more in Chap. 4). Moreover, with the delegation of administration of public education, key schools and popular schools collaborated with other stakeholders to make new channels for student selection. These practices further intensified *Zexiao* in urban China.

3.2.3 Parents' Aspirations

Public discussion after 2000 continuously indicated parents' aspirations regarding their children's education as one of the main reasons for *Zexiao* (He, Xu, & Wang, 2005, May 24; Wen, 2005, May 31; Zhang, Shi, & Shen, 2005, May 25).

There were reasons which stimulated parents' aspirations for taking part in *Zexiao*. Firstly, parents' aspirations rose with the fierce social competition in both the education transition and labor market (Li, 2007; Qu & Yang, 2007). In 2003, in an interview reported by *Wen Hui Bao*, a parent said:

> Due to the fierce competition for human resources, we must take part in *Zexiao*. It is the fact that without being able to go to a good primary school it is difficult to go to a good junior high school. Then it will be difficult to go to a good senior high school and a good university. As a result, it will be difficult to find a good job! (Lu, 2003, September 1, translated by the author)

The interview with the parent above presented the formula "university degree = good jobs = better income = social prestige" regarding people's understanding for investment in education. The monetary reward through education fuels parents' enthusiasm to invest in their children's education.

Secondly, parents' aspirations were stimulated by the One-Child Policy (Niu, 2005, November 29; Yang, 2005, December 5). Because of this policy, parents wish to devote anything to their children. *Beijing Ribao* showed parents had consensus that "My child should not be left behind at the starting line!" It deeply influenced parental decisions in choosing schools for their children (Bang, 2010, November 5). Moreover, the traditional consensus, such as "He who excels in study can follow an official career" and "Education can change one's life," pushed parents to actively take part in *Zexiao* (Di & Chai, 2007, July 30).

Interestingly, on the other hand, interviews I conducted with stakeholders in Beijing also showed some critiques on parents' aspirations. To be more specific, the mismatch between parents' aspirations for their children's education and their capacity ultimately led to the existence of *Zexiao*. Principals from different schools argued that parents' choices in *Zexiao* might not best meet their children's needs.

According to an interview with the principal of School F in Beijing, most decisions made by parents might not be appropriate for their children. Parents had an aspiration to send their children to good quality education offerings without considering whether this decision is appropriate for their children or not. She further illustrated:

> In fact, most parents did not really understand why they chose the school for their kids. They just felt that it was a good school as it used to be the key school. And their kids must go to good schools. Regarding whether the schools were really appropriate for their kids, in fact, parents did not think too much.... Obviously, most parents just wanted to try their best to send their kids to the best schools while they did not think whether these schools were appropriate for their kids or not.[6] (Interview with Principal of School F, November 7, 2011, translated by the author)

Similarly, the principal of School G explained, "the motivation for *Zexiao* actually comes from parents without considering their children's conditions."[7] In other words, parents' aspirations for *Zexiao* are often caused by the mismatch between parents' aspirations for children's education and their children's capacity/wishes for their own education.

3.2.4 Newly Emerging Discussions

The main difference between the discussions in the 1990s and after 2000 is that there were emerging critiques which demonstrated systematic issues in educational and social systems as the main reasons for *Zexiao* after 2000. These issues included the mismatch between economic and education development, systematic exchanges between power and education resources and the limited government's capacity. Moreover, interviews with school principals, scholars, staff members from local education authorities, parents, and staff members from private tutoring institutes in Beijing specified these emerging issues with Beijing's characteristics. In the following part, I provide a concrete analysis on these issues.

---

[6] The principal of School F also pointed out that the mismatch between parents' expectations and their children's capacity in *Zexiao* was often misled by the public media. According to her, "*Zexiao* represents a concept of consumption. It is very normal. The point is not whether people choose or not. Rather it is which choice is more appropriate for students. I think the media sometimes misleads parents and the public. They mainly focus on the word *Ze* (choice). But, they neglect to discuss why and what they choose.... In my opinion, the media should discuss more on how to wisely and appropriately choose schools." This interview was conducted on November 7, 2011.

[7] Interview with the principal of School G was conducted on October 27, 2011.

3.2.4.1 Mismatch Between Economic Development and Education Development

The rapid economic development stimulated individuals' demand for education which was represented by *Zexiao* in much of urban China. The growth of private investment in education is increasing in recent years. It seems that the government-dominated education system is being replaced or challenged by the emerging demands for self-determined education. An increasing number of parents is involved in the decision-making process for their children's education. The public education system cannot best accommodate all of these needs. Due to the limited capacity of the public school system to accommodate the demand for education from migrant children, there was an increasing number of migrant children who were involved in *Zexiao*. The public discussion on *Zexiao* showed that it was largely the mismatch between economic development and education development in the country rather than the imbalanced educational development which stimulated *Zexiao*.

3.2.4.2 Education for What?

Regarding *Zexiao*, Cheng (2011) gave emphasis on the shift of demand for education from the state to individuals. Considering the monetary reward from education, parents were willing to pay money to send their children to schools which they preferred instead of following the government-designated school assignment. In this way, *Zexiao* represented an increasing demand for individuals' development through education. *Zexiao* also raised the question on "*Zexiao* for what?" and "Education for what?"

Public discussion started to give special emphasis on the purpose of basic education to illustrate the deeper structural reasons for *Zexiao*. It showed that *Zexiao* is caused by the unclear objective of public basic education in urban China with the accompanying rapid social change.

Scholar B from Peking University clarified that the current development of *Zexiao* presented the overly emphasized needs for education from parents and the society while neglecting the basic needs of children. In other words, basic education in China does not always give serious concern on children's needs for the basic education. He further analyzed that:

> What is basic education? Basic education is the education which can satisfy the needs for people's lives, personal growth, and social needs. However, the social needs are completely different from their children's needs. And the latter is what we neglect in the education sector and society. ... Our current methods of children's cultivation and *Zexiao* for children do not take into account children's basic needs as basic human needs. Originally, it should be taken into consideration in education, while currently it has become something that is outside of education. Parents just send children to schools. They do not expect children to think of other things. ... Our education is doing something that we would like children to know, to do and to be. Consequently, there is a large number of children who do not know what they really want to do. (Interview with Scholar B, November 4, 2011, translated by the author)

Considering Deng's modernization theory and the idea of creating a harmonious society through education, the role of education is closely aligned with the needs of the nation's development. In contrast, the value of education for each individual's development is often neglected and replaced by the value of education for national development.

Moreover, Scholar C from East China Normal University in Shanghai highlighted the unclear objective of basic education (compulsory education) as distorted by the exam-driven education ideology and the utilitarian doctrine in education. The exam-driven basic education is often overly emphasized by the public. He further explained:

> After the implementation of the Open Door Policy, the human resources strategy in China pushed the pressure down from required university entrance exams to lower levels of education. Recently, this situation has become more serious. People have reached a consensus that "In order to attend a good quality junior high school, it is necessary to attend a good quality primary school. Then, in order to become an elite member of society, individuals must climb up the high status on the social ladder and receive good income in this society. It is thus necessary to attend a key senior high school and a key university. The utilitarian doctrine has been vividly presented in China's education sector. ... One of the reasons for *Zexiao* is that compulsory education in China does not always have a clear objective. Compulsory education for children in the early stages should cultivate their interests in the study, cultivate their good living habits and customs. And it should be a happy education experience. However, modernization, education development, talented persons and human resource development have been closely linked. And the basic education system has been driven by an exam-oriented education and utilitarian doctrine. (Interview conducted on November 24, 2011, translated by the author[8])

The utilitarian doctrine in China's education sector can be linked with the discussion on the monetary rewards as the main impetus for education in China (see Chap. 1).

Besides these, Director A of a private tutoring institute showed a negative attitude toward the monopoly of public basic education which influenced *Zexiao* in urban China. Although the central government firmly expressed a negative attitude toward *Zexiao* through the slogan "Public schools do not enroll Zexiao students. Go to minban schools for Zexiao," *the* majority of participants conducted *Zexiao* in popular public schools since these schools often have better teachers and receive more privileges in terms of school development from the education authority.[9] In Wen's opinion, without a well-developed private education system as a competitor and supplement for public basic education, parents will continue being involved in the public sector school selection process. Consequently, it will be difficult to alleviate *Zexiao* in urban public schools in the current Chinese context.

---

[8] The statement of School C was collected during the Symposium on *Zexiao* Fever, which was hosted by the 21st Century Education Research Institute on November 24, 2011.

[9] According to Lin (2006), most elite private schools have been met with discriminatory measures from the government, such as exclusion from consideration for model schools and refusal to recognize their teachers' seniority when the teachers want to return to public schools. In contrast, the education authority maintains advantages of key schools by distributing highly qualified teachers and establishing much better facilities and equipment.

3.2.4.3 Migrant Children

The public discussion raised the issue regarding the increasing number of migrant children in urban China was one of the reasons for *Zexiao*. Yet, this was not a major issue that was widely reflected in the mainstream discussion by the public. With the rapid urbanization, a growing number of internal migrants flowed into urban areas. Due to the limited capacity of accepting migrant children in urban public schools, there was a competition among these children and their parents for public education in receiving areas (Liu, 2012). Without *hukou* in receiving areas, paying *Zexiaofei* became the only way for migrant families to enroll their children in public schools. As Jie Mao, Representative of the National People's Congress, argued:

> …due to the imbalanced development in regional education development, an increasing number of migrants and the limited capacity of accepting migrant children in public schools in urban areas have become reasons for the rise of *Zexiaofei*. (Xinhuashe, 2008, March 9, translated by the author)

Also, the *hukou* system is a key reason for migrant children's *Zexiao* (Chen, 2005). Due to the proximity-based compulsory education in China, without local *hukou*, it is difficult for migrant parents to enroll their children in urban areas. Therefore, migrant parents have to take part in *Zexiao* in order to enroll children in public schools. The need for the reform of the *hukou*-based compulsory education is still not fully addressed by the government. Meanwhile, the mismatch between supply and demand for migrant children's education in urban China not only intensified *Zexiao* among migrant parents but also among local parents. According to Director A of a private tutoring institute, the increasing number of migrant children in urban public schools pushed parents in Beijing to send their children to popular schools which do not have many migrant children.[10] It further intensified *Zexiao* in urban public schools.

3.2.4.4 Systematic Exchange Between Power and Education Resources

After 2000, there was an increasing critique on the exchange between power and educational resources in urban China. Public discussion indicated that the systematic exchange between power and education resources was another reason for *Zexiao*. According to *Nanfang Zhoumo* in 2004, an interview with Professor Dongping Yang from the Beijing Institute of Technology showed that *Zexiao* was caused by the systematic exchange between power and education resources or money and education resources in the process of the industrialization of education.[11]

---

[10] The interview was conducted on October 30, 2011.

[11] According to Yang (2006, p. 106), the industrialization of education refers to the systematicalized activities that the education system and schools at all levels generated profits and enlarged educational resources through utilizing a market mechanism and approaches from the 1990s. It happened under the background of significant lack of educational financing. To some extent, these activities supplemented the limited educational fund and enlarged educational resources.

On the one hand, the limited education resources became a big market. On the other hand, our education system could not accommodate the current demands on education. The combination of these two effects created an "education resource rent seeking" which seriously distorted the meaning of education and ultimately led to corruption (Yang, 2004, October 7).[12]

Regarding the exchange between power (*guanxi*) and education resources in Beijing, Scholar B, from Peking University, critically and poignantly asked:

> Who can do *Zexiao* in Beijing? People who have money can take part in it. People who have good scores can participate in *Zexiao*. The score-based *Zexiao* sounds relatively fair. However, it is still difficult if you only have a good score. You also must have money, power, and *guanxi*. People without these still cannot do *Zexiao*.... *Zexiao* is not a rights-based competition. The equality for some people negatively influences the equality for others in education. Therefore, the limited good quality education resource is dominated by those who have advantages. Those who do not own any advantages have to go to the schools that are in relatively bad condition. The stratification raises some people up while pushing a large number of people down. (Interview conducted on November 4, 2011, translation by the author)

A similar argument was made by the Director from School H in Beijing. He sharply demonstrated that *Zexiao* was initiated by people with power and money. Moreover, his argument also showed that there was a rise in demand for *Zexiao* from people without absolute power and other advantages. The Director addressed that:

> We need to ask: who did *Zexiao* first? ... You know, of course, it is not ordinary people! It is the people who have power. They can take part in *Zexiao* through their power. And policy making leaves spaces for people with power to achieve it. ... Hence, you can guess who will not agree with the full implementation of proximity-based education transition? ... People with power and money will not agree. Because such an approach will directly influence their children's education transition. ... And the whole society will not agree.... Because most parents wish to send their children to go to the limited popular schools. (Interview conducted on May 10, 2011, translated by the author)

Although parents without power (*guanxi*) were not willing to "voluntarily" accept the predetermined exclusion regarding choice for their children's education, they still had to face various barriers which were predetermined in the process of *Zexiao*. Experience in *Zexiao* of Parent 1 from a primary school in *Dongcheng* District showed the predetermined exclusion of parents without power or money. She specified:

> The education transition to junior high schools does not depend on students' capacity nor their comprehensive evaluation. It totally depends on parents' *guanxi*.... Except for those geniuses, other children have to depend on their parents. As ordinary people, if you just

---

Meanwhile, the charge of high tuition and unauthorized charge of fees occurred. These distorted the meaning of education and intensified corruption in the education sector. The quality and reputation of education were badly influenced.

[12] According to *Jiancha Ribao*, in 2008, one principal of a Beijing primary school committed corruption by acquiring 1.4 million RMB, which was charged from educational donations (Bai, 2011, June 22). In 2008, corruption committed by a principal from a popular Beijing school was reported by the media. The corruption included more than 100 million RMB. And most of it was charged as an educational donation from parents (Chen & Wang, 2008, August 17).

follow the official school admission procedure, then finally your children can only go to the assigned schools…you know that is really a matter of luck! I mean children go to popular schools through school assignment…. Recently, I realize that *Zexiao* is not for ordinary families. You take part in each stage of *Zexiao* works with passion. But, finally, your children still have to go to the assigned schools… and without *guanxi*, it is quite difficult! (Interview conducted on May 18, 2011, translated by the author)

In contrast to powerless parents who are excluded from *Zexiao*, parents who worked for powerful work units often received support from their employers in terms of their children's education. Through exchange between power and education resources among these work units and popular schools, parents working in such places could enroll their children in popular schools. In 2005, in *Nanfang Zhoumo*, one article on education transition corruption showed a vivid picture of the exchange between power and education resources for *Zexiao* in detail. It noted:

One popular school was often monitored and reported negatively by the media, which badly influenced the school's reputation in public. One year, an editor of a newspaper contacted the principal for requesting enrollment of two students to this school. The principal took it as an opportunity for a "DEAL". He accepted the request. And at the same time, he required an editor to pay for *Zexiaofei* and give more positive reports about the school. The editor accepted everything without hesitation. In the following five years, there were continuously positive reports to boost this school in various aspects, such as quality education practice, excellent academic achievement on entrance exams to senior high schools, etc…. One journalist explained that since his child was accepted by this school through the "DEAL" between the editor and the principal, as an exchange, he had to write and boast about the principal and the school. (Wu 2005, April 28, translated by the author)

The example above highlights the exchange between powerful parents' work units and access to popular schools. Such exchange brings mutual benefits to both schools and employees in the powerful work units. One principal of a popular school pointed out that it was necessary to enroll some memo students since it brought benefits for schools, such as the government's investment and *guanxi* for school development (Xiaowei Li, 2007, June 19).

Work units—especially those with political and economic power—could provide a guarantee for the access to popular public schools for employees' kids. The public discussion showed the power of co-founding work units in terms of *Zexiao* works, especially in Beijing. As Director of School H added:

China Aerospace Science and Technology Corporation (Affiliation of PLA) is our co-founding work unit. Also, No. 304 Hospital (an army hospital) also has a co-founding sponsorship with us. Co-founding fees are a type of school income. As an exchange with the co-founding fee, we enroll students from our co-founding work units. Well, I am not sure the details of the fees or enrollment number…. As I know, both co-founding sponsor fees and *Zexiaofei* will be paid to the local education authority directly. Part of the money will be paid back to school side. But, I am not sure the exact number. (Interview conducted on May 10, 2011, translated by the author)

Xu's statement above also showed the legalization of charging co-founding fees and *Zexiaofei* through government permission. Furthermore, an interview with the principal of School E in Beijing showed a kind of non-monetary exchange between a co-founding work unit and a public school. This exchange benefited both individuals and interest groups. He clarified,

> We have co-founding work units as partners. But it is different from those who have sponsorships. Our co-founding work units do not have any sponsorship with us. We just collaborate and support each other through exchanging "conveniences". We provide some school seats to children from these work units. As an exchange, we get support from these work units. For instance, police stations can assist our school security. (Interview with Principal of School E, May 16, 2011, translated by the author)

Obviously, co-founding-based *Zexiao* showed the exchange between the public education resources and public funds from influential work units for the schooling of their employees' kids. As a result, the public resources were utilized for collective (group) interests. In other words, the government's institutions and state-owned work units have the capacity to dominate the access to good public schools for the benefit of their employees through establishing co-founding relationships with good public schools and paying the sponsor fees. The privileged groups kept the advantage position for their children's school transition by utilizing their political, social, and economic capital.

In addition, an interview with the principal of School F showed the political position of Beijing as the capital city of China was one special reason for the popularity of power-based *Zexiao* in Beijing. Professor Yang, president of the 21st Century Education Research Institute, pointed out that "Co-founding collaboration" between popular schools and government institutions, large-scale state owned enterprises aims at accommodating needs for their children's quality education. Considering the special characteristics of Beijing which have a large number of state organizations, how to limit their privileges in terms of public school admission is a big challenge for the alleviation of *Zexiao* (21st Century Education Research Institute, 2011). There is considerable political pressure for the best quality public schools to absolutely obey the orders. One principal of a popular junior high school in Beijing indicated that:

> Every year, every good school receives memos from upper administration offices for their children's education transition. Also, we get pressure from co-founding work units as well. You know, Beijing is a very special place. Central administration offices are all located here. So, we have the responsibility to serve them. The Ministry of Foreign Affairs, Police Stations, etc.… Can we say "No" to any of them? [shaking her head and bitterly smiling]. (Interview with Principal of School F, November 7, 2011, translated by the author)

Regarding co-founding students in Beijing, Director A of a private tutoring institute firmly showed his argument on the link between these work units and education transition to popular schools. In his opinion, the school admission by co-founding agreements presented the privilege for the minority in public education, which originally was known as a public good for all members of society. This approach vividly presented that good education resources were dominated by the privileged groups in Chinese society. A recently published report on *Zexiao* in Beijing further critically demonstrated the challenges for Beijing to solve *Zexiao* due to its special position in China (21st Century Education Research Institute, 2011). According to this report, there was a common understanding that education sector in Beijing should

3.2 After 2000: The Imbalanced Educational Development

accommodate any needs from the central government. The real barrier to achieving balanced education development is the interest of the privileged groups. They prefer to keep the gap between public schools in order to dominate their privilege to enroll their children in good schools. They try to establish new rules in public school admission to lead the distribution of quality education resources for their own profits. Therefore, how to take a stance against and restrict privileges are a challenge for the Party and the municipal government of Beijing.

3.2.4.5 The Limited Government's Capacity

After 2000, there were critiques on the limited capacity of government in terms of alleviation of *Zexiao* in the discussion at both the central and local levels (Di & Chai, 2007, July 30; Yang, 2004, October 7). More importantly, since *Zexiao* could generate various profits for the government and schools, the attitude of the government or their willingness to alleviate *Zexiao* also deeply influenced policy making and policy implementation.

Interviews with various stakeholders showed similar opinions on the gap between policy making and policy implementation which caused the failure in the alleviation of *Zexiao*. According to a journalist from Sohu.com, it was necessary to strengthen the policy implementation instead of simply making them. The "black box" in the process of public school admission should be open and kept transparent.[13] Scholar A from the National Institute of Education Science considered the failure in the alleviation of *Zexiao* as the result of the failure in policy implementation. He clarified:

> the policies were not implemented strictly by the government. The dysfunction of the government or passive role of the government can be considered as the core reason for the failure in the alleviation of *Zexiao*. In terms of education resource distribution, in fact, they still give more to some former key schools. It intensifies the pro-key school policy and elite education ideology. More importantly, another vital question is whether the *Compulsory Education Law* is really taken as a rigid law or a flexible law? If we really take *Zexiao* as a behavior which breaks the *Compulsory Education Law*, then probably, it will be easier for us to change the current complicated situation. Have you ever heard who was put into jail because he broke the *Compulsory Education Law* by taking part in *Zexiao*? [laughing]. (Interview with Scholar A, April 28, 2011, translated by the author)

One of the examples regarding the limited government's capacity was the alleviation of school admission by Olympic math. Since Olympic math could generate profits for various groups, the Olympic math fever was not easily cooled down. In contrast, it became a widely accepted channel for *Zexiao*. As Mingyuan Gu, President of the Chinese Education Society, pointed out, the failure in the alleviation of Olympic math fever sometimes was caused by the opposition from various interest groups and parents (Gu, 2009, August 22). Some schools, in order to get a better education transition

---

[13] The interview with the journalist from Sohu.com was conducted through email exchange between the journalist and the author.

ratio, forced students to learn Olympic math and generated profits. A math teacher from Shanghai also complained that Olympic math was heated by pursuing various profits in the society (Yongmei Yang, 2004, February 18). One specialist in teaching Olympic math specified that there were at least three types of profits generated by Olympic math schools. Firstly, it provided a platform for schools to select students with talent in math. Secondly, it boosted school reputation and enrollment. Finally, it generated profits through collecting tuition (Ye, 2004, January 11). A professor at Shandong University also stated that Olympic math became utilitarian. Schools promoted it for their reputation. And parents sent children to the Olympic math classes in order to help them gain eventual admission into key schools (Fan, 2005, March 17). There was a "profit chain" of Olympic math which intensified Olympic math fever for *Zexiao* (Li & Liang, 2009). An interview conducted by the *China Youth Daily* specified the meaning of the "Profit Chain." A teacher who taught Olympic math for nearly 10 years confessed that there was an "Olympic Math Economy" valued in 200 million yuan in China. One education specialist pointed out that Olympic math training classes collaborated with some junior high schools to pursue the common profits generated by the training (Xinling Li, 2009, April 1). Accordingly, the "Profit Chain" connected Olympic math schools, Olympic math teachers, parents, and key schools.

Regarding the alleviation of school admission by Olympic math, public discussion demonstrated that the lack of monitoring intensified *Zexiao*. In 2009, Dongping Yang, professor of the Beijing Institute of Technology, wrote about Olympic math education on his blog to show his doubt on the government's monitoring system on the alleviation of school admission by Olympic math. In the article titled "Down with the Evil of Olympic Math Education", he doubted dysfunctional government monitoring capacity in the prohibition of Olympic math education. And he argued the government should be responsible for the Olympic math issue and the link with public school admission.[14] A Deputy Director of the Education Bureau of Chengdu also addressed the necessity to establish a powerful monitoring mechanism to alleviate school admission by Olympic math (Xinhuashe, 2009, November 15).

Moreover, the endless charge of the unauthorized school fees, such as *Zexiaofei* or education donations, can be considered as the result of the limited capacity of the government. Former director of the education supervision office in *Chaoyang* District, Beijing, called this failure a result of "the indulgence of the Government." Director A of a private tutoring institute further analyzed the lack of a monitoring system on policy implementation as the core reason for the endless charge of *Zexiaofei*. He pointed out that:

> China is a single-power dominated society. The monitoring function almost does not work if it challenges "the absolute power"… I do not think we have a lack of policies… we have enough policies, but the implementation [of the policies] cannot be fully and correctly made. The core reason is the lack of monitoring. And the establishment of this system depends on the willingness of policy makers and policy implementers… (Interview with Director A, October 30, 2011, translated by the author)

---

[14] Dongping Yang's Blog, "Down with the Evil of Olympic Math Education" uploaded on April 15, 2009. Retrieved from http://blog.sina.com.cn/s/blog_492471c80100cn8h.html. Accessed on March 15, 2012

3.2 After 2000: The Imbalanced Educational Development

Meanwhile, the result of alleviation of the charge of the unauthorized school fees also depended on the will of the government, particularly the local government. With the legalization of the fee charge by the local education authority, school admission by money became the "casting couch" in public education transition in urban China. The Director from School H in Beijing gave his reasonable statement for charging *Zexiaofei* in the school admission process. He said:

> Since compulsory education should be free, the charge of unauthorized fees was illegal. But, you know, it is reasonable, especially when the fee charge is legalized by the local education authority.[15] School side administrators believe that you need to pay since your kids use our education resources.... I do not think it is an unauthorized fee charge. ... If it is the fee charge between principal and individual parents personally, then it is illegal. Since it [the fee charge] is an act of the state... [smiling and looking at the voice recorder]...you know... it is just acceptable. (Interview with the Director, School H, May 10, 2011, translated by the author)

The statement above showed the positive attitudes of school leaders toward the charge of fees for students which was stimulated by the local education authority's legalization of the unauthorized fee charge for school admission. It also presented the ideology of considering public education as a commercial good emphasized in an education reform influenced the school principal's opinion on *Zexiaofei*. The principle of efficiency as a priority in economic and educational reform became the firm argument for school principals to charge *Zexiaofei*.

Interviews also showed the limited capacity of the government in solving the conflict between balanced education development and the exam-driven education. On the one hand, government policies aimed to promote a balanced education development. On the other hand, at the school level, there still exists competition among public schools through exam results (education transition ratio) as the criterion for boosting their own reputation. More importantly, a good reputation in terms of education transition ratio could attract more students and parents to come. A staff member at the Education Training and Research Center in *Dongcheng* District, Beijing, doubted the current policies regarding the balanced education development and remedial class. She argued that:

> Recently, I am confused the conflict between balanced education development and the increasing remedial classes. On the one hand, policy promotes the balanced development of schools. On the other hand, at the school level, many schools, especially the good ones, are adding more classes for students in order to compete with other schools through exams. I am not sure whether they really attempt to alleviate the gap between public schools or they still want to select good students and separate schools... you know, the latter will absolutely stimulate *Zexiao*!... And it is also happening in our district. (Interview conducted on November 7, 2011, translated by the author)

Accordingly, the limited capacity of government is considered as the force which shaped the development of *Zexiao* in urban China. The limited capacity of government in the alleviation of Olympic math intensified the school admission by Olympic

---

[15] The legalization of the charge of *Zexiao* can also be found through an interview with the principal of School F. According to her, the rate of return of *Zexiao* fees from the local education authority to schools was 85 percent in *Dongcheng* District (Interview was conducted on November 7, 2011).

math. The limited capacity of government in the abolishment of school admission by *Zexiaofei* encouraged parents with money to invest for their children's education. And the limited capacity of government in terminating the exam-driven education system pushed public schools to boost and keep school reputation through *Zexiao*-based student selection in order to achieve high education transition ratio to the upper level of education.

The analysis above shows that the imbalanced distribution of the limited government investment was considered as the original reason for *Zexiao* after 2000. Due to the legalization of *Zexiaofei*, school admission by money kept stimulating parents' aspirations to enroll their children in popular schools. Due to the imbalanced distribution, key schools (or demonstration schools) are given more privileges in school construction, student selection, and teachers' welfare. The pro-key school distribution of education resources intensified the gap between public schools and further stimulated parent's aspirations for *Zexiao*. Also, the innovation of conversion of public schools to *minban* schools generated more school income through charging legalized school fees (and *Zexiaofei*). In order to meet the needs for quality education, local education authorities invented diverse channels for public school admission. Since these channels generated diverse profits, they widely received support from various stakeholders, such as parents, public schools, and private tutoring institutes. Public schools could collect better performing students through collaboration with private tutoring institutes. The admission by pre-admission training classes and Olympic math classes provided a platform for public schools to screen students. Furthermore, the public discussion also identified that parents' aspirations, generated by the one-child policy and fierce competition in education transition and the labor market, were the forces which affected negotiations on *Zexiao* among stakeholders in public school admission to junior high schools.

Moreover, in the public discussion after 2000, there were increasing discussions indicating that the systematic problems in the education sector and the limited capacity of government also had an influence on *Zexiao*. Firstly, the discussion touched upon the mismatch between economic development and education development. They argued that the unclear objective of education and inappropriate response to the increasing needs of migrant children for education caused *Zexiao*. Secondly, public discussion criticized the exchange between power and education resources called as "Education resource rent seeking" in public school admission. The admission by memo and the one by co-founding agreement provided a platform for people with privileges to enroll their children in popular schools. These approaches stimulated parents' aspiration to utilize any possible *guanxi* (private based or work unit based) for their children's education transition. Finally, public discussion showed the limited capacity of government in terms of alleviation of Olympic math class, the termination of *Zexiaofei*, and the lack of monitoring system in public school admission deteriorated *Zexiao*. In addition, analysis of public discussion showed the political position of Beijing-stimulated power-based *Zexiao* in this city. The privileged groups with *guanxi* and money kept their advantages in

3.2 After 2000: The Imbalanced Educational Development

public school admission to junior high schools in Beijing. This process intensified inequality in public education in urban China.

In summary, analysis of public discourse showed that the negotiation on *Zexiao* among stakeholders was shaped by diverse forces, mainly including parents, public schools, private tutoring institutes, government and systematic issues, and local historical, political, and cultural characteristics. *Zexiao* was formed by the increasing demand for good quality education from parents. Meanwhile, it was also shaped by appetites for interests in *Zexiao* from diverse stakeholders, such as public key schools, the local education authorities, private tutoring institutes, and powerful work units. Moreover, the analysis showed that there was an increasing mismatch between individual demand for education and current supply of public education, the mismatch between government policy making and policy implementation, and the mismatch between economic development and education development. In other words, *Zexiao* was shaped by the mismatch between education development and social change in China. In addition, through the analysis, public discussion showed that public school admission to junior high schools in urban China was significantly influenced by parents' socioeconomic status rather than children's own capacities. In other words, children from privileged families have more opportunities to get access to the limited good quality education resources compared with children from the disadvantaged groups. Equality in public compulsory education is seriously challenged by *Zexiao*.

The analysis above indicated a shift of the public discussion on *Zexiao* from a profit-oriented development model in the 1990s to a more balance-centered development model in China in the 2000s. The continuity of these discussions showed there is domination of the power and privileges of institutions and individuals in public school admission to secondary education in urban China during two historical periods. The power and privileges were formulated through the legalization of privileges and social advantages, commercialization of public education resources, and institutional exclusion of the powerless at both the school and individual levels. The discontinuity of the discussions suggests there was an increasing concern on the imbalanced development which further deteriorated the domination of privileges and social advantages. With the promotion of the market economy and the doctrine of efficiency as a priority, the imbalanced development in the public education sector has been violently abused as a platform for the privileged and the power to exchange power and money for access to good public education resources. Multilayered inequalities, such as privilege in student selection between key schools and regular schools and access to public education between local families and migrant families, were constituted in the stratified public school admission to secondary education.

References

21st Century Education Research Institute. (2011). Beijingshi *"xiaoshengchu" Zexiaore de zhili: luzaihefang?* (Where is the way for alleviation of *Zexiao* fever in transition to junior high schools?). Beijing, China: 21st Century Education Research Institute.

Appleton, S., & Song, L. (2008). The myth of the "New Urban Poverty"? Trends in urban poverty in China, 1988–2002. In J. R. Logan (Ed.), *Urban China in transition* (pp. 48–65). Oxford, UK: Blackwell Publishing.

Ba, D. (1994, October 29). [Aoshu] re gai jiangjiangwen le ([Olympic math] time for cooling down). *China Education Daily*, p. 4.

Bai, C. (2011, June 22). 'Gongjianfei' liaodao yipi zhongxiaoxue xiaozhang (Co-founding fee-corruptions of principals in primary and junior high schools). *Jiancha Ribao*, p. 8.

Bang, H. (2010, November 5). Guangkao hongtou wenjian guanbuzhu *Zexiao*fei (Red title documents does not work for *Zexiao*fei). *Beijing Ribao*, p. 16.

Bao, D. (1996, March 11). '*Zexiao*sheng' xianxiang gai shache le (Time for terminating '*Zexiao* Sheng'). *China Education Daily*, p. 2.

Bi, Q. (1996, March 11). Zhongdian fuchi boruo xuexiao- zhongxiaoxue *Zexiao* shoufei wenti taolun pingshu (Supporting poor performing schools: Discussion on the charge of *Zexiao*fei in compulsory education). *Renmin Ribao*, p. 11.

Central Committee of the Chinese Communist Party. (1993). *Decision of the central committee of the communist party of China on some issues concerning the establishment of the socialist market economy*. Beijing.

Chen, H., & Wang, F. (2008, August 17). Zhangwai zijin chao yiyiyuan 'zhongguanchunsanxiao' xiaozheng tanwuan kaiting (A court session for corruption by the principal of 'zhongguancun No.3 Primary School' started). *Fazhi Ribao*. Retrieved September 19, 2012, from http://society.people.com.cn/GB/42733/7679018.html

Chen, T. (2005). Dui 'jinzhi *Zexiao*' zhengce de xianshixing fenxi (Analysis on policies opposing *Zexiao*). *Jiaoxue yu guanli* (Journal of Teaching and Management), *3*, 5–7.

Cheng, S. (2011). Jiyu yiwu jiaoyufa de zhongxiaoxue *Zexiao* xianxiang yanjiu (Research on *Zexiao* by compulsory education law). *Jiaoxue yu guanli* (Journal of Teaching and Management), *3*, 3–5.

Di, F., & Chai, W. (2007, July 30). Tangchu yitao youzhi ziyuan gongxianglu (A way for sharing quality education resources). *China Education Daily*, p. 2.

Dong, C. (1997, July 31). Tigao renshi zouchu wuqu (To improve understanding and escape from mistakes). *China Education Daily*, p. 1.

Du, H. (1986, August 23). Yao chedi jiejue chaoshou xuesheng zafei wenti (To deal with over charge school fees). *China Education Daily*, p. 1.

Fan, C. (2004, March 15). Jiejue '*Zexiao*' guanjian zai junheng ziyuan (Key to deal with "*Zexiao*": Balancing resources). *China Education Daily*, p. 2.

Fan, X. (2005, March 17). 'Aoshu': biecheng gongli zhuyi 'qiaomenzhuan' ('Olympic math' open sesame for utilitarianism?). *China Education Daily*, p. 1.

Gu, M. (2009, August 22). Aoshuban gai jiaoting le! (Time for stopping Olympic math classes!). *China Education Daily*, p. 3.

He, Y., Xu, Y., & Wang, Y. (2005, May 24). *Zexiao* beihou de jiaoli (Negotiation at the back of *Zexiao*). *Renmin Ribao*, p. 11.

Ji, J. (1997, August 16). Caiqu youxiao cuoshi jiada zhili lidu (To take effective measures, to strengthen control). *China Education Daily*, p. 1.

Jiao, X. (2003, May 22). Guifan shoufei yange guanli (To regulate fee charge with strict control). *China Education Daily*, p. 2.

Li, B. (2005). Urban social change in transitional China: A perspective of social exclusion and vulnerability. *Journal of Contingencies and Crisis Management*, *13*(2), 54–65.

Li, F. (2007). Yiwu jiaoyu jieduan *Zexiao* helixing chutan (Rationality of *Zexiao* in compulsory education). *Journal of the Chinese Society of Education*, *10*, 37–40.

References

Li, J. (1997, July 18). Jiaqiang jiandu yancha weiji (To strengthen monitoring and check disciplinary violation). *China Education Daily*, p. 1.

Li, X. (2007, June 19). Youdao zhaoshengshi, 'tiaozi' miantianfei (School admission comes, memo flies). *China Education Daily*, p. 8.

Li, X. (2009, April 1). Aoshu zhe haidao weihe yuejiaoyuechangkuang (Olympic math is becoming crazy). *China Youth Daily*. Retrieved June 14, 2010, from http://zqb.cyol.com/content/2009-04/01/content_2604906.htm

Li, Y., & Liang, R. (2009). Xiaoxue aoshure de lengsikao (To deeply think of olympic math for primary education). *Jiaoyu tansuo* (Education Exploration), *221*(11), 52–53.

Lin, J. (2006). Educational stratification and the new middle class. In G. A. Postiglione (Ed.), *Education and social change in China* (pp. 179–198). Armonk, NY: East Gate Book.

Liu, J. (2012). Light and shadow of public education for migrant children in urban China. In C. C. Yeakey (Ed.), *Living on the boundaries: Urban marginality in national and international contexts* (Vol. 8, pp. 79–115). Bingley, UK: Emerald Group Publishing Limited.

Lu, J. (2003, September 1). *'Zexiao'* feng yinchu gangashi (Issus caused by *'Zexiao'*). *Wen Hui Bao*, p. 6.

Luo, C., & Lai, Q. (1992, December 3). Zhongxiaoxue shoufei de sikao (Considering fee charge in compulsory education). *China Education Daily*, p. 2.

Ministry of Education. (2002). *Notice on consolidating the school operation administration of basic education*. Beijing.

Ministry of Education. (2007). *Opinions on the implementation of standardization of school fees and further rectification of the charge of unauthorized schools fees*. Beijing.

Ministry of Education. (2009). *Instructive opinions on strengthening the specification of administration of primary schools and junior high schools*. Beijing.

Ministry of Education. (2010a). *Opinions on instruction of rectifying the charge of unauthorized fees in Zexiao of compulsory education*. Beijing.

Ministry of Education. (2010b). *Opinions on applying the scientific outlook on development to further promote balanced development of compulsory education*. Beijing.

Ministry of Education, & State Council for Rectifying. (2002). *Opinions on further rectifying the unauthorized education charge*. Beijing.

Ministry of Education, National Development and Reform Commission, State Council Office for Rectifying, Ministry of Supervision, Ministry of Finance, National Audit Office, & General Administration of Press and Publication. (2003). *Opinions on implementation of rectifying the charge of unauthorized school fees*. Beijing.

Ministry of Education, State Council Office for Rectifying, Ministry of Supervision, National Development and Reform Commission, Ministry of Finance, National Audit Office, & General Administration of Press and Publication. (2008). *Opinions on the implementation of standardization of school fees and further rectification of the charge of the unauthorized schools fees*. Beijing.

Ministry of Education, State Council Office for Rectifying, Ministry of Supervision, National Development and Reform Commission, Ministry of Finance, National Audit Office, & General Administration of Press and Publication. (2009). *Opinions on the implementation of standardizing the charge of education fee to further rectify the charge of the unauthorized school fees*. Beijing.

Ministry of Education, State Council Office for Rectifying, Ministry of Supervision, National Development and Reform Commission, Ministry of Finance, National Audit Office, & General Administration of Press and Publication. (2010). *Opinions on the implementation of standardization of school fees and further rectification of the charge of the unauthorized schools fees*. Beijing.

Ministry of Education, State Council Office for Rectifying, Ministry of Supervision, National Development and Reform Commission, Ministry of Finance, National Audit Office, & General Administration of Press and Publication. (2011). *Opinions on the implementation of standard-*

ization of school fees and further rectification of the charge of the unauthorized schools fees. Beijing.
National Congress of Communist Party of China. (2006). *Decisions on Construction of Harmonious Society*. Beijing.
National development and reform commission, & Ministry of Education. (2005). *Notice on making good preparation for standardizing the fee charging of converted schools*. Beijing.
National People's Congress. (2006). *Compulsory education law of the People's Republic of China*. Beijing.
Niu, Y. (2005, November 29). Zexiaore weihe [gaoshao] butui (Persistent fever for *Zexiao*). *Wen Hui Bao*, p. 6.
Pu, W., & Jian, P. (1995, August 19). ZhilichuzhonghexiaoxueZexiaoshenggaoshoufei (Managing over fee charge of *Zexiao* student in primary and junior high schools). *China Education Daily*, p. 2.
Qu, S., & Yang, K. (2007). *Zexiao* jiaoyu yu geti renli ziben jilei (*Zexiao* and human resources accumulation for individuals). *Jiaoyu yu jingji* (Education and Economy), *4*, 11–14.
Sonoda, S. (2008). *Fubyodokoka tyugoku* (Unequal state: China). Tokyo, Japan: Chuokoron-shinsha.
State Council. (1994). *Opinions on implementation of outline of education reform and development in China*. Beijing.
State Council. (1998). *Opinions on the experiment of reform of school system in compulsory education stage*. Beijing.
State Council. (2001). *Decision on reform and development of basic education*. Beijing.
State Council. (2004). *Regulations for the implementation of minban education promotion law*. Beijing.
State Council. (2007). *Outline of eleventh five year plan for national education development*. Beijing.
State Council. (2010) *The national guidelines for medium- and long-term educational reform and development (2010–2020)*. Beijing.
State Council Office for Rectifying, & Ministry of Education. (2001). *Opinions on further rectifying the unauthorized education charges*. Beijing.
State Education Commission. (1993a). *Notice on rectification of the charge of the unauthorized fees in primary schools and middle schools*. Beijing.
State Education Commission. (1993b). *Notice on strengthening management of the charge of school fees in primary schools and middle schools*. Beijing.
State Education Commission. (1993c). *Indication on reducing heavy academic burden of student in compulsory education and full improvement of education quality*. Beijing.
State Education Commission. (1994a). *Notification on strengthening management of contests and awarding activities for students in primary education and secondary education*. Beijing.
State Education Commission. (1994b). *Opinions on full implementation of education policy and reduction of the heavy burden of primary and middle school students*. Beijing.
State Education Commission. (1994c). *Opinion on fully implementing education plan, reducing course burden of students in primary and junior high schools*. Beijing.
State Education Commission. (1995a). *Opinions regarding the implementation of rectification of the charge of the unauthorized fees*. Beijing.
State Education Commission. (1995b). *Notice of further promotion and improvement of junior high school admission reform*. Beijing.
State Education Commission. (1995c). *Notice on appraisal and designation of 1000 demonstration senior high schools*. Beijing.
State Education Commission. (1996). *Opinions on the implementation of the rectification of the charge of unauthorized fees in primary schools and middle schools*. Beijing.
State Education Commission. (1997a). *Opinions on the rectification of the charge of unauthorized fees in primary schools and middle schools*. Beijing.
State Education Commission. (1997b). *Some principle opinions on standardizing the school operation at the present compulsory education stage*. Beijing.

References

State Education Commission. (1997c). *Opinions on standardizing the school operation at the present compulsory education stage*. Beijing.
The World Bank. (2012). *China 2030*. Retrieved from Washington, DC: The World Bank.
Wang, Y. (2005, November 7). Zexaio nanti: shiheng de 'jiaoyuluanxiang' (Zexiao: imbalanced education in a mess). *China Education Daily*, p. 3.
Wang, Z. (1997, July 30). Zexiaoxuzonghezhili (Comprehensive management on *Zexiao*). *China Education Daily*, p. 1.
Wen, B. (2005, May 31). Gongping youxian haishi xiaolv youxian? (Equality and efficiency, which should be the priority?). *Renmin Ribao*, p. 11.
Wen, H. (2003, July 21). Xiwang youyitian buzai *Zexiao* (One day there will be no *Zexiao*"). *China Education Daily*, p. 1.
Weng, W. (2003). *Jiaoyu gongping yu xuexiao xuanze zhidu* (Education equality and school choice policy). Beijing, China: Beijing Shifan Daxue Chubanshe.
Whyte, M. K., & Guo, M. (2009). How angry are Chinese citizens about current inequalities? Evidence from a national survey. In K.-b. Chan, A. S. Ku, & Y.-w. Chu (Eds.), *Social stratification in Chinese societies* (pp. 17–54). Leiden, The Netherlands: Brill.
Wu, F. (2005, April 28). Zhaosheng fubai yihai yidai (Corruption in school admission destroys a generation). *Nanfang Zhoumo*, p. B14.
Xi, W. (1993, October 7). Xiaomen neiwai yousilu (Concerns on inside and outside of schools). *China Education Daily*, p. 1.
Xia, L. (2004, February 24). Ruhe rang '*Zexiao*' buzai yuyanyulie (What caused the endless '*Zexiao*'). *China Education Daily*, p. 2.
Xiao, S. (2009, December 15). *Zexiao* wenti jiushi zhengwei shifou zuowei de wenti (*Zexiao*: A problem of government?). *China Youth Daily*, p. 2.
Xinhuashe. (2008, March 9). *Zexiao*fei, heshi chengwei lishi (*Zexiao*fei: When it will become history?). *China Education Daily*, p. 2.
Xinhuashe. (2009, November 15). Cong xuanba jianzi dao wangren peilian (From elites selection to thousand training partners). *China Education Daily*, p. 2.
Xinxiaoxibao. (2009, August 16). Biegei *Zexiao*fei pishang hefa waiyi (Do not legalize *Zexiao*fei). *China Education Daily*, p. 2.
Yang, D. (2004, October 7). Bianxi 'jiaoyu chanyehua' (Ascertaining industrialization of education). *Nanfang Zhoumo*, p. C20.
Yang, Y. (2004, February 18). Aoshu zhengzai chengwei xianjing? (Olympic math: A fall-trap?). *China Education Daily*, p. 3.
Yang, Y. (2005, December 5). Jiaoyu junheng fazhan xueyao tizhi chuangxin (Balanced educational development needs innovation of system). *China Education Daily*, p. 7.
Ye, S. (2004, January 11). Jingcheng xiaoxuesheng qimo gangkaomang (Busy with exams: life of primary school students in Beijing in the end of the semester). *China Education Daily*, pp. 1–2.
Yu, Q. (1996, February 1). Women shi zeyang jiejue *Zexiao* wenti de" ("How we dealt with *Zexiao*"). *Renmin Ribao*, p. 5.
Zeng, S., & Yi, H. (1996, July 30). Jianjue zhizhi yiwu jiaoyu jieduan zhongxiaoxue luanshoufei (To terminate the charge of unauthorized fees in compulsory education without hesitation). *China Education Daily*, p. 1.
Zhang, J., Yu, J., Yu, L., Li, C., Zhao, H., & Bao, J. (2003, October 26). Toushi zhongxiaoxuexiao shoufei wenti (Looking through the fee charge in compulsory education). *China Education Daily*, p. 3.
Zhang, Z., Shi, F., & Shen, L. (2005, May 25). *Zexiao*feng jiaodong aoshure (Olympic math fever heated by *Zexiao*). *Renmin Ribao*, p. 11.
Zhao, C. (2009). *Zexiao*fei yu quanli xunzu lunxi (Analysis on *Zexiao*fei and power rent seeking). *Jiaoxue yu guanli, 8*, 14–15.

Chapter 4
Where There Is a Policy, There Is a Countermeasure

Abstract With the rapid social change in Chinese society, the Chinese government launched a series of educational policies for supporting national development. Policies on public school admission in compulsory education (Grades 1–9) have been amended at both the central and local levels to accommodate national needs. Meanwhile, local governments (at the city and district levels) also released their regulations on public school admission in compulsory education to meet requests from the central government and demands from local interest groups. This chapter interprets how gaps of policies on public school admission to junior high schools at central and local levels came out and shaped inequalities in admission to public lower secondary education at the school level. It reviews policy changes from the 1980s to 2011 in public school admission to uncover the diversity of public school admission policy at different administration levels. Moreover, it analyzes the interaction between the central and local governments to visualize how the power relationship between governments at different levels shaped the implementation of public school admission policy at the lower secondary education level. Analysis of interviews with stakeholders, such as school principals, local education officials, scholars, and managers of private tutoring institutes, is utilized to explain further how policy making and implementation affect the practice of student placement to public junior high schools in Beijing.

With the establishment of the new Chinese government in 1949, the government has given special focus on national education development. It has become a priority of the government to promote basic education for all since then. The proximity-based admission to public schools at the education level also became the main principle to enroll students to primary and junior high schools in China. This principle was even more strictly followed during the Cultural Revolution in the 1960s and the 1970s (Kusuyama, 2009; Li, 2009). With the end of the Cultural Revolution, the central government started launching a series of regulations to guarantee this principle. In 1980, the Central Committee of the Communist Party and the State Council jointly launched a statement to emphasize the necessary efforts for relocating schools in order to provide proximity-based public education (Central Committee of Chinese Communist Party & The State Council, 1980). In 1983, the government demonstrated it should gradually abolish an entrance exam for admission to junior high schools. And they also emphasized the importance of proximity-based school admission to free the overburdened students (Ministry of Education, 1983). It was until 1986 that the proximity-based admission to primary and junior secondary schools was officially presented in the first *Compulsory Education Law* in China. In 1986, the *Compulsory Education Law* gave the proximity-based admission to basic education (G1–G9) a legal status to guarantee the basic right of Chinese citizens to receive basic education by the central government. It also led to a reform of admission to public lower secondary education. In the same year, the government declared the abolishment of its entrance exam to public junior high schools. And they reemphasized the proximity-based admission to junior high schools (National People's Congress, 1986; State Education Commission, 1986). With a universalization of primary education, from 1993, the State Council further promoted a gradual reform of entrance exams to secondary education and tertiary education (State Council, 1993; State Education Commission, 1994a). Since then, the government kept giving a strict tone on the implementation of the proximity-based admission to public junior high schools. However, with the decentralization of public education to local governments, researchers also identify that there is a big gap in terms of implementing the proximity-based admission to public junior high schools between the central government and local governments. And there are diverse approaches introduced to admission to public junior high schools at the local level (21st Century Education Research Institute, 2011; Kusuyama, 2009; Li, 2009; Liu, 2013).

Similar to the development stages of public discourses on *Zexiao*, research shows that public discussion on policy change regarding the proximity-based admission to junior high schools followed a similar pattern. The issues of proximity-based admission were often mentioned together with the issue of the charge of the unauthorized school fees and the rise of students' burden in education in the 1980s and the 1990s. From 2000, it was always discussed with the issues of educational exclusion of disadvantaged groups and the rise of inequalities in public school admission (Li, 2009; Liu, 2015).

By following the development stages of public discourses on the proximity-based admission to junior high schools, this chapter presents how the central government and local governments interacted in the implementation of public school admission policy at the lower secondary education level. It also visualizes how policy making and policy implementation affected the practice of student placement to public junior high schools through mapping public discourses on public school admission through analyzing policy documents, newspapers, and interviews.

4.1 A Non-choice Public School Admission in China

According to the *Compulsory Education Law* of the People's Republic of China (National People's Congress, 2006), school-aged children should be admitted to nearby schools without any kind of selective examinations and streaming; and local authorities should provide enough school places for school-aged children in their areas. According to the law, the admission to primary education and lower secondary education should be made without an exam, be free, and follow the principle of proximity. Based on the principle of proximity, normally, parents send their children to the public schools which belong to the catchment area assigned by the respective local education authority (Wu, 2012). School catchment area refers to a geographic area in a county or district in which a public school can normally enroll children of the residents in that area.[1] Every public school has its own catchment area when it comes to public school admission.

The admission to public primary schools is normally based on the school catchment areas assigned by the local education authorities. In general, parents have to show household registration certification (*hukou*) and the actual living address certificate which can prove the child's registration belongs to the school catchment area.[2] As to the admission to public junior high schools, mainly, it also follows the principle of proximity without any selective examination. The local education authority designates an individual junior high school to several primary schools based on the school catchment areas. (If there is only one junior high school within one school catchment area, then all students from the primary schools in this area are enrolled automatically in the junior high school.) Recently, some local governments innovated diverse approaches for achieving equal education transition without breaking the proximity-based junior high school admission process. Within these approaches, the school lottery system (*diannaopaiwei*) is the most widely practiced one. Students in primary schools are randomly assigned to junior high schools by a computer system within the designated school district. However, since this system cannot guarantee to send children to a better school in one school district, it is not welcomed by parents and students (21st Century Education Research Institute, 2011; Lai, 2007; Li, 2009). The following section gives a review of school admission policies at different government levels to present the similarities and differences in the implementation of school admission in the 1990s and after 2000.

4.2 School Admission Policy: The 1990s

Public discussions showed that school admission policies were one of the forces that shaped *Zexiao* in urban China. On the one hand, the government kept emphasizing on "free, no screening, and proximity-based compulsory education," which

---

[1] As a resident, each student has to show their household registration (*hukou*) which belongs to the school catchment area. The *hukou* system was established in the late 1950s. It separates China into rural and urban areas. And it is closely related to different privileges to various social welfares, such as access to health care, public education, housing, and so forth (Wu & Treiman, 2004).

[2] According to Wang (2009 p. 19) and Wu (2012), in urban areas, if the residence certificate of the applying child is not registered in the same area as their parents or guardians, or as their actual living address, it is up to local education authorities to decide their school designation.

prohibited certificate-based[3] student selection in public school admission. With the same stance on the implementation of proximity-based school admission, the local governments left policy space to accommodate diverse needs for school admission in accordance with the local context. On the other hand, the government gave public schools privileges to select students based on certificates and students' achievements made both inside and outside of schools. As a result, the gap between policies at the central government level and at the local level left a space for policy makers and other stakeholders to interact in school admission to accommodate diverse needs.

4.2.1 Government Documents

Review of government documents showed emphasis on the implementation of a no entrance exam and proximity-based public school admission policy in the 1990s. At the same time, a series of documents were promulgated to ban public school admission based on talent contests for students at the compulsory education level.

With the implementation of the *Compulsory Education Law* in 1986, the entrance exams to junior high schools were gradually abolished in urban China (National People's Congress, 1986). At the same time, the proximity-based public school admission was repeatedly addressed in government documents. In 1993, the no entrance exam-based admission to junior high schools was addressed by the government (State Education Commission, 1993). The reform of junior high school admission delegated the administration of primary school graduation exams from the district to the school level in 1994. Furthermore, the education authority firmly promoted the no-entrance-exam policy and the principle of proximity-based junior high school admission. Nevertheless, there was a gap in terms of policy implementation between the central and local government levels. In 1995, although most provinces in China had already implemented the policies of no entrance exam and proximity-based junior high school admission, *Zexiao*-based school admission rapidly emerged in some urban schools (State Education Commission, 1995).

A new trend emerged when public schools performed their admission reviews. For example, with the gradual abolishment of the entrance exam to junior high schools, there was limited room for public schools to select students they preferred. In order to choose the best-performing students, some public schools linked certificates of contests or competitions with public school admissions. However, the government showed firm opposition to the new trend. In 1991, the State Education Commission pointed out that the certificates students received from contests or competitions intensified heavy burdens for students and teachers. The State Education Commission also emphasized that results of competitions should not be linked to school admissions (State Education Commission, 1991). In 1994, the government addressed the issues on Olympic math schools and classes that increased the workload for students and the charge of unauthorized fees. These schools and

---

[3]Certificate refers to child's talents and achievements received in after-school curriculum programs.

classes were required to close as soon as possible (State Education Commission, 1994a). Furthermore, contests or awarding activities were not allowed to link with public school admission (State Education Commission, 1994b).

4.2.2 Beijing's Policy

Review of the policy of school admission to junior high schools in Beijing showed that the municipal government followed the central government's policies. They abolished entrance exams to junior high schools, separated talent contests from admission to junior high schools, phased out school recommendation-based admission to junior high schools, and gradually reduced the public school gap in order to implement proximity-based school admission. On the other hand, the review showed the municipal government left policy space to accommodate needs for *Zexiao* from special groups. Moreover, there were diverse approaches for admission to public junior high schools during this period.

The proximity-based school admission was promoted with the abolishment of the unified graduation exams at the primary education level. However, the municipal government allowed public primary schools to recommend some well-performing students to some designated public junior high schools (Beijing Municipal Education Bureau, 1993, 1994; Beijing Municipal Education Committee, 1996). Moreover, in 1994, the policy allowed the district education administration to accommodate the demand for *Zexiao* from students without well-performing records (Beijing Municipal Education Bureau, 1994). The policies also provided advantages in school admission to special social groups, such as the children of education urban youth sent to the countryside during the Cultural Revolution, Taiwan residents, and postdoctoral scholars (Beijing Municipal Education Bureau, 1993). The approach for admission to public junior high schools became more diverse in the late 1990s. Students with special talents in arts, sports, and science had opportunities to go to designated public schools (Beijing Municipal Education Committee, 1998, 1999). With the commercialization of the public education sector, there were increasing private junior high schools and enterprise-based schools opening to the public through exams and tuition payments. In addition to these, there are increasing converted schools which were allowed to charge tuition to enroll students at the secondary education level.

4.2.3 Public Discussion

The public discussion review showed that key schools were given privileges to charge *Zexiaofei* and select students in their admission process. The analysis revealed that, due to limited education funding, there was a link between *Zexiaofei* and public school admission. As addressed in government documents, there was also a clear link between certificates received from contests and public school admissions. Particularly, students who had certificates from the Olympic math contest would receive direct or indirect enrollment by key schools. The *China Education Daily* reported the incidents as follows:

> In many documents of local education authorities, it regulates that students who received awards in Olympic math contests at different levels can be directly enrolled by key schools or get additional scores for education transition. In some places, it regulates that students who earned awards in Olympic contexts at various levels can be directly enrolled in junior high schools. With the abolishment of the entrance exam to junior high schools, school admission at the junior high school level is based on the principle of proximity. In order to go to key schools, it is important to have necessary "special talents".... With the high expectation on Olympic schools for education transition, various types of Olympic schools came into being. (Ba, 1994, October 29, translated by the author)[4]

Accordingly, the fever of Olympic math training and other special talent trainings were stimulated by student selection criteria of key schools.

The public discussion also illustrated that competition results became key criteria in key schools' admissions and student selection. For example, many key schools used Olympic math scores as the main criteria for selecting students. The *China Education Daily* described the situation in 1994:

> There is a student selection competition among key junior high schools in Beijing. In order to select good students, those schools hold Olympic schools or classes to select students. This competition even changed into different strange shapes. In order to enroll good students, some key schools signed an agreement with students. In Olympic schools owned by some key schools, students can be enrolled directly into the key school. Also, key primary schools and key junior high schools collaborated with each other on the school transition. The linkage became closer compared with the policy regulated. (Ba, 1994, December 19, translated by the author)

The analysis of the interaction between government documents and public discussions on the school admission policy indicated a mismatch between the public school admission policy and the actual practice of public schools, particularly key schools. The disparity in school admission among public schools was caused by the pro-key school admission policy. Certificates or results in the competition of students became the key criteria for key schools to choose students they preferred. The student selection by key schools intensified *Zexiao*.

4.3 School Admission Policy: After 2000

Similar to the discussion in the 1990s, the discussion after 2000 continuously considered the delegation of the administrative responsibility of compulsory education to the local government as the force that broke proximity-based public school admission and ironically stimulated the aspirations of the local education authority

---

[4] Similar arguments are also found in the *China Education Daily*, February 28, 1995 (Bao, 1995, February 28).

4.3 School Admission Policy: After 2000   103

to best accommodate needs for public school admission to junior high schools. Meanwhile, public discussion showed that public schools and other stakeholders innovated diverse channels in public school admission by utilizing the loophole of the policy left by the local government. These channels, such as the admission by school recommendation and by accepting students with special talents, intensified *Zexiao* in urban China.

4.3.1 Government Documents

After 2000, the government continuously addressed proximity-based public school admission (Ministry of Education, 2000, 2002, 2004; National People's Congress, 2006; State Council, 2010). Public schools at the compulsory education level were not allowed to admit students through exams or special selection. And they were not authorized to charge *Zexiaofei* to enroll students. Educational donations to public schools were not allowed to be linked with school admission (Ministry of Education et al., 2010, 2011). Moreover, the central government continuously emphasized the local (province, city, and district) governments and educational authorities have the main responsibility for constructing a balanced development of compulsory education and implementing the principle of proximity in public school admission. With the delegation of administration of compulsory education to the local governments, the central government kept encouraging the local governments to reduce the gap among public schools to achieve a balanced development of public education. They also emphasized that the local educational administration should comprehensively implement proximity-based school admission at the compulsory education level (Ministry of Education, 2006; Ministry of Education et al., 2010; National People's Congress, 2006).

4.3.2 Beijing's Policy

In contrast to the stance of the central government, a review of government documents on admission to public junior high schools in Beijing showed the delegation of authority on admission to public junior high schools to the local level left space for making diverse channels for admission to public junior high schools. It may accommodate the various demands for education transition. Conversely, it may also intensify *Zexiao* and cause inequality in compulsory public education. The review showed that the municipal government applied the central government's stance regarding equality and balanced development of public schools to admission policies to public junior high schools. On the other hand, they also emphasized that admission approaches should be relevant to the context at the district level. There was wider policy space utilized by the district educational administration to accommodate the local need for admission to public junior high schools. As a result, there were diverse options for public school admissions at the district level which were against the school policies at the municipal level (Beijing Municipal Education Committee, 2000, 2003, 2004, 2005, 2006, 2007, 2008, 2009, 2010, 2011). As shown in Table 1.1, there were more than ten channels for admission to public junior high schools in eight districts of Beijing in 2010. Recommendation-based school admission returned to the list of admission channels. The proportion of enrollment of special talented students through exam-based selection was much bigger than the municipal level (21st Century Education Research Institute, 2011). Co-founding-based school admission was officially shown on the policy documents. These were against proximity-based school admission that was addressed by the Beijing Municipal Education Committee. Moreover, these diverse admission channels fostered *Zexiao* development in Beijing.

4.3.3 Public Discussion

The public discussion after 2000 illustrated that the public school admission policy broke the balance of student distribution among public schools, which led to the imbalanced school development and intensified *Zexiao* (Bao & Chu, 2001, May 11). In contrast to the proximity-based public school admission promulgated by the *Compulsory Education Law* of 2006, various channels were innovated by the local education authority and public schools to meet the increasing demands for quality education. Besides the *Zexiaofei*-based school admission which existed from the 1990s, the channels for *Zexiao* became diversified after 2000. These channels for *Zexiao* presented as the interaction among stakeholders regarding the mismatch between demand and supply for school admissions. Besides the *Zexiaofei*-based option, public discussion indicated that student's achievement-based *Zexiao* became the mainstream channel for school admission after 2000. Mainly, this option included admission by school recommendation and admission by special talents. In the next section, I analyze public discourse on the relationship between these channels for school admission and their impact on *Zexiao*.

4.3.3.1 Admission by School Recommendation

The public discussion showed that the admission by school recommendation was an authorized (by the education authorities at the city or district level) channel for accommodating the needs from students in public school admission. However, since this channel was exam-based and depended on the subjective evaluation of students' academic performance, it stratified students and excluded low academic achievers but with good ethics from popular schools. More seriously, since this channel was linked to school promotion and student selection, it distorted the equality in compulsory education and made education more utilitarian.

The interviews I conducted with some scholars and relevant stakeholders showed diverse attitudes toward the admission by the school recommendation approach.

4.3 School Admission Policy: After 2000

According to Scholar A, the purpose of this approach was to accommodate diverse needs from the local education authority, public schools, and parents in Beijing. It was the result of negotiation among these stakeholder groups. He further explained:

> Both admissions by school recommendation and admission by special talents are authorized approaches in the current school admission process at the district level in Beijing. *Zexiao* does exist in these approaches. However, there is no rule to follow. ... In the past, the full computer lottery system-based school admission was not widely accepted. So, what shall we do? The solution should be widely accepted. Moreover, at the same time, it should be functional for student selection. Therefore, education authorities just provided various choices for parents and students to choose. You know, I do not think these stimulated *Zexiao*. In fact, they are just solutions for education authorities to alleviate the conflicts in the process of *Zexiao*. Or we can say it is a compromise indeed. (Interview with Scholar A, April 28, 2011, translated by the author)

In contrast to Scholar A's neutral attitude toward the admission by school recommendation, a former director of the education supervision office in one district of Beijing offered some negative comments about the channel. He believed this channel stratified students into different groups, which was against the *Compulsory Education Law*. In his opinion, students who were not recommended by schools were invisibly labeled as "not excellent students." Such channels would not only raise the burden of both parents and students but also affect students' attitudes toward their future lives. An office manager of School H shared the same view. He argued admission by school recommendation made compulsory education into a selective education process, and it was against the *Compulsory Education Law*.[5] Furthermore, the manager pointed out that the criterion utilized in the admission by school recommendation should be more objective and scientific. In most of the interviews I conducted in Beijing, stakeholders opposed the approach of taking "three excellence students"[6] as one of the most important criteria in the evaluation of the recommended students. They raised various weaknesses of the "three excellence student" evaluation. For example, the principal of School G in Beijing pointed out that the "three excellence student" evaluation was not comprehensive enough since it overemphasized students' academic achievements without giving a comprehensive evaluation on students' ethics and physical development. The director of Private Tutoring Institute A thought "three excellence students" were easily affected

---

[5] Interview with the manager of School H was conducted on May 10, 2011.

[6] In 1953, Mao Zedong gave the first definition of "three excellence students" in a statement for the Communist Youth League. He asked young people to achieve "good health, good study, and good work" (Mao, 1969). According to Chinanews.com, this evaluation of students was abolished during the Cultural Revolution. Then, it reemerged after the "lost ten years" (Retrieved from http://tv.sohu.com/20080916/n259584866.shtml, accessed on April 12, 2011). In 1982, the Ministry of Education and the Central Committee of Youth League promulgated the approach for selecting three excellence students in secondary education. The criterion should follow the students who are selected due to excellence in terms of morals (*de*), study (*zhi*), and health (*ti*) (Ministry of Education, 1982). According to CPC Beijing Municipal Committee, Beijing started evaluation of three excellence students beginning in 1979. Three excellence students selected in primary schools could be directly enrolled by key junior high schools (CPC Beijing Municipal Committee, 1979).

by subjective factors, such as teachers' biases and teacher-parent relationship.[7] The principal of School I in Beijing shared a similar opinion that people's biases influenced the evaluation of "three excellence students." She specified that:

> In fact, this evaluation causes various issues. We need to take care of teachers' feelings, pay attention to the corruption… you know, in order to let children become "three excellence students," parents give gifts to head teachers… and also we need to take care of children's feelings and parents' feelings. The evaluation will affect children. Some of them really care about the results. … (Interview with Principal of School I, October 25, 2011, translated by the author)[8]

The quote above shows that the evaluation of "three excellence students" in public schools was inked with teacher-parent relationships and parents' socioeconomic status. To some extent, "three excellence students" or "school recommendation students" became one type of "educational resource rent seeking" for public schools, teachers, and parents. It can be considered as a platform for "profit exchange" between public schools, teachers, and parents. And the participation in this exchange depends on the socioeconomic status of parents.

Parent 1 from a primary school in *Dongcheng* District of Beijing took admission by school recommendation to key schools as a predetermined process. In *Dongcheng* District, "three excellence students" was the prerequisite for students to gain school recommendation. As Parent 1 explained, "Although the recommendation process looked fair, there were loopholes for schools and parents to reach the results they preferred." She further explained the necessity for parents to take the initiative in this process:

> As parents, if we do not fight for the opportunity, then our children may not be selected. You know, for the head teacher, a "small gift" [gift at a low price] from parents generally does not work at all. You know, we [parents without high socioeconomic status] have very few chances! This year the school recommendation ratio is about 20% of the total enrollment. However, you know, there is no guarantee for accepting all recommend students in the admission process.[9] (Interview with Parent 1, Primary school in *Dongcheng* District, May 18, 2011, translated by the author)

---

[7] This interview was conducted on October 30, 2011.

[8] According to the principal of School I, problems caused by evaluation of "three excellence students" are quite complicated. In fact, the various evaluations have their reasons to exist. Now, if a child can be selected as a "three excellence student," then he or she can save 50,000 yuan or 100,000 yuan for parents! This title can change his life. To some extent, it is a reliable option for children to find out an access to popular schools. This evaluation also increases many management difficulties for participating schools. For these evaluations, we need to have four meetings among teachers. And finally, once the result is announced, school side has to accept parents' questions and arguments. Furthermore, sometimes the evaluation process is difficult to manage. The number of students given by the education authority sometimes is difficult to distribute to each class. For instance, if we have to select seven or eight students from three classes, it is difficult to balance. It may even deteriorate the relationship between teachers and school leaders.

[9] A similar problem was also mentioned by the principal of School I. According to this principal, in Xuanwu District, the enrollment ratio of school recommendation students was about 87% in 2010. It means that not 100% of school recommendation students can be successfully enrolled by key schools (Interview with the principal of School I was conducted on October 25, 2011).

According to *Guangming Ribao*, the quota of school recommendation student is determined by the education authority in each district. Since school recommendation students should be all round developed, the admission by school recommendation approach intensified the competition in school transition (Zhang, 2011, May 10).

The principal of School G showed a negative attitude toward the link between "three excellence students" and school admission to junior high schools. In his opinion, the "three excellence student" title was just an honor for students. The link with school admission made the title very utilitarian. In other words, students might pretend to be good for becoming a "three excellence student" in order to be recommended to key schools.[10] In addition, according to the director of Private Tutoring Institute A, the "three excellence student" evaluation often excluded students with good capacity but did not seriously obey the school disciplines. Thus, such an evaluation became a barrier for those students to access to key schools.[11]

4.3.3.2 Admission by Special Talents

With the school admission reform in the 1990s, admission by special talents at the compulsory education level was innovated by local education authorities to meet the increasing demand for sending children to popular schools. Public discussion illustrated that this option became a channel for parents to choose schools for their children. With the abolishment of the entrance exam to junior high schools, students had to take more extracurricular classes to get certificates to meet the requirements of popular schools for school admission (Xiaoxin Wu, 2008). The interviews with parents conducted by the media showed that many of them had to spend a lot of money and sent their children to various after-school classes. These classes could enable their children to become more competitive in the admission by acquiring special talents. The interviews with parents showed that the main reason for doing so was to send their children to popular schools. One parent said:

> The reason for [my child] taking the Music Level Exam is because of the current school admission process. Some schools showed they enroll special talent students based on their certificates. (Shi, 2004, February 17, translated by the author)

Another parent said:

> if my child can get awards in music instrument contests, then, it will be helpful for my child to be recommended to a key senior high school or taking special talent student tests given by key senior high schools. (Jinri Zaobao, 2007, September 23, translated by the author)

The interviews above indicated that the after-school classes or special training for cultivating children's interests became utilitarian for sending children to popular schools.

---

[10] The interview with the principal of School G was conducted on October 27, 2011.
[11] The interview with the office director of a private tutoring institute was conducted on April 20, 2011.

Moreover, admission by special talents was also widely considered as a convenient approach for public schools to select students in accordance with their interests. Schools which were authorized to enroll special talent students could enroll any student they needed.[12] They could select students by tests authorized and scheduled by the local education authority. One principal said that these schools could do anything for the students they preferred (Ye, Chai, & Bao, 2006, June 13). In other words, the government-authorized approach could be considered as a platform for popular schools to select students. Obviously, it is against the *Compulsory Education Law* in China. Meanwhile, it intensified the competition in school admission involving schools, students, and parents.

In addition, public discussion showed that the lack of criteria for student evaluation was also one reason for schools to emphasize the importance of certificates approving various special talents of students. In contrast to the *hukou*-based school admission to junior high schools, popular schools took initiatives to take various certificates as a kind of criteria for student selection (Su, 2005, November 8). Accordingly, the student selection by popular schools generated a certificate fever for school admission and intensified *Zexiao* as a result. Meanwhile, it seems that school admission by special talents became key school-initiated student selection. Both parents and students were forced to follow the rules.

4.3.3.3 Admission by Olympic Math and PETS

One of the rules is to select students based on achievement in Olympic math study. In contrast to the prohibition on school admission by Olympic math, public discussion showed that Olympic math was closely linked with school admission at the practice level. According to public discussion, achievement in Olympic math as a special talent was widely accepted as a channel for enrollment of special talent students. The link between Olympic math and public school admission stimulated parents' aspirations for sending their children to Olympic math training classes. On the other hand, this link connected various stakeholders for their own interests through *Zexiao*, such as key schools and private tutoring institutes.

For parents, the Olympic math was passport for children's education transition to popular schools. One parent showed the close link between Olympic math and school admission. And the achievement in Olympic math of pupils can save *Zexiaofei* for their parents in school admission to junior high schools (Wang, 2005, April 17). Another parent from Beijing explained that the purpose of sending children to Olympic math was to enroll a child into an experiment class in key schools (Chai, 2005, March 2). Furthermore, the enlargement of enrollment in higher education was also considered as an external reason for the Olympic math fever in

---

[12] According to an interview with the principal of School E, public schools which can enroll special talented students should be authorized by the local education authority. Mainly, the former key schools are those which are qualified to be selected as such a type of school. The interview was conducted on May 16, 2011.

Zexiao at the compulsory education level (Li & Liang, 2009). As introduced in Chap. 1, in order to send children to key universities in China, parents believe *Zexiao* is one step in preparation for the entrance exams to universities. The director of Private Tutoring Institute B took Olympic math class as a platform for students and parents to get access to key schools. Standing behind the private tutoring institute, she argued that it was unfair to close Olympic math classes as they accommodate the needs of parents and students.[13] Meanwhile, the director of Private Tutoring Institute A argued that the Olympic math-based *Zexiao* is unfair if it needs parents to invest both time and money in the relevant training. Relatively, it excluded disadvantaged groups from this channel for *Zexiao*.

For schools, Olympic math was considered as one criterion to select students. News about Olympic math study in Beijing showed the link between Olympic math and school admission to junior high schools. It caused the boom of Olympic math study (China Education Daily, 2003, September 28). Furthermore, student selection for key schools is closely dependent on the collaboration between private tutoring institutes and key schools. It intensified school admission by Olympic math. An interview with a parent in the fieldwork illustrated a close link between Olympic math, private tutoring institutes, and key schools in school admission. She mentioned that:

> My son took part in two Olympic math classes in two private tutoring institutes.[14] Since both of these schools are so-called "Golden Classes", we sent our son to study there. I heard that one of the schools recommended 91 students who studied in this private tutoring school to key schools as special talent students in *Dongcheng* District last year (2010).[15] You know, this private tutoring school is becoming popular in recent years in Beijing. Key schools in this (*Dongcheng*) District all invited their director to interview students who applied these key schools. And some key schools even invited this school to organize entrance exams for them to select students. So ... (laughing)... you can see the relationship and the link with education transition.... (Interview with Parent 1 from primary school in *Dongcheng* District, May 18, 2011, translated by the author)

---

[13] This interview was conducted on April 30, 2011.

[14] One of the private tutoring institutes in this conversation has been listed on the exchange market in China. According to independent scholar Feng Wen, nowadays, there are four private tutoring institutes which have been listed on the exchange market in China. The main reason for the rise of these institutes' success is closely linked with the exam-oriented education. Since there are needs for Olympic math for education transition to public junior high schools, these private tutoring institutes identified the needs and responded efficiently. Mainly, private tutoring institutes in China are just supplements for school education at the basic education level. Their role is to strengthen what schools teach in the class. Without changing the education structure on the policy and systematic level, it is impossible for private tutoring institutes to change. The student selection-based collaboration between key schools and some private tutoring institutes is understandable. Since there is profit involved, there is collaboration (Interview with the Director of Private Tutoring Institute A was conducted on October 20, 2011).

[15] Parent 1 heard this information from other parents whose children studied Olympic math in the same institute as Parent 1's son did. According to Parent 1, parents always shared rumors about school admission policies, enrollment numbers in specific key schools, and strategies for going to key schools.

In my fieldwork, although the director of Private Tutoring Institute B in Beijing denied their collaboration with key junior high schools, she clarified that private tutoring institutes provided a platform for parents and junior high schools to make a mutual selection. Exams held by private tutoring institutes were taken as a criterion for selecting students by some key schools. It became an approach for key schools to select students they expected. Meanwhile, the Olympic math-focused exam for student selection by key schools further intensified Olympic math for *Zexiao*. According to this director, some public junior high schools, especially the key schools, took knowledge of Olympic math as the main part in their entrance tests. These tests were much more difficult than what students learned from the required school curriculum. In order to meet the needs for making children well prepared for these tests, it was necessary for parents to send their children to after-school programs held by private tutoring institutes. In other words, the mismatch between the required school curriculum and the tests for student selection at key schools intensified the development of *Zexiao* by achievement in Olympic math.

In addition, the public media also reported that the direct reason for Olympic math in China was the economic profits generated through the link between Olympic math and education transition (China Education Daily, 2009, May 31). Considering the cost spent on Olympic math training classes, relevant textbooks, and contests, there was a tremendous amount of benefits generated by Olympic math.

Meanwhile, interviews with the director of Private Tutoring Institute A showed that the lack of appropriate evaluation criteria for the student is the core reason for school admission by Olympic math. He confessed that Olympic math provided a relatively objective evaluation criterion for students. And to some extent, it solved the problem of equality in education. Relatively, exam-based education transition was a fair approach for students to compete for access to popular schools.[16]

Besides Olympic math, public discussion indicated that PETS became a channel for parents and students to take part in *Zexiao* as it became a standard for key schools to select students (Beijing Wanbao, 2007, May 16).[17] Scholars also stressed that the boom for *Zexiao* by PETS was caused by the popular school which took it as a criterion to select students (Wang, 2008a; Yang, 2006; Yang & Chai, 2010). Apparently, admission by special talents can be considered as the result of the mismatch between

---

[16] In the interview, Mr. Wen explained the paradox of Olympic math in terms of education transition. According to him, the Olympic math-based school admission is shaped by the lack of a standardized student evaluation system. For parents, Olympic math is an approach to send children to popular schools, especially for parents who do not have *guanxi* and money. Therefore, when Professor Dongping Yang publicly showed his firm opposition to Olympic math and its link with education transition, many parents stood up against him and protect their assurance for their children's good quality education (Interview with Feng Wen was conducted on October 20, 2011). A similar argument can also be found on the *China Education Daily*, March 1. 2005. According to the *China Education Daily*, Siming Zhang, math teacher, Affiliated High School of Peking University, pointed out that the narrow student selection standard made Olympic math a standard for student selection (Bao, Zhang, & Chai, 2005, March 1).

[17] China Youth Daily, November 24, 2005. Retrieved from http://33te.com/education/edu_news/051214224518389638530.shtml, accessed on March 13, 2012.

public school admission and the demand for quality education from parents and students. Meanwhile, it is also intensified by the motivation of popular schools for student selection. In other words, admission by special talents became a platform for mutual selection between parents and public schools.

4.3.3.4 Admission by Pre-admission Training Class

The public discussion showed that pre-admission training classes as a channel for *Zexiao* were stimulated by the lack of reliable student evaluation criteria in the current public school admission. The pre-admission training class is considered as the result of public school admission reform. The principal of School F specified that:

> the abolishment of the unified entrance exam to junior high school led to a school admission without a standard for student selection. It stimulated the market of the pre-admission training classes. As a result, key schools are always oversubscribed since many students apply to such schools. Therefore, these schools have to select good students through exams. Since some private tutoring institutes just provide such training and guarantee the access to key schools with collaboration with key schools, the pre-admission training classes become more popular.... (Interview with Principal of School F, November 7, 2011, translated by the author)

This approach became a platform for key schools to select students they preferred through collaboration with private tutoring institutes. It intensified the imbalance in student distribution between public schools and *Zexiao* in urban China. A government official from the Ministry of Education pointed out that it was necessary to alleviate the phenomenon of *"Zhankengban"* since some schools (key schools) have already taken it as a tool for selecting students (Chun, 2011, February 24). According to the *China Education Daily*, an interview with a parent showed *"Zhankengban"* became a tool for key schools' student selection. The parent reported:

> For popular junior high schools, school recommendation students should be best from primary schools. However, due to the different levels of primary schools, the best students recommended from different primary schools are different (in terms of quality). Since acquiring good quality students is the main objective for popular junior high schools, principals from such schools say that they have their own ways to select good students. Their own way is to hold selection exams by training institutes. Then based on the results, schools will select students. The most popular training institutes have a close relationship with those key schools. Therefore, only those who attend their classes can have the opportunity to take such exams. (Wang, 2008b, July 6, translated by the author)

According to the *Beijing Ribao*, in order to send children to go to popular schools, parents have to enroll children to *"Zhankengban"* through entrance exams. Then, students will be screened and selected by key schools through several rounds of the exams. Interviews I conducted with the principal of School E[18] and the principal of School G[19] in Beijing indicated that the nature of the pre-admission training classes is to serve as a tool for student selection by key schools. Sometimes, in order to

---

[18] Interview with the principal of School E was conducted on May 16, 2011.

[19] Interview with the principal of School G was conducted on October 27, 2011.

avoid the influence by the sudden change of policy at the city or district level, the student selection through *"Zhankengban"* is often held before the announcement of public school admission policy announcements. In Beijing, before the announcement of the school admission policy by the municipal education authority, some popular schools have already finished their student selection through pre-admission training classes (Liu, 2009, March 25).

A series of reports showed the collaboration between parents, private tutoring institutes, and key schools by means of pre-admission training classes. The *Guangming Daily* also noted that:

> Preadmission training classes, in fact, is *Zexiao*. It is totally against the principle of proximity and the equity in compulsory education and the balanced compulsory education development. The pre-admission training class is created by parents. It includes "Gold Classes" which are held by popular school affiliated training institutes; Multifunctional Classes which are held by popular private training institutes. (Guangming Ribao, 2010, July 25; translated by the author)

As the main participants in the *"Zhankengban,"* parents shared their experiences which show collaboration between private tutoring institutes and key schools. One parent introduced:

> Now, training schools have a direct relationship with some key schools. They held selection exams for key schools granting the possibility for children who wanted to go to key schools. Exam results in these schools become important references for key schools to select children. (Beijing Youth Daily, 2009, February 15, translated by the author)

The analysis of pre-admission classes showed the close collaboration between key schools and private tutoring institutes in terms of public school admission. On the other hand, it illustrated key schools took initiatives in student selection which was against the *Compulsory Education Law*. Private tutoring institutes became the media for parents and public schools to achieve mutual selection. At the same time, they could generate profits through holding the pre-admission training classes and hosting exams for student selection by key schools. In other words, school admission to junior high schools was closely involved in the education market through student selection by key schools. The marketization of public school admission generated profits for key schools, private tutoring institutes, and individual families. Meanwhile, this process also excluded families without relevant resources to enroll their children in key schools.

This chapter explained how gaps of policies on public school admission to junior high schools affected the practice of student placement in admission to public junior high schools in urban China. The analysis of government policies on school admission at central, municipal, and district levels between the 1990s and the 2000s showed that three levels of educational administration kept a common stance on a full implementation of proximity-based admission to public junior high schools in urban China. Nevertheless, with the delegation of educational administration, both municipality and district educational administrations fully utilized policy space to innovate diverse channels of admission to public schools to accommodate needs formulated by their respective local contexts. There were always countermeasures created by the district educational administration to enroll students without following the proximity-based school admission policy. It shows that delegation of educational administration to district authorities and the policy spaces left by municipal and district governments further enlarged the gaps between policy making and implementation of proximity-based admission to public junior high schools. Moreover, the analysis indicated that a policy space at the municipal level provided stakeholders at the district level advantages in admission to public junior high schools. A pro-key school admission policy authorized the key schools to select students through payment of *Zexiaofei*, school recommendation, and special talents training of students. Furthermore, a collaboration between public key schools and private tutoring institutes provided a platform for key schools and prosperous families to practice mutual selection in admission to public junior high schools. This chapter told us how policy space left at the district level forced the diversification of channels for admission to public junior high schools. Also, it further presented how proximity-based school admission was reshaped by the delegation of education administration to local governments and the commercialization of public education in urban China.

References

21st Century Education Research Institute. (2011). *Beijingshi "xiaoshengchu" Zexiaore de zhili: luzaihefang?* (Where is the way for alleviation of *Zexiao* fever in transition to junior high schools?). Beijing, China: 21st Century Education Research Institute.

Ba, D. (1994, December 19). [Aoshu] re gai jiangjiangwen le ([Olympic math] time for cooling down). *China Education Daily*, p. 1.

Bao, D. (1995, February 28). Weishenme tingban aoxiao (ban) (Why the Olympic math school (class) should be closed?). *China Education Daily*, p. 1.

Bao, D., & Chu, Z. (2001, May 11). *Zexiao*sheng wenti zhende jianbuduan? (*Zexiao* cannot be alleviated?). *China Education Daily*, p. 6.

Bao, D., Zhang, G., & Chai, W. (2005, March 1). "Zhuanjia shijiaoxia de 'aoshure'" ("The views of specialists on "Olympic Math Fever""), *China Education Daily*, pp. 1–2.

Beijing Municipal Education Bureau. (1993). *Interim provisions on education transition to junior high school*. Beijing.

Beijing Municipal Education Bureau. (1994). *Notification of opinion of the further reform of school admission to junior high school in Beijing*. Beijing.

Beijing Municipal Education Committee. (1996). *Opinions on reform of junior high school admission*. Beijing.

Beijing Municipal Education Committee. (1998). *Opinion on education transition to junior high school in Beijing*. Beijing.

Beijing Municipal Education Committee. (1999). *Notification of education transition to junior high school in Beijing*. Beijing.

Beijing Municipal Education Committee. (2000). *Notification of education transition to junior high school*. Beijing.

Beijing Municipal Education Committee. (2003). *Notification of education transition to junior high school*. Beijing.

Beijing Municipal Education Committee. (2004). *Notification of education transition to junior high school*. Beijing.

Beijing Municipal Education Committee. (2005). *Notification of education transition to junior high school*. Beijing.

Beijing Municipal Education Committee. (2006). *Opinions on primary school and junior high school admission.* Beijing.
Beijing Municipal Education Committee. (2007). *Opinions on primary school and junior high school admission.* Beijing.
Beijing Municipal Education Committee. (2008). *Opinions on primary school and junior high school admission.* Beijing.
Beijing Municipal Education Committee. (2009). *Opinions on primary school and junior high school admission.* Beijing.
Beijing Municipal Education Committee. (2010). *Opinions on school admission at compulsory education level.* Beijing.
Beijing Municipal Education Committee. (2011). *Opinions on school admission at compulsory education level.* Beijing.
Beijing Wanbao. (2007, May 16). *Jinkao quanguo gonggong yingyu dengji jiefang shiwan haizi* (Permission for 100,000 kids for PETS). Retrieved July 15, 2011, from http://edu.sina.com.cn/yyks/2007-05-16/112482660.html
Beijing Youth Daily. (2009, February 15). Peixunbanansongshengyuan, Xiaoshengchuqianguize? (Student Selection through private tutoring class, a casting couch in admission to the junior high school?). *China Education Daily,* p. 2.
Central Committee of Chinese Communist Party, & The State Council. (1980). *Decision on several issues concerning universalization of primary education.* Beijing.
Chai, M. (2005, March 2). Cong 'aoshu' xianxiang shuokaiqu (Starting from 'Olympic Math'). *China Education Daily,* p. 1.
China Education Daily. (2003, September 28). Shang aoxiao wei shengxue? (Olympic School for Education Transition?). *China Education Daily,* p. 2.
China Education Daily. (2009, May 31). Fanlan de aoshu zhende wuren nengguan? (No one can govern Olympic math?). *China Education Daily,* p. 2.
Chun, C. (2011, February 24). Zhuolizhi "*Zexiaofei*" "Zhankengban" (Making efforts to prevent "*Zexiaofei*" and "Zhankengban"). *China Youth Daily,* p. 6.
CPC Beijing Municipal Committee. (1979). *Decision on problems of improvement of education quality in primary and secondary education.* Beijing.
Guangming Ribao. (2010, July 25). Zhankengban Weihejinerbujue (Why Zhankengban cannot be eliminated). *China Education Daily,* p. 2.
Jinri Zaobao. (2007, September 23). Yiban haizi xue yueqi zhiwei kaoji jiafen (About 50% of kids study musical instruments for scores). *China Education Daily,* p. 2.
Kusuyama, K. (2009). *Gendai Tyugoku Syotyutokyoiku no tayoka to seito kaikaku* (The diversification and schooling system reform of elementary and secondary education in China). Tokyo, Japan: Toshindo Publishing Co., Ltd
Lai, F. (2007). *The effect of winning a first-choice school entry lottery on student performance: Evidence from a natural experiment.* New York: New York University. Retrieved July 12, 2011, from http://ncspe.tc.columbia.edu/working-papers/OP139.pdf
Li, J. (2009). *Yiwu jiaoyu jieduan jiujin ruxue zhengce fenxi (Analysis on proximity-based school admission in compulsory education).* Shanghai, China: Xue Lin Chu Ban She.
Li, Y., & Liang, R. (2009). Xiaoxue aoshure de lengsikao (To deeply think of Olympic math for primary education). *Jiaoyu tansuo* (Education Exploration), *221*(11), 52–53.
Liu, H. (2009, March 25). Xiaoshengchu Zhengceweidingceshixianxing (Selection exam occurred before Policy on Admission to Junior High Schools launched). *Beijing Ribao,* p. RJ063.
Liu, J. (2013). *The development of inequality in public school admission: Public discourses on Zexiao and practices in Urban China.* PhD Nagoya, Japan: Nagoya University. Retrieved May 24, 2014, from http://ir.nul.nagoya-u.ac.jp/jspui/bitstream/2237/18153/1/k10080.pdf
Liu, J. (2015). Understanding inequality in public school admission in urban China: Analysis of public discourses on *Zexiao*. *Asian Education and Development Studies, 4*(4), 434–447.
Mao, Z. (1969). *Maozhuxi lun jiaoyu geming* (Mao Zhuxi's educational revolution). Beijing.

References

Ministry of Education. (1982). *The trail for evaluation of three excellence student among students in secondary education*. Beijing.
Ministry of Education. (1983). *Opinions on further improving education quality of regular junior high schools*. Beijing.
Ministry of Education. (2000). *Urgent notice of reduction of over heavy burden of primary school students*. Beijing.
Ministry of Education. (2002). *Notice on consolidating the school operation administration of basic education*. Beijing.
Ministry of Education. (2004). *2003–2007 Action plan for invigorating education*. Beijing.
Ministry of Education. (2006). *Opinions on implementation of compulsory education law and further regulations on administration in compulsory education*. Beijing.
Ministry of Education, State Council Office for Rectifying, Ministry of Supervision, National Development and Reform Commission, Ministry of Finance, National Audit Office, & General Administration of Press and Publication. (2010). *Opinions on the implementation of standardization of school fees and further rectification of the charge of the unauthorized schools fees*. Beijing.
Ministry of Education, State Council Office for Rectifying, Ministry of Supervision, National Development and Reform Commission, Ministry of Finance, National Audit Office, & General Administration of Press and Publication. (2011). *Opinions on the implementation of standardization of school fees and further rectification of the charge of the unauthorized schools fees*. Beijing.
National People's Congress. (1986). *Compulsory education law of the People's Republic of China*. Beijing.
National People's Congress. (2006). *Compulsory education law of the People's Republic of China*. Beijing.
Shi, X. (2004, February 17). Yaoxiangbugongli zhende tingnan (Difficult to be away from utilitarian). *China Education Daily*, p. 2.
State Council. (1993). *Outline of the reform and development of China's education*. Beijing.
State Council. (2010). *The national guidelines for medium- and long-term educational reform and development (2010–2020)*. Beijing.
State Education Commission. (1986). *Notice on reform of junior high school admission in the place where middle school education has been popularized*. Beijing.
State Education Commission. (1991). *Notice on strengthening management of competitions for students in primary schools and junior high schools*. Beijing.
State Education Commission. (1993). *Indication on reducing heavy academic burden of student in compulsory education and full improvement of education quality*. Beijing.
State Education Commission. (1994a). *Opinions on full implementation of education policy and reduction of the heavy burden of primary and middle school students*. Beijing.
State Education Commission. (1994b). *Notification on strengthening management of contests and awarding activities for students in primary education and secondary education*. Beijing.
State Education Commission. (1995). *Notice of further promotion and improvement of junior high school admission reform*. Beijing.
Su, L. (2005, November 8). 'Zhengshu' zachenglejin 'mingxiao' de qiaomenzhuan (Certificates: Open sesame for access to well-known schools?). *China Education Daily*, p. Weekly.
Wang, S. (2005, April 17). 'Aosai' peixun heshi zhenzheng xiaoshi? ('Olympic tests': When the end comes?). *China Education Daily*, p. 1.
Wang, J. (2008a). *Jiaoyu: Cong junhen zouxiang gongping (Education: From balance to equality)*. Beijing, China: Beijing Normal University Publishing Group.
Wang, J. (2008b, July 6). Xiaoshengchuliuxingbing (Epidemic in admission to junior high schools). *China Education Daily*, p. 3.
Wu, X. (2008). The power of positional competition and market mechanism: A case study of recent parental choice development in China. *Journal of Education Policy, 23*(6), 595–614.

Wu, X. (2012). School choice with Chinese characteristics. *Comparative Education, 48*(3), 347–366.

Wu, X., & Treiman, D. J. (2004). The household registration system and social stratification in China: 1955–1996. *Demography, 41*(2), 363–384.

Yang, D. (2006). *Zhongguo jiaoyu gongping de lixiang yu xianshi* (The wish and reality of educational equality in China). Beijing, China: Peking University Press.

Yang, D., & Chai, C. (2010). *Zhongguo jiaoyu fazhan baogao 2010* (Annual report on China's education 2010). Beijing, China: Social Sciences Academic Press (China).

Ye, S., Chai, W., & Bao, D. (2006, June 13). Pushuomili 'xiaoshengchu' (Puzzle: education transition to junior high schools). *China Education Daily*, p. 1.

Zhang, J. (2011, May 10). 'Tuiyou' zhengce jiaju xiaoshengchu jingzheng jiazhang haizi doulei" ("School recommendation intensified competition for education transition to junior high schools and made parents and kids tired"). *Guangming Ribao*, p. 6.

Chapter 5
The Key Schools and *Zexiao*

Abstract A key school system, started in the 1950s, stratified the public school system in China into key schools and regular schools. Despite an "official abolishment" of the system in the late 1990s, this system led to an enlargement of gaps in development between key schools and regular schools. On the other hand, the limited access to the key schools was commercialized by local educational administrations to seek rent for generating fund to develop the local public education sector. This caused competition for admission to key junior high schools in urban China. In this chapter, the author will review the history of the key school system and the expansion of gaps between public schools. Then, he will explain how stratification of the public school system and commercialization of the limited access to the key schools formulated inequality in admission to public junior high schools in urban China through analyzing the public discourses. In the end, he will untangle a rise of collusion between the key schools and cram schools in student selection for admission to public lower secondary education in urban China by analyzing interviews with school principals and managers of cram schools in Beijing.

Those who have experience in studying in the Chinese education system must have heard about the term "key school." Millions of parents wish to enroll their children in such schools as they believe that these schools provide a better quality of education compared with other regular schools. As Chinese (especially in urban context), since we were young, we had already been taught that we had to do our best to enter into key schools if we want to have a bright future. As a culture, key schools have been widely recognized as "good schools." Students inside of these schools are socially labeled as "good students." And teachers of these schools are well known as "qualified teachers." Students and teachers who are not in such schools are taken as the "not excellent." Consequently, the key school system led to a stratification of public school system. Key schools are not only the examples for regular schools to learn from but also considered the brand of quality and excellent. Therefore, the limited access to these schools became targets of competition among parents for sending their kids to these schools. With the influence of elitism in Chinese society, key schools were able to keep their privileges in terms of school development, student selection, and teacher assignment. Since the 1990s, a commercialization of quality public education resources which aimed at generating additional revenue for public education investment started. The reform gave privileges to the key schools, and the schools began charging school fees and making student selections for school admission. These strengthened the advantages of the key schools and enlarged the gaps between public schools. Furthermore, through collaboration with private tutoring institutes, these "good schools" competed with each other to select better-performing students in school admission. The competition and the collaboration further broke the balance of school development and deteriorated inequality in public school admission.

This chapter gives a review of the development of a gap between public schools formed by the key school system. Furthermore, it presents results of analysis of public discourses on the gap between public schools to indicate how the gap between public schools affected public school admission. The subsequent section then introduces how key schools and private tutoring institutes worked together to select students for admission to junior high schools. Finally, the chapter concludes by summarizing how admission to public junior high schools in urban China was shaped by a stratification of public school system, commercialization of public education resource, and collusion for student selection for *Zexiao* between public schools and private tutoring institutes.

5.1 The Key School System

While the interregional disparity and the disparity between rural areas and urban areas objectively occur, the disparity among schools within a city or a school catchment area has been created deliberately (Qin, 2008). One of the main reasons for this disparity is the reemergence of the key school system. There is an obvious disparity between key schools and ordinary schools. The initial reason for establishing key schools was to concentrate limited resources on building a few limited high-quality schools, so as to train human resources effectively for socialist construction. Compared with ordinary schools, key schools have better equipment, more highly qualified teachers, more funding, and more able pupils selected by examination. The direct result of the key school system is the disparity between key schools and ordinary schools. Disparities among schools occur not only between key schools and ordinary schools but also among ordinary schools and among key schools. Schools are divided into different divisions by education administration and by communities, intentionally or unintentionally. Key schools vary at provincial (metropolitan area or autonomous region) level or city level or district level or county level; ordinary schools can also be divided into the adequate, or the weak, or the very weak. Disparities are seen in the promotion rate, teacher quality, student resources, financial resources, reputation, school buildings, teaching facilities, libraries, staff welfare, bonuses, etc. (Qin, 2008, p. 335). According to Wu (2008), a dual-track system, including regular schools and key schools, has been in existence in China for more than half a century.

5.1 The Key School System

The history of the key school system should be tracked back to the early 1950s. In 1953, Mao Zedong raised the discussion about the establishment of key junior high schools in the meeting of CPC Central Political Bureau. Based on the decision made in this meeting, in May 26, 1953, the Ministry of Education announced the *Notification of promoting the establishment of Senior High Schools and Complete High Schools to improve education quality*. The notification asked local education administrations to select one or two from junior high schools as the key schools at secondary education level. Experiences from these schools should be used to promote other schools. In the 2nd National Education Conference held in 1953, 194 junior high schools within the country were selected as the key high schools, which was 4.4% of the total number of high schools. This number increased to 487 in 1963 (Encyclopedia of China Publishing House, 1984). In terms of key primary schools, by the notification on the construction of key primary and secondary schools announced by the Ministry of Education in 1962, the selected key primary schools were expected to perform as a good example for other schools in order to improve the overall education quality. By 1981, excluding Shanghai, there were 5,271 key primary schools in China (Encyclopedia of China Publishing House). Less than 5% of public schools are key schools (Lin, 2006, p. 186). There were 4,016 key public junior high schools nationwide in 1981, which was 3.8% of the total number of key schools (Ke, Chen, & Ren, 2013, p. 66; Kusuyama, 2009, p. 164). According to Henze (1992, p. 116), in 1988, about 2.6% of all entrants in lower secondary schools attended key schools; this was also the case for 2.8% of the total enrollment and 3.4% of the graduates.

Although it was abolished during the Cultural Revolution,[1] the key school system was reintroduced in the era of the post-Cultural Revolution (Lewin & Hui, 1989; Rosen, 1983). Compared with regular schools, key schools have more well-trained teachers, better equipment, and much greater funding, as well as a bigger number of enrollment of well-performing students (Kusuyama, 2010; Lin, 2006; Pepper, 1990; Tsang, 2000; Wu, 2009; You, 2007). At the same time, due to the constant governmental investment in both infrastructure and human resources, it has been almost impossible for the regular schools to follow the key schools as a model. In the National Educational Work Conference in April 1978, Deng Xiaoping gave an important speech on the quality, order, and discipline, education and economic development, and teacher status. He pointed out that "the construction of key lower secondary schools is one of the crucial strategies for cultivating people for modernization" (Encyclopedia of China Publishing House, 1984).

---

[1] During the Cultural Revolution, the key schools were called "little treasure house pagoda schools" by the Red Guards. The key schools were declared to cultivate the sons and grandsons of dragons: "They put intellectual cultivation in the first place and results of examinations in command. They fanatically pursue a high rate of promotion into higher schools." Students of the 1 August Boarding School for the children of leading cadres appealed to Red Guard units to release them from the prison which was turning them into "revisionist saplings." Once their school had served the revolutionary cause by housing the children of cadres working in the white areas; now it was a privileged institution, a Shangri-la for the children of powerful party personnel. School authorities had followed the road of British and Soviet aristocratic boarding establishments and never admitted the children of workers or peasants (Cleverley, 1985, p. 169).

Regarding the key school system, many scholars showed their concerns. For example, Lewin and Hui (1989) argued that key schools are not equitable since they confer advantages on the already educationally advantaged. They are justified by the need to concentrate scarce resources. Their current status reflects the balance of ideological debate on the relative importance of nurturing the next generation of intellectuals and experts at the expense of marginal improvements in school quality for the majority. You (2007) argued key schools aimed to distinguish between top students and ordinary students on the basis of scores so that those who managed to compete for admission to top schools at the next levels could get access to better education and became elites of the country. Hawkins (1983, pp. 35–38) explained the key school system as an elitist concept which is justified in terms of the need to identify and train China's most talented youth in order to speed the process of modernization, thus eventually benefiting the entire society. Furthermore, Fei Xiaotong, a prominent educator in the Chinese People's Political Consultative Conference, with his colleagues, gave concerns on the negative side effects associated with the key primary and secondary schools. They argued that the key schools could never train enough personnel to meet the needs of a modernized nation; on the other hand, the concentration of resources in these schools demoralized the majority of students attending the ordinary schools, who found themselves generally ignored. This contributed to relatively high (for China) dropout rates and a low educational standard for those who graduate. They argued that the key school system contributed to the "new illiteracy" (Rosen, 1983, p. 329). Pepper's studies on key school after the Cultural Revolution showed that key school system caused student segregation and polarization of public schools (Pepper, 1990, 1996).

With the increasing criticism of the key school system which led to a polarization between schools and students, the government claimed to abolish the system in 1997 (State Education Commission, 1997a). However, with the development of decades, those former key schools have already acquired strong attraction and deep influence on well-performing students and parents who have education aspiration (Lin, 2006; Nanbu, 2012). In urban China, most of the oversubscribed schools are the former key schools. In 1995, the government made the decision to select and construct 1,000 "Demonstration senior high schools" (*shifanxinggaozhong*) (henceforth abbreviated as "demonstration schools") in the late 1990s. These schools comprised only about 4% of China's public schools (Lin, 2006, p. 190) and can be considered as the continuation of the key school policy (Wu, 2008; Yang, 2006; You, 2007). Since the criteria for evaluating the demonstration schools are quite high, the most qualified schools would not surprisingly be those former key schools.[2] On the other hand, in order to accommodate the increasing demand for the good quality schools from parents, the Ministry of Education encouraged those former key schools, especially those at compulsory education level, to change into "converted

---

[2] For example, in 2001, Beijing planned to establish 60 demonstration senior high schools. From 2002 to 2010, 74 senior high schools have been evaluated as the demonstration senior high schools. Interestingly, the former key schools awarded in the 1980s by Beijing Municipal Government became the demonstration senior high schools.

5.1 The Key School System

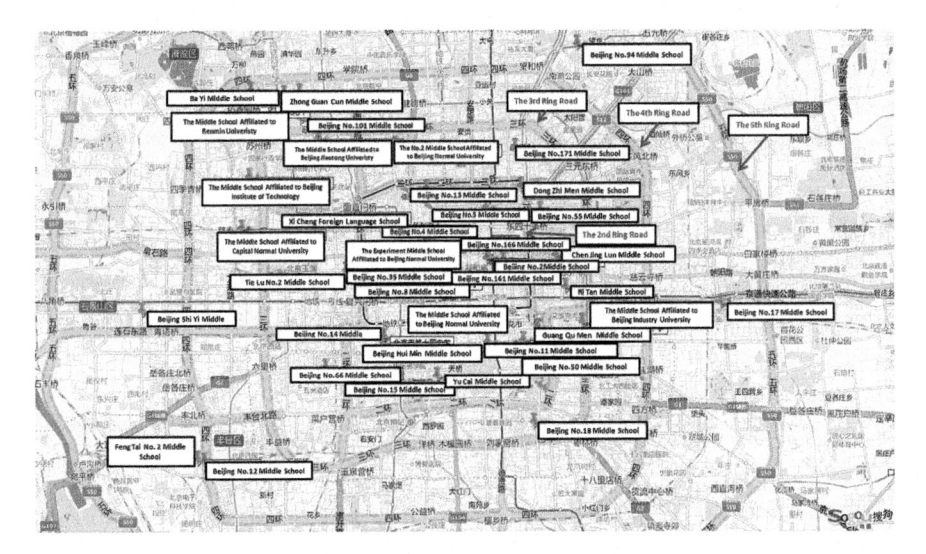

Fig. 5.1 Demonstration schools within the 5th Ring Road of Beijing, 2011 (Source: Compiled by author based on information collected from Beijing Municipal Education Committee)

schools"[3] by using their reputation (Wu, 2008). Because of the limited education funding, the main purpose of establishing those "converted schools" is to raise more funds by charging school fees from parents. The collected funds will be redistributed by education authority to the left behind schools for their construction. Moreover, by utilizing the established reputations, some key schools set up "offspring" schools which are affiliated with the former key schools. These schools could use facilities, teachers from parent former key schools. And because of the merits they get from parent former key schools, generally, these schools can charge high school fees to generate financial resources for bonuses and school improvement projects (Lin, 2007; Tsang, 2000, 2003; Wu, 2008). Although these schools were required to turn to real *minban* schools or truly public schools in 2006, in the transition, together with the former key schools, the present demonstration schools, they have already become the main target schools for parents and students who want to take part in *Zexiao*.

The key school system and the establishment of demonstration schools broke the balance of distribution of education resources in urban China. Figure 5.1 shows the

---

[3] According to Wu (2008), "converted school" refers to school-operating-system reformed piloting school. A converted school is one that used to be a public school run at government expense but has now been converted to a quasi-private/quasi-public institution that charges fees for its services. Tsang (2003) introduced that in a survey conducted in Beijing, people-run government-assisted schools consists of the following types: schools affiliated with existing key government schools, people-run schools converted from dysfunctional government schools, schools formerly run by enterprises, new pilot schools in small residential districts, and people-run schools converted from traditional private schools.

Table 5.1 Distribution of demonstration schools and distribution of registered population in Beijing (2008)

District	Demonstration school	Registered population (10,000)	Severed population/per demonstration school(10,000/per school)
Beijing	**74**	**1,229.9**	**16.6**
Dongcheng	7	61.9	8.8
Xicheng	9	78.3	8.7
Chongwen	5	33.5	6.7
Xuanwu	6	53.7	9.0
Chaoyang	7	181.8	26.0
Fengtai	4	103.6	25.9
Shijingshan	3	35.7	11.9
Haidian	11	209.9	19.1
Fangshan	4	76.5	19.1
Tongzhou	3	64.9	21.6
Shunyi	3	57.4	19.1
Changping	2	51.2	25.6
Daxing	2	58.7	29.4
Mentougou	1	24.1	24.1
Huairou	1	27.7	27.7
Pinggu	2	39.7	19.9
Miyun County	3	43.1	14.4
Yanqing County	1	28.0	28.0

Source: Beijing Municipal Education Committee

location of demonstration schools within the 5th Ring Road of Beijing.[4] These schools are mainly located in the center of and areas which have many higher education institutions. Comparatively, the northern part of Beijing has more demonstration schools than the southern part of Beijing. The interdistrict imbalanced distribution of education resources may identify students' mobility and *Zexiao*. As Table 5.1 indicated, the distribution of demonstration schools in Beijing did not correspond to the distribution of the population in Beijing. Districts, such as *Chaoyang* District and *Fengtai* District, with bigger populations, have less number of demonstration schools than districts with small populations. The imbalance in school allocation caused competition for sending children into the key schools or demonstration schools among parents. On the other hand, it also led to competition for student selection among public schools.

The section above briefly reviews the transformation process of the key school system in urban China. Also, it shows this system broke the balance in the distribu-

---

[4] According to Beijing Municipal Education Committee, there are 74 demonstration schools in Beijing by 2011. Retrieved from http://www.bjedu.gov.cn/publish/portal0/tab40, accessed on October 15, 2012.

tion of education resources in urban China. In the following sections, I explain how stratification of public schools and commercialization of public education affected public junior high school admission by mapping out a discussion by the government and the public from the 1990s to the 2000s about the gap between public schools.

5.2 The Gap Between Public Schools

The analysis of discussion on the gap between public schools follows the framework of public discourses on *Zexiao* presented in Chap. 3. There are two stages of the discussion on the gap between public schools which is related to public school admission. Discussion in the 1990s, the first stage, mainly took place around the theme of the unauthorized charge of school fees. However, in the second stage, the discussion after 2000 shifted to the theme of imbalanced educational development. The following sections present interaction between the government and the public in the discussion about the gap between public schools and *Zexiao* in admission to public junior high schools in the 1990s and after 2000.

5.2.1 The Discussion in the 1990s

In the 1990s, the gap between public schools was discussed from the perspective of the key school system and the perspective of school conversion reform. The analysis of the government document showed the government recognized the risk of school conversion reform fostering *Zexiao* and the key school system intensifying the unauthorized charge of school fees for school admission. However, they did not directly clarify the relationship between the gap between public schools (particularly the key school system) and *Zexiao*. In contrast, the gap between public schools was discussed as one of the forces which formed *Zexiao* in urban China through newspaper reports representing the public discussion.

5.2.1.1 Government Documents

The analysis of government documents on the gap between public schools showed the government's paradoxical attitudes toward the abolishment of key schools and the establishment of demonstration schools which led to gaps among public schools. More gaps were created, while some public schools converted to *minban* schools[5] to diversify the school system for the purpose of generating funds to supplement

---
[5] According to Tsang (2003, p. 165), people-run schools are schools sponsored and managed by a community of people or a collective organization and funded by resources from the community or financial assistance from the state, etc.

limited government education investment.[6] Consequently, those issues further enlarged the gaps among public schools.

As mentioned above, the key school system was reintroduced with the implementation of the *Open Door Policy* in the late 1970s. With an important role in cultivating necessary human resources to boost China's economy and modernization, the key school system was taken as one of the most important strategies in China's educational reform. By focusing on governmental investment in a limited number of public schools, it would be relatively efficient to cultivate needed human resources for China's modernization. Meanwhile, government documents in the 1990s showed increasing concern about the key school system deteriorating the balanced development between key schools and regular schools.

On one hand, review of government documents showed the government's concerns of the key school system challenging the balanced development of public schools. As indicated in *Instruction of reducing course burden of students in compulsory education and fully improving education quality*, the existence of the key school system was considered one of the main causes of students' excessive workload in compulsory education. In the same document, the government showed a clear stand against the separation of key schools (classes) and non-key schools (classes) in public compulsory education (State Education Commission, 1993a, 1993b). In 1994, in the *Opinions on fully implementing education plan, reducing course burden of students in primary and junior high schools*, the State Education Commission reemphasized that there should be no separation between key schools (class) or non-key schools (class) in compulsory education. Furthermore, the government also showed concerns about the gaps between key and regular schools in the aspects of government investment, school condition, teacher quality, leadership, and school administration (State Education Commission, 1994, 1995a). In addition, they urged reducing the gap between key schools and non-key schools. In *Opinions on standardizing the school operation at the present compulsory education stage* issued in 1997, the government expressed firm opposition to the key school system, including key classes, advanced and regular classes in compulsory education (State Education Commission, 1997a).

On the other hand, the government attempted to strengthen the position of key schools in urban society. For instance, the government document *Opinions on the implementation of the outline of education reform and development in China* issued in 1994 showed that the government planned to establish 1000 demonstration senior high schools nationwide (State Council, 1994). The State Education Commission announced the details of development and evaluation of these 1000 demonstration senior high schools in 1995 (State Education Commission, 1995b). According to the criteria, without long-term all-round development,[7] it seems difficult for regular schools to meet the

---

[6] According to Wu (2008, p. 597), "converted school" is short for "school-operating-system reformed piloting school." A converted school refers to one that used to be a public school run by government but has been converted to a quasi-private/public institution that charges fees for its services.

[7] Here, the all-round development refers to both development of school infrastructure and development of human resources.

5.2 The Gap Between Public Schools

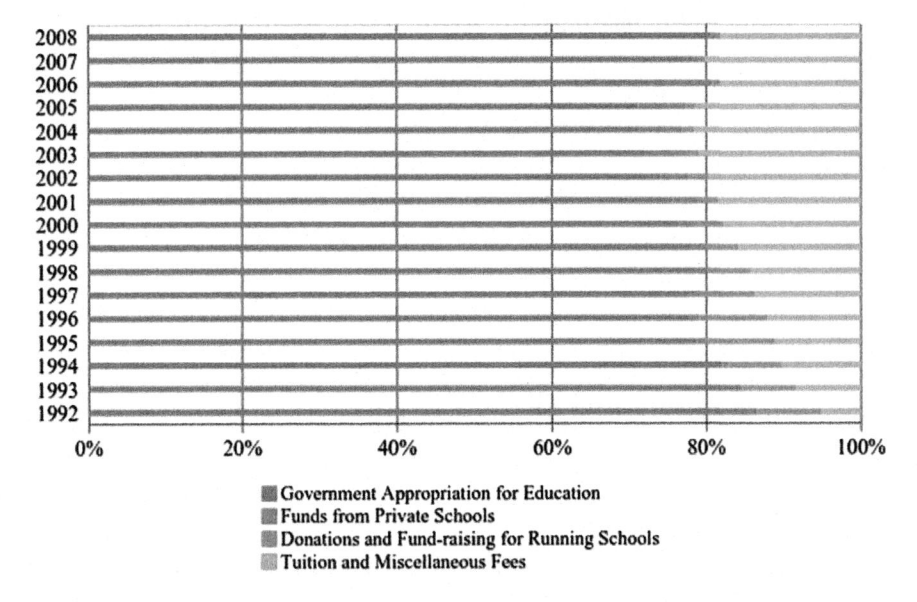

Fig. 5.2 Diversification of educational fund (1992–2008) (Source: China Education Yearbook 1992–2009, author edited)

requirements to participate in the evaluation to become demonstration schools. As Wu (2008) argued, there's no doubt that the former key schools would meet the criteria and be designated as demonstration schools. Yang (2006) pointed out that the government's policy stimulated the development of a new round key schools. Consequently, the policy further intensified the gaps among public schools.

Moreover, review of government documents identified that conversion of the public school to *minban* (people run) school was one of the forces that further enlarged the gaps among public schools and fostered *Zexiao*. In 1992, the 14th Communist Party of China (CPC) Congress announced that the objective of economic reform in China was to establish the socialist market economic system. In order to support the economic reform, there was a need for the education system to shift into a new model which could accommodate the economic development. Therefore, the education system reform was given the green light in 1993. According to the *Outline for the reform and development of China's education* released in 1993, with the ongoing reforms of the economic system, the political system, and the science and technology system, the education system reform should take comprehensive measures to change the government-monopolized system (State Council, 1993). This system should be changed by gradually establishing a system that involves the government as the main body with collaboration from other social parties (State Council, 1993). Figure 5.2 indicates the rise of collaboration between government and other social parties in terms of educational investment. In the

Opinions on Implementation of Outline for the reform and development of China's education released in 1994, the government clearly defined the new type of the school-run system as follows:

> Basic education is mainly run by the government. Meanwhile, based on the related laws and policies, the diverse types of school system by enterprises and other social forces are encouraged. In places where the condition is good enough, it is possible to implement government-run people-assisted and people-run government-assisted schools. School-run enterprises-owned schools can also be run by social forces under the supervision of local government (State Council, 1994).

Government policies in 1996 and 1997 emphasized the reform of the school-run system. The conversion of public schools to government-run people-assisted schools (*gongbanminzhuxuexiao*), people-run government-assisted schools (*minbangongzhuxuexiao*), community participated schools (*shequxuexiao*), and other private schools were recommended (State Education Commission, 1996, 1997b). Even though the reform of the school-run system supplemented the lack of education investment in public education and supported education development, the conversion of public schools to *minban schools* was taken as a tool by some well-known public schools to generate additional school revenue charging students and parents unauthorized school fees. Ironically, it resulted in furthering the practices of *Zexiao*.

The government recognized the role school conversion played in intensifying the unauthorized charge of school fees, further enlarging the gap between public schools and fostering *Zexiao*. However, they did not directly elaborate on the relationship between the reform and the development of *Zexiao* in urban China. Rather, they believed that the school conversion reform, in general, alleviated the pressure from *Zexiao*. It is the practice of generating additional school revenue by converting some well-known schools which intensified *Zexiao*. In 1998, State Council released *Opinions on the experiment of reform of school system in compulsory education stage*. In this document, the government addressed the problems caused by the reform of school-running system as follows:

> Although the reform of the school running system has a positive effect on rectification of the charge of the unauthorized school fees and eases the pressure from *Zexiao*, there are some problems in this reform... mainly, some good quality schools converted into people-run government-assisted schools to charge high fees for compulsory education; some good quality public schools open a "school within a school," "people-run class inside of school" or "two systems in one school;" some demonstration schools still select students by examination; some schools charge unauthorized school fees, which is very serious in some cases; there are still many low-performing schools at the local level. As a result, the public is unsatisfied with public education. And it fosters *Zexiao* as a result. (State Council, 1998)

The analysis of government opinions on the gap between public schools indicated that the gap was caused by the key school system which stratified the public school system. Then, it was intensified by both the selection of demonstration schools to further keep the advanced status of the key schools and the conversion of public schools to *minban* schools to generate additional school revenue. Facing the situation of limited educational investment from the government, generating more funds through the public school conversion system became much more important than releasing the pressure from *Zexiao* caused by the gap between public schools. Moreover, the failure in alleviating the conversion of well-performing public schools to *minban* schools also intensified the gap between public schools and further heated up *Zexiao*.

5.2.1.2 Public Discussion

Similar to the government documents, the public discussion on *Zexiao* in the 1990s focused on the gap between public schools which was caused and intensified by the key school and demonstration systems. The public discussion, mainly represented in the newspaper articles, indicated that the gaps within public schools in urban China stimulated the charge of unauthorized *Zexiaofei* which further intensified *Zexiao*. However, the review shows that there was not much relevant discussion on the conversion of public schools to *minban* schools and *Zexiao* by the public in the 1990s despite this being presented by the government documents as a reason for *Zexiao*.

Due to some historical reasons and limited state investment, the key school system, representing an elite education ideology, divided public schools based on factors such as school facilities, teacher quality, and education quality. Parents were motivated to participate in *Zexiao* (Luo & Lai, 1992, December 3; Wang, 1997, July 30; Zhang, 1997, July 24). In 1996, *Renmin Ribao*, representing the voice of the central government, pointed out that *Zexiao* was caused by the key school system. It also confirmed that the central government believed that local education authorities were responsible for creating an imbalance among public schools, which led to the intensification of *Zexiao* and pro-key schools funding strategies. It further clarified as follows:

> In the late 1970s and the early 1980s, in order to recover from the Culture Revolution and cultivate human resources for country's construction quickly, a number of key schools in primary and lower secondary education were established. Those schools were given priorities in the aspects of school finance, human resources, and student selection. By training quality students, those key schools made great achievements and contributions to China's construction. However, in the past decade, some local governments overemphasized the role of those key schools and ignored other schools, which enlarged the gap between public schools in terms of school condition, education quality, and student quality. As a result, *Zexiao* developed gradually. (Bi, 1996, March 11, translated by the author)

Newspaper reports showed that the abolishment of key schools unexpectedly pushed local governments to establish demonstration schools or "experiment schools" to keep the advantaged position for the former key schools. Consequently, the gaps among schools in the same region were enlarged artificially, which, continuously stimulated parents' interests in choosing schools for their children (Bi, 1996, March 11; Dong, 1997, July 31).[8] In addition, authorized by local education

---

[8] The similar analysis of reasons for *Zexiao* can also be found from a letter written by a retired teacher in Beijing to *China Education Daily*. The teacher believed the reasons for *Zexiao* included the imbalanced school development and the high expectation for children's education (Huang, 1996, August 4).

authorities, key schools were given privileges to charge *Zexiaofei*, which deteriorated the alleviation of charging unauthorized school fees and intensified *Zexiao* (Li, 1997, July 18).

5.2.2 The Discussion After the 2000s

The discussion after the 2000s, as introduced in Chap. 3, took place under the theme of imbalanced social development, including the public education sector. Analysis of government documents and the public discussion on *Zexiao* after 2000 indicated the key school system, and its conversion intensified the gap between public schools in urban China which caused *Zexiao*. Moreover, with the promotion of commercialization of public education resources, the privileges in charging school fees authorized to key schools and popular schools by the government also intensified *Zexiao* in urban China. In addition, profits in school admission generated by the effect of key school and its conversion stimulated people's aspiration to take part in *Zexiao*. Compared with the public discussion on *Zexiao* in the 1990s, the discussion after 2000 gave a comprehensive analysis on issues regarding the gap between public schools. The discussion uncovered more detailed reasons for causing the gaps, such as privileges of key schools given by the government in terms of school development and public school admission, the transformation of the key school system to demonstration school system, and the gap between the converted public schools and the regular public schools.

5.2.2.1 Government Documents

Review of government documents showed that there were three perspectives which intensified the gap between public schools and *Zexiao*. They included the key school system, converted schools, and improvement of weak schools.[9] Firstly, although the government abolished the key school system officially in 1997, the government recognized that there was a continuous influence of key schools on public compulsory education. They repeatedly showed their firm opposition toward the existence of key school system and key classes as well (National People's Congress, 2006; State Council, 2010).

---

[9] According to the Ministry of Education (1998), the weak schools refer to public schools in big and medium size cities which are not well managed, with low teaching quality, not sound social reputation, and not receiving trust from parents and students. These are caused by relatively bad teaching condition, weak school leadership, weak teaching teams, and problems in terms of student admission.

Secondly, conversion of public schools into *minban* schools, especially from key schools to *minban* schools, was considered one of the main reasons stimulating parents' zeal for *Zexiao*. These schools have privileges in charging high school fees to enroll students. It pushed parents to be willing to pay for the high school fees. The government document issued in 2002 showed concerns about the reason that public key schools or popular schools desired to change their status to *minban* schools, stating that:

> Public primary schools and junior high schools with high quality of education, teaching level and good social reputation are public education resources through a long-term accumulation. They should not be converted into *minban* schools or converted for the reason of charging high school fees. (Ministry of Education & State Council for Rectifying, 2002, translated by the author)

In order to moderate parents' zeal for *Zexiao*, the government issued a couple of policies between 2004 and 2005 to terminate the conversion of public key schools to *minban* schools (National development and reform Commission & Ministry of Education, 2005; State Council, 2004). There were two options for dealing with conversion of public schools. Schools could choose to turn into real *minban* schools, or the school could change their status back into public schools. Schools were required to complete the transactions by 2009 (Ministry of Education et al., 2009).

Thirdly, the existence of low-performing public schools in the public school system is another reason for intensified *Zexiao*. The government desired to improve low-performing schools and provide public education with quality and balance among public schools in order to accommodate educational needs from the society (Ministry of Education, 2002, 2009, 2010; State Council, 2007).

Apparently, the government gradually recognized that the gaps between public schools fostered *Zexiao* in public school system. The analysis of government documents also showed their firm stance on reducing the gaps. However, the analysis of public discussion below shows the different stories contrasting government opinion.

5.2.2.2 Public Discussion

The public discussion identified that the gap between public schools as a result of the imbalanced educational development intensified *Zexiao* in urban China (Fei, 2000, July 10; Hua, 2000, September 19; Yuan, 2007, November 12; Zhao, 2006, April 13).[10] The interviews I conducted with school principals, scholars, and other stakeholders in Beijing also showed the gap between the public schools, particularly

---

[10]According to *China Youth Daily* December 15, 2009, result of a survey conducted by *China Youth Daily* among 30 cities showed 63.9% of the participants in the survey believed the big gap between schools was the main reason for *Zexiao*. It also indicated that 75.8% of participants involved in this survey chose school gap caused charge of high *Zexiao* fee was considered as the more serious educational inequality phenomenon in China (Xiao, 2009, December 15).

the gap caused by the key school system, severely affected the balanced education development. As a result, it fostered *Zexiao* in Beijing.

The interview conducted with Scholar A from the National Institute of Education Sciences indicated that a localized implementation of the key school policy was one of the reasons for *Zexiao*. In contrast to the policy on the abolishment of key schools by the central government, the local governments took action to protect such schools and considered such schools a card for exchanging profits between stakeholders. According to Scholar A, this policy was not implemented appropriately and led to imbalance at the local level despite its original purpose of selecting key schools as model schools for low-performing schools to learn from and achieve school improvement. Instead, it caused stratification of public schools. Although the key school system has been terminated by the government since the late 1990s, the transformation of key schools to demonstration schools kept the advantage and popularity of key schools in the eyes of the public. The establishment of demonstration schools from the mid-1990s negatively influenced the alleviation of *Zexiao* in Beijing. Moreover, key schools became the fund and profit generator for local governments. As the scholar explained:

> ... those [key]schools at the compulsory education level still have significant influence. Those schools are given special focus by a local authority. And, definitely, they are also the focus for parents. Although the term "key school" has been eliminated, local governments still treat those schools differently. Some policies and evaluations still give favor to those schools..... Some local government officials even use key schools as resources to boost their power. Key schools became a card for a local government to exchange profits with stakeholders. And these [what I mentioned above] stimulated the public's aspiration for *Zexiao*.... (Interview with Scholar A, April 28, 2011, translated by the author)

Interviews with school principals and staff of local education authorities in Beijing provide a diverse explanation on reasons for *Zexiao* caused by the key school system.

Interviews with school principals in Beijing showed more privileges were given to key schools in terms of student selection, teacher hiring, and welfare. These caused imbalanced development among public schools. In other words, the imbalanced development between public schools in Beijing mainly referred to the gap of "soft power (students' qualities, teachers' qualities, and teachers' welfare)" between schools. The vice principal of School F[11] in *Dongcheng* District analyzed that there was no big difference in terms of infrastructure between key schools and non-key schools since all schools followed the same standard made by the government. The big gap between the two types of schools mainly referred to students' quality and teachers' quality. According to the former principal of School E,[12] although the computer lottery system in school admissions was to balance the educational devel-

---

[11] School F is public school in Dongcheng District. Although this school is not a key school, it is popular as a popular school among parents in Dongcheng District. The interview was conducted on November 7, 2011.

[12] School E is a converted school which means that school changed its status from a public junior high school to a converted school in 1996. The school is located in the Chongwen District of Beijing. The interview was conducted on May 9, 2011.

opment through distributing students with balanced quality, the imbalance of student distribution still existed among junior high schools due to the fact that some key schools could choose not to participate in the system. In reality, key schools were allowed to pick qualified student before the computer lottery system started. Mrs. A, a teaching and research staff from the Education Training and Research Center in the *Dongcheng* District of Beijing, clarified that student distribution reflected the pro-key school process, a practice that negatively influenced the balance of student quality between key schools and regular schools. She said that:

> When I was a teacher in School F, the student distribution was equal. At that time, key schools around us averagely enrolled four or five classes. Since they had the privileges to select quality students in this district, School F could only enroll the so-called "second-class students". How about now? You know, the enrollment in key schools was enlarged. In recent years, they had enrolled an average of 8 or 10 classes…On the one hand, the enrollment of key schools has been doubled. On the other hand, comparing with previous years, School F enrolls less good quality students … the imbalance of student quality between schools is getting worse…. (Interview conducted on November 7, 2011, translated by the author)

The case above showed that the non-key schools were discriminated by the pro-key school admission policy. The practice of students' selection enlarged the gap between key schools and regular schools, which further fostered *Zexiao* in the urban public school system.

Furthermore, the imbalance of teachers' distribution and teachers' welfare between key schools and regular schools in the same or different school districts also contributed to the imbalanced educational development in Beijing, which led to more serious issues such as more parents wanted their children to go to key schools and more teachers changed jobs and worked for key schools.

The former head of the Educational Supervision Office in one district of Beijing pointed out that there was a big gap of teachers' welfare between key schools and regular schools. Key schools regularly offered teachers incentives such as rice, eggs, and other life necessities (such as shampoo, tissue paper).[13] In contrast, non-key schools had very little to reward their teachers. Consequently, key schools or schools located in affluent areas became the "haves," and underperforming schools became the "have nots." The turnover of teachers affected parents' decisions for their children since they would like their children to enroll in schools that had more quality teachers. Scholar A explained that the imbalanced teachers' distribution among public schools and between districts deeply affected the balanced educational development and intensified *Zexiao*. Although the government attempted to make some adjustments to prevent teachers from turning over, Scholar A argued that the non-

---

[13] Regarding the gap of welfare between schools, former vice principal of School A told a real story. One teacher of School A moved to a key school at city level. The salary was several times compared with the one in School A. Every academic year, teachers in this key school were required to go abroad for self-study tour. The cost of domestic tour could not be covered by school side. Teachers in this key school were asked to buy laptop. School side only covered the laptop which was over 10,000 yuan. This story shows a big gap of teachers' welfare between key school and regular school (the interview was conducted with former vice principal of School A on April 18, 2011).

civil servant status of teachers was the main reason for the rotation of teachers. He further clarified the difficulties:

> …being different from Japan that makes public school teachers civil servants at the national level, teachers in China are just employees of their schools… in order to make a teacher rotation within a district, we need to make teachers civil servants at the district level. In order to narrow down the gap of teachers between districts, we need to make teachers civil servants at the city level…However, here is a problem! According to district-based compulsory education administration, it is not appropriate to upgrade teachers' management at the city level…therefore, it is difficult to balance the teacher quality between districts… the only solution is to make teachers as civil servants at national level…however, due to the gap between urban and rural areas, it is still not easy to fulfill this goal…. (Interview with Scholar A, April 28, 2011, translated by the author)

Scholar A's analysis on teacher rotation system indicated that it would be difficult to fulfill the balance in the quality of teachers in public schools without a systematic reform of employment system in public education of China.

Interviews I conducted with school principals also showed that the demonstration school system further broke the balance among public schools in terms of distribution of financial resources, teachers' distribution, and student selection. Head teacher from School D[14] agreed that the transformation of a key school to demonstration school[15] excluded many children from entering popular schools through the regular process of public school admissions. The demonstration school system broke the balance of educational resource distribution in each district, as well as the balance in the distribution of human resources and students between public schools.

Moreover, the complicated relationship between key schools and the newly designated demonstration schools was taken as a reason for *Zexiao*. With the transformation of key schools to demonstration schools in urban China, key schools were required to separate junior high school departments from the senior high school departments. The latter became the newly established demonstration schools. Some junior high school departments of key schools became branches of the demonstration schools. Those schools were allowed to become *minban* schools. However, according to Scholar A, at least in Beijing, the link or collaboration between newly established branch schools and the demonstration schools still existed. And the collaboration continuously influenced parents' decision on *Zexiao*. The open enrollment[16] at the newly established branch schools or the newly converted *minban* schools could be considered quality control in student selection for demonstration schools. In other words, demonstration schools were able to

---

[14] School D is a demonstration school in *Xicheng* District.

[15] According to Scholar A, the demonstration school refers to senior high school. This type of school used to have both junior high school department and senior high school department. In order to become demonstration schools, they are required to separate the junior high school part from the newly designated demonstration schools. The interview with Scholar A was conducted on April 28, 2011.

[16] Open enrollment in this study means enrollment of students from the whole city of Beijing. According to Scholar A, only demonstration schools and some converted schools have such privilege.

5.2 The Gap Between Public Schools

select well-performing students from affiliated junior high schools. This policy attracted many parents to be willing to send their children to those affiliated junior high schools in order to get access to the demonstration schools. Such student selection process was considered a cause of imbalanced student distribution among public schools. As a result, it also intensified the competition for *Zexiao*. This process represented not only competition between parents but also competition among public schools, particularly the demonstration schools.

In addition, the imbalance of education development was caused by the gap between converted schools and regular schools. According to the former principal of School E, the conversion[17] allowed those schools to charge school fees and open special education programs. School E established a special English education program and became popular among parents. According to the principal of School E, the school planned to enroll around 240 students at most in 2011.[18] In contrast, they received more than 1,000 applications.[19] With the privilege to hold entrance exam to select a student, the schools could enroll better students than other regular public schools. This enlarged the gap of student quality between schools. Moreover, the gap further stimulated parents' participation in *Zexiao* process. A director of a private tutoring institute viewed the reform of conversion of public schools as a mistake made by the government. In his opinion, it just aimed to supplement the lack of government investment in education through collecting fees from parents. It also aimed to generate more social welfare for teachers and the education sector as a whole.[20]

---

[17] The conversion of public schools to *minban* schools started from 1996 in Beijing. According to current principal of School E, the purpose of establishing these converted schools was originally to collect more funds for schools by charging tuition fees. By 2003, there were about 50 converted schools in Beijing. With the rapid economic development and increase of education investment, in 2008, Beijing education authority required these schools to make decision to return to public school system or become fully *minban* schools. In Beijing, 90% of the converted schools chose to return to public school system. Currently, these schools are still given authority to select students by themselves. The full implementation of the proximity-based school admission will start in the coming several years (Interview with principal of School E was conducted on May 16, 2011). As to the reform of converted schools in Beijing, vice principal of School G in Chaoyang District considered it as the unification of education resource within Beijing by Beijing education authority. In order to balanced teacher's salary, it will be easier to make reform in the same system (Interview with vice principal of School G was conducted on October 27, 2011).

[18] Since the school had to accept 80 school recommendation students based on the admission policy for local schools, the number of students for open enrollment was 160 only.

[19] The popularity of School E was represented by interview with Parent 6 from School B whose son went to take the entrance exam to School E in 2011. According to the parent, there were at least 700 or 800 students who took part in the entrance exam held by School E. In contrast, the enrollment plan in School E was 200 in 2011. The interview with this parent was conducted on May 13, 2011.

[20] Interview with the director of a Private Tutoring Institute A was conducted on October 30, 2011. He started independent research on China's education from 1992. His research interests include entrance exams to university, education transition to secondary education, preschool education, equality in education, and sustainable education development. The director's blog often shows some firsthand data regarding basic education in China. It has become popular blog for parents and education research institutions to understand various perspectives of China's education.

Another director of a private tutoring institute in Beijing showed a positive view on the gap. She firmly believed that key schools could become examples for regular schools to improve school management and educational quality. Moreover, she pointed out that key schools provided high achievers with opportunities to key universities. And those students could become the elites for China's future.[21] Obviously, the director held the view that the elite education ideology was the right choice for urban China. Moreover, she believed that the key school system was useful for elite student selection in public schools, especially those popular schools.

The analysis of public discussion, particularly through the interviews conducted in Beijing, indicated that the conflict between government's policies on the abolishment of key schools and the establishment of demonstration schools and the conversion of public schools to *minban* schools caused the imbalanced development of public schools. Consequently, it forced stakeholders to take part in *Zexiao*. The analysis showed that key schools, demonstration schools, converted schools, local education authorities, and individual families became the stakeholders in *Zexiao*. *Zexiao* presents collective profits among these stakeholders in public school admission.

5.3 Collusion for Student Selection

Analysis of the public discussion after 2000 demonstrated that there is an emerging collusion between private tutoring institutes and the popular key schools through pre-admission training (*Zhankengban*) to select students in public school admission in urban China. As introduced in Chap. 2, this approach, as part of achievement-based *Zexiao*, also has become one widely accepted channel for parents to send children to popular schools. On the other hand, the collusion illustrated key schools held privileges in student selection which was against the *Compulsory Education Law*. Chapter 3 showed student selection hosted by the key schools was prohibited by the government. Within this context, private tutoring institutes especially the big scale ones, as new stakeholders, became the media for parents and key schools to achieve mutual selection through hosting pre-admission training classes. At the same time, they could generate profits through holding the pre-admission training classes and hosting exams for student selection by key schools. The collusion generated mutual profits for key schools, private tutoring institutes, and individual families. However, it also excluded students whose families did not have relevant resources from the access to the key schools.

---

[21] The interview with office director of private tutoring institute was conducted on April 20, 2011. This institute was established in 1994. Until May 2012, this institute has established branch schools in 12 cities in China. In Beijing, until May 2012, it has 93 branches. It has been selected as one of the most influential private tutoring institute by mass media for years. For more information, please refer to the link, http://www.juren.com/.

5.3 Collusion for Student Selection

Interview with principal of School F showed that pre-admission training class became a platform for key schools to select students they preferred through the collusion with private tutoring institutes. He specified that:

> ...Key schools are always oversubscribed since many students apply to such schools. Therefore, these schools have to select better-performing students through exams. Since some private tutoring institutes just provide such training and guarantee the access to key schools with collaboration with key schools, the (pre-admission training) class becomes popular.... (Interview with Principal of School F, November 7, 2011, translated by the author)

A government official from the Ministry of Education pointed out that it was necessary to alleviate the phenomenon of *Zhankengban* since some schools (key schools) have already taken it as a tool for selecting students (Chun, 2011, February 24). An interview with a parent conducted by *China Education Daily* also showed *Zhankengban* had become a tool for key schools' student selection. The parent analyzed:

> ...For popular junior high school, school recommendation students should be best from primary schools. However, due to the different level of primary schools, the best students recommended from different primary schools are different (in terms of quality). Since the good quality student is the main objective for popular junior high schools, principals from such schools say that they have their own ways to select good students. Their own way is to hold selection exam by training institutes. Then based on the result, schools will select students. The most popular training institutes have a close relationship with those key schools. Therefore, only those who attend their classes can have the opportunity to take such exams. (Wang, 2008, July 6, translated by the author)

According to *Beijing Ribao*, in order to send children to popular schools, parents have to enroll children in *Zhankengban* through entrance exam. Then, students will be screened and selected by key schools through several rounds of the exam. Interviews conducted with principal of School E[22] and principal of School G[23] in Beijing indicated the nature of the pre-admission training class as a tool for student selection by key schools. Sometimes, in order to avoid the influence by the sudden change of policy at city or district level, the student selection through *Zhankengban* often took place before the announcement of public school admission policy. As a case in point, some popular schools in Beijing have already finished their student selection through pre-admission training classes before the announcement of the school admission policy by the municipal education authority (Liu, 2009, March 25).

A series of reports showed the collusion between parents, private tutoring institutes, and key schools in terms of pre-admission training class. *Guangming Ribao* analyzed that:

> Pre-admission training class, in fact, is *Zexiao*. It is totally against the principle of proximity and the equity in compulsory education and the balanced compulsory education development. Pre-admission training class is created by parents. It includes "Gold Class" which is held by popular school affiliated training institutes; Multifunctional Class which is held by popular private training institutes. (Guangming Ribao, 2010, July 25; translated by the author)

---

[22] Interview with principal of School E was conducted on May 16, 2011.

[23] Interview with principal of School G was conducted on October 27, 2011.

As the main participants in the *Zhankengban*, parents shared their experiences which showed collusion between private tutoring institutes and key schools. One parent introduced:

> ...Now, private tutoring institutes have direct relationship with some key schools. They held selection exam for key schools in training schools and won possibility for children who wanted to go to key schools. Exam results in these schools become important reference for key schools to select children. (Beijing Youth Daily, 2009, February 15, translated by the author)

In addition, there is a close collusion between private tutoring institutes and key schools in student selection through Olympic math training classes held by private tutoring institutes. An interview held with a parent in my fieldwork illustrates the close link between Olympic math, private tutoring institutes, and key schools in school admission. She related:

> My son took part in two Olympic math classes in two private tutoring institutes.[24] Since both of these schools are so-called "Gold Class", we sent our son to study there. I heard that one of the schools recommended 91 students who studied in this private tutoring school to key schools as special talent students in *Dongcheng* District last year (2010).[25] You know, this private tutoring school is becoming popular in recent years in Beijing. Key schools in this (*Dongcheng*) District all invited their director to interview students who applied these key schools. And some key schools even invited this institute to organize entrance exams for them to select students. So ... (laughing)... you can see the relationship and the link with school admission.... (Interview with Parent 1 from primary school in *Dongcheng* District, May 18, 2011, translated by the author)

In my fieldwork, Director of Private Tutoring Institute B in Beijing denied their collusion with key junior high schools in student selection. However, she clarified that private tutoring institutes provided a platform for parents and junior high schools to make a mutual selection. Exams held by private tutoring institutes were taken as a criterion for selecting students by some key schools. It became an approach for key schools to select students they expected. Meanwhile, the Olympic math exam for student selection by key schools further intensified achievement in Olympic math

---

[24] One of the private tutoring institutes in this conversation has been listed on the exchange market in China. According to a director of private tutoring institute, nowadays, there are four private tutoring institutes which have been listed on the exchange market in China. The main reason for the rise of these institutes' success is closely linked with the exam-oriented education. Since there are needs for Olympic math for education transition to public junior high schools, these private tutoring institutes identified the needs and responded efficiently. Mainly, private tutoring institutes in China are just supplement for school education at basic education level. Their role is to strengthen what schools teach in the class. Without changing the education structure on the policy and systematic level, it is impossible for private tutoring institutes to change. The student selection-based collaboration between key schools and some private tutoring institutes is understandable. Since there is profit, there is collaboration (Interview with Director of Private Tutoring Institute A was conducted on October 20, 2011).

[25] Parent 1 heard this information from others parents whose children studied Olympic math in the same institute as Parent 1's son did. According to Parent 1, parents always shared rumors about school admission policies, enrollment number in specific key schools, and strategies for going to key schools.

for *Zexiao*. According to this director, some public junior high schools, especially the key schools, took knowledge of Olympic math as the main part in their entrance tests. These tests were much more difficult than what students learn from the school curriculum. In order to meet the needs for making children well prepared for these tests, it was necessary for parents to send their children to after-school programs held by private tutoring institutes. In other words, the mismatch between school curriculum and the tests for student selection at key schools intensified the development of achievement-based *Zexiao* by achievement in Olympic math. Meanwhile, children from families who could not afford the cost of private tutoring or training classes were excluded from the selection.

In summary, this chapter, through analyzing public discourses on the gap between public schools, can clarify two questions: (1) How does the gap between public schools affect public school admission? (2) How do the popular schools work with private tutoring institutes to select students in public school admission? A key school system distinguished public schools into good schools and regular schools from school investment, student selection, and teacher assignment. And it stratified public schools. These caused the gap between public schools. Although the government showed their attitude against the system since the 1990s, as commercialization of the gaps could generate additional fund to supplement the limited public school finance, the system was not officially abolished until the late 1990s. However, the following reforms, such as demonstration school nomination and conversion of public school, kept and enlarged the gap between key schools and regular schools and further stimulated privilege abuse in public school admission. Consequently, it led to competition among parents for enrolling their children in the key schools. Also, the findings indicate there is a rise of collusion between popular schools and private tutoring institutes for student selection in school admission which accommodated parents' demand for the limited access to the key schools. On the other hand, the collusion also caused educational exclusion of families which could not afford pre-admission training classes for getting their children prepared for the student selection in school admission. With the influence of elitism and marketization on Chinese society, the gap between public schools, as an imbalance of educational development in Chinese society at the school level, caused inequality in public school admission. And the inequality was further deteriorated by the collusion for mutual selection among the private tutoring institutes, popular public schools, and individual families.

References

Beijing Youth Daily. (2009, February 15). Peixunbanansongshengyuan, Xiaoshengchuqianguize? (Student Selection through private tutoring class, a casting couch in admission to the junior high school?). *China Education Daily*, p. 2.

Bi, Q. (1996, March 11). "Zhongdian fuchi boruo xuexiao- zhongxiaoxue Zexiao shoufei wenti taolun pingshu" ("Supporting poor performing schools: Discussion on the charge of Zexiaofei in compulsory education"). *Renmin Ribao*, 11.

Chun, C. (2011, February 24). Zhuolizhi "Zexiaofei" "Zhankengban" (Making efforts to prevent "Zexiaofei" and "ZhanKengban"). *China Youth Daily*, 6.
Cleverley, J. (1985). *The schooling of China*. Sydney, Australia: George Allen & Unwin Australia Pty Ltd.
Dong, C. (1997, July 31). Tigao renshi zouchu wuqu (To improve understanding and escape from mistakes). *China Education Daily*, p. 1.
Encyclopedia of China Publishing House. (1984). *China education yearbook*. Beijing, China: Encyclopedia of China Publishing House.
Fei, X. (2000, July 10). Zexiao, yige chenzhong de huati (Zexiao, a serious topic). *Chongqing Ribao*, p. 9.
Guangming Ribao. (2010, July 25). Zhankengban Weihejinerbujue) (Why Zhankengban cannot be eliminated). *China Education Daily*, p. 2.
Hawkins, J. N. (1983). *Education and social change in the People's Republic of China*. New York: Praeger Publisher.
Henze, J. (1992). The formal education system and modernization: An analysis of development since 1978. In R. Hayhoe (Ed.), *Education and modernization* (pp. 103–140). Oxford, UK: Pergamon Press.
Hua, W. (2000, September 19). Mingxiao aini bu rongyi (How should I love you: The well-known schools?). *China Education Daily*, p. 1.
Huang, C. (1996, August 4). "Zexiao" xianxiang toushi (Looking through "Zexiao"). *China Education Daily* p. 1.
Ke, Z., Chen, S., & Ren, Y. (2013). Comparison of Principals' leadership behaviors in the key and the ordinary schools. *Beijing Daxue Jiaoyu Pinglun* (Peking University Education Review), *1*(1), 63–82.
Kusuyama, K. (2009). *Gendai Tyugoku Syotyutokyoiku no tayoka to seito kaikaku (The diversification and schooling system reform of elementary and secondary education in China)*. Tokyo: Toshindo Publishing Co., Ltd.
Kusuyama, K. (2010). Tyugoku ni okeru gimugyoiku kyoiku seido no tanryokuka to situ hosyo (The flexibility and quality assurance of Compulsory Education System in China). *Hikaku kyoiku kenkyu* (Comparative Education), *41*, 49–62.
Lewin, K., & Hui, X. (1989). Rethinking revolution; reflections on China's 1985 educational reforms. *Comparative Education*, *25*(1), 7–17.
Li, J. (1997, July 18). Jiaqiang jiandu yancha weiji (To strengthen monitoring and check disciplinary violation). *China Education Daily*, p. 1.
Lin, J. (2006). Educational stratification and the new middle class. In G. A. Postiglione (Ed.), *Education and social change in China* (pp. 179–198). Armonk, NY: East Gate Book.
Lin, J. (2007). Emergence of private schools in China. In E. Hannum & A. Park (Eds.), *Education and reform in China* (pp. 44–63). Oxon, UK: Routledge.
Liu, H. (2009, March 25). Xiaoshengchu Zhengceweidingceshixianxing (Selection exam occurred before policy on admission to junior high schools launched). *Beijing Ribao*, p. RJ063.
Luo, C., & Lai, Q. (1992, December 3). Zhongxiaoxue shoufei de sikao (Considering fee charge in compulsory education). *China Education Daily*, p. 2.
Ministry of Education. (1998). *Opinions on strengthening the construction of weak schools in big and medium-size cities and managing well each school*. Beijing.
Ministry of Education. (2002). *Notice on consolidating the school operation administration of basic education*. Beijing.
Ministry of Education. (2009). *Instructive opinions on strengthening the specification of administration of primary schools and junior high schools*. Beijing.
Ministry of Education. (2010). *Opinions on instruction of rectifying the charge of unauthorized fees in Zexiao of compulsory education*. Beijing.
Ministry of Education, & State Council for Rectifying. (2002). *Opinions on further rectifying the unauthorized education charge*. Beijing.

References

Ministry of Education, State Council Office for Rectifying, Ministry of Supervision, National Development and Reform Commission, Ministry of Finance, National Audit Office, & General Administration of Press and Publication. (2009). *Opinions on the implementation of standardizing the charge of education fee to further rectify the charge of unauthorized school fees.* Beijing.

Nanbu, H. (2012). Bunkakugo tyugoku ni okeru sainokyoiku no tenkai (The development of gifted education program in China under the policy of diffusing education). *Hikaku kyoiku kenkyu (Comparative Education), 45*, 52–65.

National development and reform commission, & Ministry of Education. (2005). *Notice on making good preparation for standardizing the fee charging of converted schools.* Beijing.

National People's Congress. (2006). *Compulsory education law of the People's Republic of China.* Beijing.

Pepper, S. (1990). *China's education reform in the 1980s.* Berkeley, CA: Institute of East Asian Studies University of California at Berkeley.

Pepper, S. (1996). *Radicalism and education reform in 20th-century China.* Cambridge, UK: Cambridge University Press.

Qin, H. (2008). School choice in China. *Frontier Education in China, 3*(3), 331–345.

Rosen, S. (1983). Education and the political socialization of Chinese youths. In J. N. Hawkins (Ed.), *Education and social change in the People's Republic of China* (pp. 97–133). New York: Praeger Publishers.

State Council. (1993). *Outline of the reform and development of China's education.* Beijing.

State Council. (1994). *Opinions on implementation of outline of education reform and development in China.* Beijing.

State Council. (1998). *Opinions on the experiment of reform of school system in compulsory education stage.* Beijing.

State Council. (2004). *Regulations for the implementation of minban education promotion law.* Beijing.

State Council. (2007). *Outline of Eleventh Five Year Plan for National Education Development.* Beijing.

State Council. (2010). *The national guidelines for medium- and long-term educational reform and development (2010–2020).* Beijing.

State Education Commission. (1993a). *Indication on reducing heavy academic burden of student in compulsory education and full improvement of education quality.* Beijing.

State Education Commission. (1993b). *Notice on rectification of the charge of the unauthorized fees in primary schools and middle schools.* Beijing.

State Education Commission. (1994). *Opinion on fully implementing education plan, reducing course burden of students in primary and junior high schools.* Beijing.

State Education Commission. (1995a). *Opinions regarding the implementation of rectification of the charge of the unauthorized fees.* Beijing.

State Education Commission. (1995b). *Notice on appraisal and designation of 1000 demonstration senior high schools.* Beijing, China.

State Education Commission. (1996). *Opinions on the implementation of the rectification of the charge of unauthorized fees in primary schools and middle schools.* Beijing.

State Education Commission. (1997a). *Opinions on standardizing the school operation at the present compulsory education stage.* Beijing.

State Education Commission. (1997b). *Opinions on the rectification of the charge of unauthorized fees in primary schools and middle schools.* Beijing.

Tsang, M. C. (2000). Education and National Development in China since 1949: Oscillating policies and enduring dilemmas. *The China Review*, 579–614.

Tsang, M. C. (2003). School choice in the People's Republic of China. In D. N. Plank & G. Sykes (Eds.), *Choosing choice* (2001st ed., pp. 164–195). New York: Teachers College Press.

Wang, J. (2008, July 6). Xiaoshengchuliuxingbing (Epidemic in Admission to Junior High Schools). *China Education Daily*, p. 3.

Wang, Z. (1997, July 30). Zexiaoxuzonghezhili (Comprehensive management on *Zexiao*). *China Education Daily*, p. 1.

Wu, X. (2008). The power of positional competition and market mechanism: A case study of recent parental choice development in China. *Journal of Education Policy, 23*(6), 595–614.

Wu, X. (2009). *The power of market mechanism in the school choice in China: An empirical study*. Retrieved May 15, 2011, from http://www.unige.ch/fapse/ggape/seminaire/programme/progjeudi12/Wu.pdf

Xiao, S. (2009, December 15). *Zexiao* wenti jiushi zhengwei shifou zuowei de wenti (*Zexiao*: A problem of government?). *China Youth Daily*, p. 2.

Yang, D. (2006). *Zhongguo jiaoyu gongping de lixiang yu xianshi (The wish and reality of educational equality in China)*. Beijing, China: Peking University Press.

You, Y. (2007). A deep reflection on the "key school system" in basic education in China. *Frontier Education in China, 2*(2), 229–239.

Yuan, Z. (2007, November 12). Jian "banxuelianheti" cu jiaoyu junheng fazhan (Establishing "Combo" for balanced education development). China Education Daily, p. 3.

Zhang, B. (1997, July 24). Mingque mubiao wenzhong qiujin (To be clear of our objectives to move forward). *China Education Daily*, p. 1.

Zhao, Z. (2006, April 13). Beijing lizheng 3nian banhao meiyisuo chuzhong (Beijing: to run each junior high school well in three years). *China Education Daily*, p. 1.

Chapter 6
Competition of Family Background with Local Characteristics

Abstract There is an increasing effect of family background on children's education in China. In this chapter, the author will investigate how family background influences the engagement of families in admission to public junior high schools in Community A of Beijing as a case study. The author will analyze experiences in admission to junior high schools based on interviews with school principals and parents of Community A to visualize how families engaged in junior high school admission by utilizing their various resources. The analysis will follow stages of admission to public junior high schools in Community A to visualize a full process of competition among parents for public school admission in urban China which are based on advantage, privileges, and local characteristics.

In the previous two chapters, we investigated policies and public school systems as forces that shaped stakeholders' participation in admission to public junior high schools in urban China. In contrast, this chapter investigated how parents engaged in admission to public junior high school in Community A in the southern part of Beijing to visualize parentocracy's effects on parents' participation in children's admission to junior high schools. Data were collected from qualitative field interviews with 26 participants from a public junior high school (School A) and a public primary school (School B) of Community A in the southern part of Beijing. The interview respondents included the principal of School A, the principal of School B, 2 retired principals of School A, 16 parents from School A, and 6 parents from School B (see Appendix 7).

This chapter briefly summarizes features of public junior high school admission policy in Community A. Then we will analyze respondents' experiences in both official and legalized unofficial approaches in public junior high schools to illustrate "parentocracy"-based *Zexiao* and pre-determined educational exclusion. Also, we will explain how local context influenced the process of admission to public junior high schools in Community A. Finally, the chapter concludes by mapping the "parentocracy"-based public junior high school admission policy in Community A.

6.1 Public School Admission Policy in Community A

The interviews I conducted in Community A indicated that diversified public school admission policies manipulated by district education authority intensified the competition in school admission to junior high schools and *Zexiao*. The participation in diverse approaches for public school admission was socially constructed by "parentocracy."

As the policy decision on school admission was delegated to the local education authority at the district level, nine options for public junior high school admission were provided in *Fengtai* District. For example, students could be admitted based on school recommendation, special talents of students, mutual selection between school and parents, *hukou* registration, assigned admission, *minban* school admission, boarding school-based school admission, and migrant children with a "Green Card" in Beijing,[1] as well as admission without a "Green Card."

Table 6.1 describes the nine admission options. According to the interviews with the vice principal of School B, in Community A, besides the three admission approaches for attending popular schools, most local primary school graduates went to the junior high school assigned to them, i.e., School A. Since boarding school and *minban* school charged expensive tuition and fees, few students from School B attended those schools.[2] As to the approach "going back to *hukou* registered school admission," local students who had *guanxi* usually transferred their *hukou* to the districts that had better education resources.[3]

In terms of school admission for migrant children, in some respects they have been excluded from the mainstream (local students') school admission. Despite migrant children being included in the special talent admission approach, they were excluded from the school recommendation approach and the mutual selection approach. In other instances migrant children were affected by their "Green Card" status, and their parents' socioeconomic status, which was against the education stressed by the *Compulsory Education Law*. The interviews with the principals of School A and B also showed biased attitudes of school officials toward public education for migrant children in Community A. The vice principal of School B showed a negative attitude toward the increasing number of migrant children in public schools. She stated:

---

[1] Green Card refers to various certificates issued by Beijing Municipal Government for residents without Beijing *hukou*. Holders and their children can have the same treatment as Beijing residents. Migrant children whose parents hold the following certificates can be treated as Beijing residents. They include (1) certificates of children of the returned educated urban youth working in countryside, (2) certificate of children of Taiwanese, (3) certificate of children of post doctors, (4) certificate of children of army officials, (5) certificate of children of overseas Chinese, (6) certificate of Beijing resident card issued by Beijing government, (7) certificate of children of employers in CSCEC-Pauly Construction Company Limited, and (8) children of employers from big-scale state-owned enterprises (Beijing Municipal Education Committee, 2005, 2006, 2007, 2008, 2009, 2010, 2011).

[2] The interview with vice principal of School B was conducted on May 12, 2011.

[3] Based on interview with principal of School A which was conducted on April 18, 2011.

6.1 Public School Admission Policy in Community A

Table 6.1 School admission options in Community A in 2011

School admission option	Definition
Admission by school recommendation	In Beijing, the local education authority allowed each school to take a very small number of students recommended by their schools. Schools that were authorized to admit students by the recommendation made their own selection criteria, such as students' unified exam scores in G5 and G6, ethics, awards of "three excellence student," and so forth. The recommendation was a four-phase process, including (1) self-recommendation, (2) class recommendation, (3) teachers' recommendation, and (4) school recommendation to the local education authority. Students who pursued this process were usually local and held Beijing *hukou*. Therefore, migrant children without "Green Card" were not eligible for this admission scheme
Admission by special talents	Based on the guidelines provided by the local education authority, only three types of students were qualified for this admission method, that is, students with outstanding skills in sports, arts, and technologies talent student. Schools that were authorized to admission special talent students administered admission exams, but the examination date was determined by Beijing Education Committee. Each student was allowed to choose two or three schools to take the exams. Migrant children with special talents and approved by the local education authority have been allowed to take this approach for junior high school admission in *Fengtai* District since 2011
Admission by mutual selection	Admission by mutual selection had been practiced in *Fengtai* District since 2010. It refers to the process in which both schools and students were allowed to choose each other. *Fengtai* District had given school districts. Community A belonged to School District 1. There were 11 junior high schools in School District 1. Local students could select 3 schools out of 11 junior high schools. At the same time, the schools also selected students who picked the schools checking students' academic achievements and comprehensive evaluation. The mutual selection process usually lasted 3 days
Boarding school admission	In *Fengtai* District, only one key school provided room and board at the junior high school level
Admission to assigned schools	Local students who did not participate in the admission processes such as by school recommendation, special talents, and mutual selection were assigned to schools by the local education authority
Going back to *hukou* registered school admission	This option is for students who study outside their *hukou* registered school districts in primary schools. These students return to *hukou* registered school districts for low secondary education
Minban school admission	This option was for students who planned to study in private junior high schools
Admission for migrant children with "Green Card"	Migrant children with one of the eight types of certificates issued by Beijing Municipal Government were treated as local students and eligible in public school admission to junior high schools
Admission for migrant children without "Green Card"	In *Fengtai* District, parents of migrant children without "Green Card" had to find schools on their own. Normally, they registered in a local junior high school first. Then their children took an entrance exam. Those who passed the exam were admitted to the public junior high schools upon meeting the admission criteria by the school

Source: Summarized from recording taken in parent meeting for the guidance of school admission by vice principal of School B on May 12, 2011

Because of the One Child Policy, the number of school-aged children in Beijing is decreasing. On the other hand, the number of migrant children is increasing rapidly. In fact, to some extent, compulsory public education in Beijing is serving migrant children. They are using many good quality education resources of Beijing… And in fact, our teachers are really suffering in teaching them…. (Interview conducted on May 12, 2011, translated by the author)

Furthermore, the interview with the principal of School A indicated that the school admission policy for migrant children at School A was against "Free, no selection exam and proximity-based compulsory education." It also broke equality in the process of admission to public junior high schools because migrant children were excluded from the mainstream public school admission. As the principal of School A described:

…different from other schools in this area, our school requires entrance exam for migrant children in order to control student quality…you know, annually, we have about 260 applications, but we only can enroll 60 migrant children. Therefore, we have to select through exams and interviews…. (Interview conducted on April 18, 2011, translated by the author)

In addition, the exclusion of migrant children from public school admission was also presented by the exclusion of migrant parents from having access to obtaining public school admission information. The data collected revealed that the public school admission policies at the district level were made to protect the benefits of local schools and local students. Conversely, the policies at the city level emphasized equal public education for all.[4] Therefore, it is difficult for schools to explain policies at the district level in detail for parents in regard to public school admission policy. The parent-teacher meeting which introduced public school admission policy simply became a platform for the pre-determined educational exclusion. According to Appendix 10, the school admission schedule of School B in 2011 failed to provide detailed information on the school admission approaches for migrant children. A migrant mother, also a business owner, from Shandong province, expressed her dissatisfaction of the parent-teacher meeting held by School B. She believed she and her husband were excluded from the public school admission process. She described her experience as follows:

…To be honest, it was a kind of waste of time in attending the parent-teacher meeting held by School B. I was hurt by their (school's) attitudes towards migrants… (her eyes were full of tears)… During the meeting, teachers did not mention school admission for migrant children at all! Within about two hours, they mainly talked about local students' school admission…you know, it is really a discrimination! …. (Interview with Parent 3 from School B, May 12, 2011, translated by the author)

The feeling of exclusion was also shared by Parent 6 from School B. The migrant parent felt angry and complained during the interview:

---

[4] According to vice principal of School B, in fact, due to population explosion in Beijing, especially for the significant growth of migrant population in Beijing in recent years, policy for migrant children in 2011 became stricter compared with previous years. School admission policy was considered a tool for preventing migrants from rapidly flowing into Beijing. However, in the parents' meeting it is difficult for school side to explain this target clearly for migrant parent. Therefore, in most of time in the parent-teacher meeting, vice principle of School B just intentionally avoided touching upon migrant children's school admission. I took part in the 2 h parent-teacher meeting held by School B on April 27, 2011.

...I might be too direct, but, you know, parent-teacher meeting held by my son's primary school was really terrible and useless. It seemed policies were just for local students. As to our migrant children, we had to find schools by ourselves. Nobody cared about us. I was so disappointed with this! (Interview conducted on May 13, 2011, translated by the author)

In summary, public school admission policy in Community A has two features: the first being, indeed, there are diverse options for parents and students to choose for their admission to junior high schools. Nevertheless, the available approaches are mainly dependent on parents' socio-economic status. It may cause inequality in public school admission. And the second, obviously, is an educational exclusion in public school admission in Community A. It is particularly presented in the school admission approaches for migrant children and the exclusion of migrant parents from access to information about school admission policy.

6.2 "Parentocracy"-based School Admission

In the following section, I examine parents' experiences in *Zexiao* and their opinions on school admission policies and approaches for *Zexiao*. Through an analysis of parents' experiences and opinions on both official and legalized unofficial approaches for public junior high school admission, this section further illustrates the "parentocracy"-based *Zexiao* and the pre-determined exclusion of migrant children from admission to public junior high schools in Community A. Table 6.2 shows the school admission schedule of School B in Community A in 2011 officially started from the middle of April to early June. An analysis of parents'

Table 6.2 School admission schedule in School B, 2011

Date	School admission
April 13–17	Checking student's basic information
April 19–20	Procedure for students whose parents have a "Green Card"
April 22–May 5	School recommendation student
May 4–5	Going back to *hukou* registered school application
May 14–15	Special talent student registration
May 17–18	Mutual selection registration
May 12	Special talent student test
May 21–22	Mutual selection[a]
June 1–6	School assignment and announcement of school admission results

Source: School admission arrangement distributed by School B for G6 students' parents, collected from parent-teacher meeting on April 27, 2011, edited by Author
[a]According to the principal of School A, in general, School A had 30 seat positions for the mutual selection approved by the local education authority. Within three days, students and School A mutually select each other. School A selects students who choose School A by taking student's learning achievement and comprehensive evaluation. (Interview with the principal from School A was conducted on April 18, 2011)

experiences and opinions in public school admission follows the school admission in Community A. Interviews with parents in School A and School B mainly talked about school recommendation-based and special talent-based school admission to junior high schools.

6.2.1 Admission by School Recommendation

The interviews with parents showed two major concerns about this admission approach. Firstly, parents felt this approach intensified exam-driven education and increased students' workload. Secondly, the selection criteria for recommendation by schools did not reflect fairness and equality in education.

In terms of the first concern, to compete for the limited quota for admission by recommendation, students were forced to study for exams, which intensified students' workload. Working as a teacher in School B, Parent 1 pointed out that the purpose of the admission by recommendation approach was to dispute better-performing students for key schools. Students who would like to pursue admission by recommendation were required to have a GPA of over 95 points (the full score is 100 points) in two locally unified exams in Grade 5 and Grade 6. Therefore, in order to perform well on the exams, parents had to send their children to various private tutors or tutoring agencies after school and on weekends. Some parents started the exam preparation when their children were in Grade 3 or Grade 4. Both parents and students felt exhausted in the process.[5] It was evident that the admission by recommendation had become exam-driven, and students' workload had been increased tremendously.

However, such achievement-based evaluation limited students' access to quality education. According to criteria of recommendation student, the learning achievement-based and *hukou*-based selection standard excluded children without high scores and without *hukou* from the access to popular schools. The interviews with parents showed concerns on the limitations of student evaluations. Parent 5, a local parent from School B, specified:

> Well, my child has got school recommendation to No.12 Middle School.[6] You know the high score and being a "three excellence student" are the two keys to becoming school recommendation student.... However, I think it is necessary to look at the overall development of our kids. Two exam scores are really not enough. They do not show everything, in fact. The daily achievement should also be given consideration. And it is really important. (Interview conducted on May 12, 2011, translated by the author)

Parent 16 from School A said that the academic achievement-based selection still could not reflect the strengths of a student.[7] Moreover, the admission by recommendation

---

[5] The Interview with Parent 1 from School B was conducted on May 10, 2011.

[6] No. 12 Middle School is the "demonstration school" in *Fengtai* District. It is said that this school is considered as the best school in this district.

[7] The interview was conducted on May 11, 2011.

approach was considered a barrier for students to go to popular schools. Parent 3's daughter was not recommended by School B due to a dissatisfied exam result in math. Thus, Parent 3 argued:

> It is really not fair. I really do not think it is a good policy. I am not sure how badly this policy will influence children who cannot be recommended. But, you know, without recommendation, it is almost impossible to get access to good schools. It is unfair to exclude children from quality schools because of a poor result of one exam. It will be a big damage for our child and her future. I think it is necessary to terminate this policy. The policy excludes children from attending good schools. And it may badly affect their future. (Interview with conducted on May 12, 2011, translated by the author)

Migrant parents expressed their mixed feelings on the exclusion of their children from the admission by recommendation approach. Parent 6, a migrant parent, from School B felt that the recommendation approach would motivate students to work harder. However, she wished migrant children could be included in that process.[8] Parent 6's view was echoed by Parent 4, also a migrant parent from School B.[9]

Furthermore, parents expressed their concerns about the transparency of the student selection in the admission by recommendation process. Parent 3, a migrant worker in Beijing, pointed out that the selection was subjective and clearly led to inequality in education.[10] Parents also showed their concerns on the effect of *guanxi* on the student selection process. Parent 2 from School A criticized the process as follows:

> This policy is really a terrible one. It is just a tool for a *guanxi* network and exchange between power, money, and access to key schools. I really dislike the policy which plans to increase the quota of school recommendation students. You know, maybe because my child is not good enough to be recommended. I do not have any feeling for it. (Interview conducted on May 4, 2011, translated by the author)

In summary, as a tool for key schools to select students, the admission by school recommendation approach excluded students who did not have good examination scores and local *hukou*. More seriously, the criteria for student selection were clearly influenced by exam-driven education and *guanxi*. Furthermore, the approach might have also caused social exclusion and intensified inequality in public school admission and education.

6.2.2 Admission by Special Talents

Since School A is not authorized to enroll special talent students by the local education authority, there is no student who entered into School A as special talent students. Nevertheless, the interviews with parents from Schools A and B showed diverse purposes for cultivating children's special talents. Meanwhile, the

---

[8] The interview with Parent 6 from School B was conducted on May 13, 2011.
[9] The interview with Parent 4 from School B was conducted on May 12, 2011.
[10] The interview with Parent 3 from School A was conducted on May 3, 2011.

interviews with parents indicated that mastery of Olympic math, English, and pre-admission training classes were critical to those who wished to enter into popular schools as special talent students. The data collected also confirmed that parents were inspired to send their children to those training classes. Consequently, the special talent-based approach intensified *Zexiao*.

As noted earlier, parents had various attitudes toward how to develop their children's special talents. Firstly, some parents did not link developing their children's hobbies to special skills. For example, Parent 2 from School A started teaching his daughter the violin when she was 4 years old. He did not expect his daughter to become a violinist but just want her to know about and love music.[11] However, some parents invested everything they had to cultivate their children's talent for their future. In order to send her child to the Central Musical Institute, Parent 11 from School A took her daughter to Beijing from Jiangsu province. She hired a professor from the Central Musical Institute to teach her daughter and paid an expensive fee. This type of investment is beyond the financial ability of most regular families in Beijing.[12] Different from Parents 2 and 11, some parents decided to trade off when there was a conflict between developing students' special talents and allowing them to have normal schooling. For example, Parent 4 from School A asked her son to give up his hobby on Chinese chess in the beginning of Grade 5, though he had been playing Chinese chess for years in primary school.[13] Parent 4 felt that playing Chinese chess would not help her son get a good job in the future. Another example, Parent 2 from School B used to take her daughter to play a Chinese traditional musical instrument. However, to prepare for the unified exams at the district level, she asked her daughter to give up her musical instrument training.[14]

As mentioned earlier, Olympic math was one of the main criteria for student selection. Some parents showed positive attitudes toward Olympic math classes since they were useful for school admission. Parents 3 from School B sent her son to an Olympic math class from Grade 1 onward. She was very positive about the Olympic math class since she believed that it could help her son with his study, and it was useful for his education transition. She said that:

> I think the main purpose of sending him to tutoring classes is to help him to touch upon knowledge widely in order to improve his exam result … I think Olympic math can help children to practice using their brains. And I do believe it is necessary for children to learn. Also, if children are able to get awards from the Olympic math competition, they will gain priority in education transition from G6 to G7. In my child's class, over 50% of the students take Olympic math. You know, teachers also recommended it. (Interview conducted on May 12, 2011, translated by the author)

---

[11] Interview with Parent 2 from School A was conducted on May 3, 2011.

[12] According to Parent 11, the musical instrument class costs between 800 and 1000 yuan per hour. And the total tuition for the training is about 50,000 yuan. According to the Beijing Statistics Bureau, the per capita disposable income of most Beijing residents in 2011 was 32,903 yuan. Therefore, the disposable income for a three-person family (two parents and one child) is 65,806 yuan. The musical instrument tuition is about 76% of the total disposable income for a normal Beijing family.

[13] Interview with Parent 3 from School A was conducted on May 4, 2011.

[14] Interview with Parent 2 from School B was conducted on May 10, 2011.

6.2 "Parentocracy"-based School Admission

Similar positive feedback on Olympic math classes was also found in the interview with Parent 9 from School A. Her child started Olympic math classes during Grade 3. Parent 9 believed that there were two main benefits from taking Olympic math classes. Firstly, it was helpful for her child's study. Secondly, it was useful for her child to have a successful admission to a good junior high school by taking Olympic math classes.[15] The interview with Parent 2 from School B showed that knowledge of Olympic math was closely linked with school admission. As Parent 2 from School B explained,

> Two years ago, I heard that the government did not allow schools to link Olympic math with school admission. Therefore, I did not send him to that class. Well, you know.... (laughing)...if they have linked again; then I am sure I will let him take it without hesitation. (Interview conducted on May 10, 2011, translated by the author)

Olympic math classes were usually offered by private tutoring institutes. According to Parent 5 from School B, since one tutoring institute guaranteed to recommend her child to a key school upon completion of the Olympic math class, Parent 5 enrolled her child in that private tutoring institute. However, after tuition was paid, the tutoring institute never mentioned again recommending her child to a key school.[16] Olympic math classes had been linked closely with admission to popular schools, which attracted parents to send their children to such classes.

Like Olympic math, mastery of English was considered another important talent for those who desired to enter popular schools to have. The interviews with respondents indicated that achievement in English study became an added assurance for children to gain access to popular schools. Meanwhile, certificates received from English contests became a critical criterion for popular schools to select students in the admission process to junior high schools.

English classes were closely linked with school admission in Community A. According to Parent 15 from School A, the reason for her child to take English classes was to get certificates, which were useful for her child's transition to junior high school.[17] To some parents, taking English at a young age also meant preparing their children for entering a good university. As Parent 4 explained,

> I sent my son to Cambridge English classes when he was in kindergarten. The class was held twice a week, two hours each time. It continued until G5.... Before graduation from primary school, we sent him to ABC English classes.[18] The tuition was 5,000 yuan per semester. My objective for sending him to English classes was just to send him to School C. Then he can go to a better university. (Interview conducted on May 13, 2011, translated by the author)

Furthermore, the government decision on the disconnection between English study and education transition made parents disappointed. It illustrated the

---

[15] The interview with Parent 9 from School A was conducted on May 5, 2011.
[16] The interview with Parent 5 from School B was conducted on May 13, 2011.
[17] Interview with Parent 15 from School A was conducted on May 5, 2011.
[18] The ABC English program is offered by ABC Education Corporation in China. The corporation was established in Beijing in 1997. It provides English learning programs from pre-school level to adult level. Retrieved from http://www.abc.com.cn/index.php/rukou, accessed to June 1, 2012.

importance of English study for children's education transition. Parent 6 from School B complained:

> We went to English classes from G3 to G5.... Yes, even taking Cambridge English.[19] But I was told by some parents that the Cambridge English was not useful for education transition to lower secondary education…to be honest, it really affected my son's motivation and mine to continue it! (Interview conducted on May 13, 2011, translated by the author)

The interviews with parents showed their paradoxical feelings for sending children to take extracurricular classes for public school admission. Parents believed that without taking any extra classes, their children's education transition and future would be in jeopardy. As Parent 6 from School A noted,

> Regarding the remedial classes, I think these kinds of classes just likes giving the seeding a hand. It is too early [for children] to learn so many things a day. I really do not believe they can remember all they learn. But it is really a paradox. If I give her a free life, then everything will become difficult. (Interview conducted on May 4, 2011, translated by the author)

The interviews with respondents showed that the pressure on students and parents for admission to public junior high schools through remedial classes in Community A also came from the local education authority and schools. Parent 1 from School B explained that the local education authority deeply influenced parents' decisions on sending their children to cram schools or private tutoring. The exam-oriented education pushed parents and schools to support private tutoring. In order to achieve expected exam results, schools recommended parents to send their children to cram schools for private tutoring. Parent 1 further explained:

> As to the cram schools, some are from the private sector, while some are operated by the local education authority. Some teachers and research staff members are from the education authority at the district level and also teach there.[20] The local education authority informs schools of any classes it offers. But, you know, these are all inside information…. Since those teachers are the ones who design the standardized exams at the district level or even at the city level, we strongly recommend our children to go in order to have a good exam result. (Interview conducted on May 10, 2011, translated by the author)

Moreover, the interviews with parents also indicated that parents' socioeconomic status determined their children's participation in Olympic math or English classes. In order to obtain certificates from Cambridge English classes, Parent 3 from School A paid tuition in the amount of 1,500 yuan per semester. Tuition for an ABC English class, according to Parent 4 from School A, was about 5,000 yuan per semester. Parent 6 paid 1,000 yuan per semester for her daughter to attend a pre-admission

---

[19] According to the homepage of the University of Cambridge, they started English for speakers of other languages examination program in 1913. From 1992, this program started in China. Cambridge Young Learners English Tests is an English exam system for young learners from 7 to 12 years old. It has three levels from starters to flyers. Retrieved from http://www.cambridgeesol-china.org/index.php, accessed on June 2, 2012.

[20] In Beijing, there are teaching and research centers at both the district and city levels. These institutes are in charge of designing unified exams at various levels. Therefore, the teachers' classes are considered as important resources for students and teachers to prepare for the exams (The information was collected from interview with Parent 1 from School B on May 10, 2011).

training class in a key school located in a neighboring district. Although it costs a lot for parents to do so, the interviews confirmed that parents of low-income families were willing to invest in their children's education. Parent 9 from School A was a factory worker. Since his wife was laid off a couple of years ago, the husband became the only provider in the family. Although the cost for their child attending an Olympic math class was high, Parent 9 still sent his son to the class. The average cost for an extracurriculum class was about one-third of the family's income.[21]

Accordingly, in addition to sending their children to Olympic math classes, parents in Community A also sent their children to English classes in order to get advantages in public school admission to popular junior high schools. The participation in such classes was stimulated by the link between achievement in English contests and public school admission criteria. Moreover, parents' participation in such approaches was also forced by the local education authority and dependent on their own socioeconomic status.

Although schools never openly informed the public that taking pre-admission training classes was one of their admission criteria, the interviews with parents in Community A showed that many parents did it anyway, especially those who planned to send their children to popular schools. The close linkage between pre-admission training classes and the access to popular junior high schools led to the fever for taking such class and then further enhanced the collaboration between private tutoring institutes and popular public junior high schools in the process of school admission and student selection.

Parent 4 from School B,[22] a migrant parent, confessed that the main reason for her to send her son to a pre-admission tutoring class was there might be a possibility for her son to be recommended by the private tutoring institute to the popular junior high school. She believed that there was a working relationship between the private tutoring institute and the popular school. She also believed that the pre-admission training class was part of the exam-based student selection by the popular school. Students took pre-admission training classes once a week to study Chinese, math, and English. Exams were determined to screen students every other 2 or 3 weeks. Those who achieved high scores on those exams were recommended by the private tutoring institutes to popular schools. Therefore, the exam results were critical for final student selection and admission to the popular school. The interview with Parent 6 from School A showed fierce competition in pre-admission training classes. She said:

> In fact, my daughter also participated in a popular junior high school's pre-admission training class. The tuition was around 1,000 yuan per semester. They followed the exam-based selection system. After one exam, some students had to "drop out" because they failed to meet the minimum standard. That was a fierce competition. Students who failed the exams would lose their opportunity for student selection by the popular school. (Interview conducted on, May 4, 2011, translated by the author)

---

[21] The interview with Parent 9 from School A was conducted on May 5, 2011.

[22] The interview with Parent 4 from School B was conducted on May 12, 2011.

The interviews with parents also confirmed that without taking pre-admission training classes, students could lose their admission opportunity to a popular school. Parent 4 from School A informed that her son failed the entrance exam to a popular school because he did not take pre-admission training class preparing for the entrance exam. However, participation in pre-admission training classes did not guarantee success in passing the entrance exam by the popular school, because *guanxi* was another important factor that affected admission to a popular school. According to Parent 4 from School A, in addition to entrance examination results, many people used *guanxi* to get their children admitted to the popular school. Therefore, the popular school selected students by utilizing both exam results and *guanxi* as admission criteria.[23]

6.2.3 School Admission for Migrant Children

The interviews with migrant parents showed that migrant children in Community A were excluded from most approaches provided in regular public school admission due to the mismatch between migrant children's conditions and the admission requirement (see Table 6.1). In principle, most migrant parents had to find children's junior high schools by themselves. Meanwhile, school admission for migrant children to junior high schools depended on migrant parents' socioeconomic status. In other words, few migrant parents might have strong *guanxi* and enough money to meet the requirements of popular schools.

The data collected showed that migrant parents did not have any or strong *guanxi*, and thus they were completely excluded from *Zexiao*. As Parent 4 from School B described, he went to several public schools and attempted to negotiate with the schools about his son's education transition. All of those schools rejected his request. He was told that since local students had problems in entering popular schools, migrant children would not be given any consideration until local students' needs were met.[24] According to Parent 13 from School A, she followed the procedures set for migrant children's school admission in Beijing and spent 3 months preparing necessary documents to meet the admission requirements. In order to make it possible, the parent applied to five schools in three districts. Only School A, a non-key school, responded. Parent 13 complained:

> I really felt angry with those schools...even though we were not qualified, we still thought it was necessary for them to let us know the result... the feeling of being neglected was really sad! But you know, we have to keep being strong since nobody will help us in this city! (Interview conducted on May 5, 2011, translated by the author)

Conversely, migrant parents with *guanxi* in Beijing could find a school for their children much easier. For example, Parent 11 from School A had *guanxi* in Beijing.

---

[23] The interview with Parent 4 from School A was conducted on May 3, 2011.

[24] The interview with Parent 4 from School B was conducted on May 12, 2011.

So, she was able to enroll her daughter in School A without any difficulty. With help from her relative living in Beijing, her daughter entered into School A quickly after arriving in Beijing.[25] Parent 6 from School B, also a migrant mother, shared her experience in looking for schools for her son. By the time when I interviewed her, her son had been rejected by three key schools in different districts. In order to send her son to a popular public junior high school, Parent 6 said she had tried to utilize any possible *guanxi*. Since she had a small company serving some local customers, she planned to ask her clients for help, which was her last resort.[26]

Besides *guanxi* in Beijing, *guanxi* in migrant's hometown could also help. Some migrant parents chose to send their children back to their hometown for secondary education. Those migrant parents recognized the difficulty in sending their children to key schools in Beijing and therefore, "voluntarily" accepted the reality by sending their children to popular schools in their hometown. Parent 3 from School B had been working in Beijing for more than a decade. They prepared for their daughter's education transition since she was in Grade 4. On the one hand, they tried to find the possibility to enroll the child in a key school in Beijing. On the other hand, they started searching for good schools in their hometown. Through help from relatives, their daughter was accepted by one of the top ten junior high schools in their province. Since they bought an apartment next to that school, their daughter was able to enroll based on the principle of proximity without paying any additional fees. Parents who did well financially and had a social network in their hometown could take this approach. By utilizing money and *guanxi* to gain access for their children to study in popular schools, migrant parents could have generated similar issues and problems in their hometown.

Findings showed that migrant children's school admission to junior high school was determined by factors such as public school admission policy at the district level and parents' social networks in both Beijing and their hometown, as well as their financial capabilities. The study also showed that the majority of migrant parents had to accept the exclusion of their children in public junior high school admission in Community A. While migrant parents with strong local social networks had some advantages for sending their children to public schools in Beijing, they also had a backup system if they had *guanxi* in their hometown.

6.3 "Legalization" of *Zexiaofei*

Besides the official channels for admission to public junior high schools, there were unofficial approaches which were widely accepted and practiced by stakeholders in the school admission process. With the rapid commercialization of public education services in China, access to quality junior high schools in China became more dependent on parents' economic resources. Although lower secondary education is

---

[25] The interview with Parent 11 from School A was conducted on May 5, 2011.

[26] The interview with Parent 6 from School B was conducted on May 13, 2011.

supposed to be free, the charge of the cost of choosing schools, called as *Zexiaofei*, was "legalized" and widely accepted by parents if they wanted to send their children to key schools. Parents' experiences in *Zexiao* show the legalization of *Zexiaofei* in public school admission to the junior high school in Community A. Moreover, their *Zexiao* experiences also revealed the "legalized exclusion" of low-income families from participating in *Zexiao* since they were unable to pay *Zexiaofei*. Meanwhile, the interviews with parents in Community A also revealed the importance of *guanxi* in *Zexiao*.

According to Parent 1 from School B,[27] the inter-districts *Zexiao* generally cost 30,000 yuan. The money should be paid to a specific account that belonged to the district education committee, which showed clear evidence that *Zexiaofei* was legalized by the local education authority.[28] Although Parent 3 from School B did not pay money for her daughter's school admission, she shared her friend's stories of paying *Zexiaofei*. She lamented that education had been commercialized too much. In order to enroll a child to a popular junior high school in a neighboring district, her friend paid 70,000 yuan as *Zexiaofei*.[29]

Furthermore, interviews showed that there is a *"guanxi* rent seeking" as well. Those who had *guanxi* with popular schools were able to make money by connecting parents with the schools. In order to buy a limited access to popular schools, parents have to pay *Zexiaofei*. In this process, parents were usually charged twice in order to get their children to be enrolled in quality schools. The interview with

---

[27] The interview with Parent 1 from School B was conducted on May 10, 2011.

[28] The "legalization" of *Zexiao* fees is also mentioned in the interview with the principal of School A. Since there is no *Zexiao* student in School A, School A did not get any income from the charge of *Zexiao* fees. According to the principal of School A, before the prohibition of *Jiedu* fees for migrant children, the charge of *Jiedu* fees from migrant children was paid directly by parents to an account that belonged to the local education authority. About 70% of the collected money from parents in School A was paid back to the school from the local education authority. The rest of the 30% was used for the reconstruction of poor quality schools in the district. This interview with the principal of School A was conducted on April 18, 2011. An interview with the ex-vice principal of School A showed that in the 1990s when School A was in the peak period of its development, the school charged 50,000 yuan, which was the highest *Zexiaofei* in the school's history. Based on the standard set up by the local education authority, in general they charged 12,000 yuan from *Zexiao* students. And at that time, the money collected was not required to be submitted to the local education authority. According to the ex-vice principal of School A, the cost for *Zexiao* sometimes was more than the *Zexiaofei* itself. In Beijing, primary school graduates' identification cards were usually transferred to assigned junior high schools by the local education authority. Students who chose *Zexiao* had to get their cards back from the assigned schools by themselves. Sometimes, the assigned schools charged a commission fee for parents to get the identification card back. In some cases, it took several thousand yuan (based on an interview with the ex-vice principal of School A, which was conducted on April 18, 2011). The vice principal of School B also shared a similar observation regarding the charge of *Zexiao* fees. She said that if it was inter-districts transition then parents were normally charged 15,000 yuan. The price had been increased to 30,000 yuan in recent years however. She pointed out that 30,000 yuan was just the amount written in an invoice; the real price of a *Zexiaofei* was hard to tell. Only the principal and parents knew the exact amounts (based on an interview with the vice principal of School B on May 12, 2011).

[29] The interview with Parent 3 from School B was conducted on May 12, 2011.

6.3 "Legalization" of *Zexiaofei*

Parent 4 from School A showed that parents would not have any access to pay *Zexiaofei* without *guanxi*. She shared her sister's story as follows:

> my sister decided to pay money in order to enroll her son in a good school. Since they did not have *guanxi*, the first step was to find someone with *guanxi* that could help them to deliver the money to the school they preferred. In order to find someone with *guanxi*, they paid 30,000 yuan to a middle man. At the same time, they paid additional money as *Zexiaofei*... it really cost a lot. (Interview conducted on May 4, 2011, translated by the author)

A similar experience was also shared by Parent 6 from School A. In order to send her daughter to a key school in a neighboring district, they paid 20,000 yuan to a middle man who negotiated with the school. However, since the *guanxi* between the middle man and the school was not "strong" enough, Parent 6 had to wait a long time for the result. Parent 6 did not get any result from the middle man until the principal of that school was arrested due to corruption.[30] It was evident that a middle man and his/her *guanxi* with a key school played a very important role in *Zexiao*, which made the process of *Zexiao* more complicated and costly. Apparently, the "legalized" *Zexiaofei* excluded families that had little money or no *guanxi* with the schools they preferred. For affluent parents with strong *guanxi*, it is a virtual assurance for them to send their children to popular schools, while disadvantaged families were excluded from a fair public school admission. Parent 14 from School A is a migrant single mother. She was excluded from *Zexiao* since she could not afford *Zexiaofei* charged by a key school in a neighbor district. She recalled:

> We went to that key school to look for a possibility.... The first question we got was whether we could pay 30,000 yuan as *Zexiaofei* or not since my daughter did not have Beijing *hukou*... (she choked with emotion) ... you know, as a single mother, it had already been over my affordability... The only choice for me was to give up my wish to providing my kid a good education and sent her to come here (School A). (Interview conducted on May 5, 2011, translated by the author)

Besides paying *Zexiaofei* directly, another type of payment for *Zexiao* was to rent a house close to an objective school. Since many parents selected schools that were far away from home, they had to rent apartments close to the desired schools. Parent 5 from School B decided to send her daughter to a key school that was far away from home. Therefore, they had to rent an apartment close to the school so they would not have to commute a long distance. The rent was about 3,000 yuan per month, which was beyond many families' affordability in Beijing.[31] Obviously, the case of Parent 5 from School B proved that the socioeconomic status was the pre-

---

[30] *Zexiaofei*-based corruption became a hot topic in urban China recently. In 2008, the principal of one famous primary school in Haidian District was arrested on charges of corruption. According to the China News Net, the unauthorized *Zexiao* fees collected by this school was more than 100 million yuan. Retrieved from http://news.xinhuanet.com/legal/2008-08/17/content_9424765.htm, accessed on April 2, 2012.

[31] According to the Beijing Statistic Bureau, the average monthly salary of people is 4,201 yuan in 2010. Retrieved from http://www.bjstats.gov.cn/, accessed on December 13, 2011. The room rent paid by Parent 5 is beyond the affordability of many families in Beijing. The interview with Parent 5 from School B was conducted on May 13, 2011.

condition for parents to participate in *Zexiao*. Regardless of what type of payment for *Zexiao*, direct or indirect, the legalization of *Zexiaofei* and the utilization of *guanxi* in *Zexiao* became widely accepted by parents to take part in *Zexiao*. In summary, the interviews with parents confirmed that preparing their children for admission to popular junior high schools had become costly and time-consuming. Moreover, the admission process failed to be fair, and it failed to provide migrant children and those of low-income families with equal education opportunities. The inequality and failure of the admission process to popular schools were also reflected by the involvement of private tutoring institutes with public schools or vice versa, as well as the involvement of the local education authority in offering and promoting pre-admission training classes, which showed a clear conflict of interests. The public school admission became a luxury for children of the rich and the powerful. The process could be described as what Brown (1990) termed "parentocracy."

6.4 The Local Context and Beyond

In Chap. 3, I presented that the public discourse analysis indicated that the imbalanced development of public schools, parents' attitudes toward their children's education, and a systematic power exchange shaped people's involvement in *Zexiao* and public school admission in China. Those findings were echoed by the interviews with parents in Community A, who complained that the imbalanced school development, parents' aspirations, and power changes further determined their involvement in *Zexiao*.

6.4.1 The Gap Between Public Schools

Similar to what was introduced in Chap. 5, an analysis of the study's interviews indicated that there was big gap in educational resources between the junior high schools in Community A and schools in neighboring districts, as well as between the two junior high schools in Community A. The gap can be categorized in terms of school facilities, student distribution, and teachers' salaries.

6.4.1.1 The Gap Between Schools in Different Districts

The interview with the retired principal of School A showed serious student mobility in Community A due to the gap between public schools in different districts. As Fig. 5.1 illustrates, there was a gap between the southern and northern parts of Beijing in terms of allocation of demonstration schools. According to the retired principal, School A used to have a full student enrollment from the five primary schools in Community A. In some years, School A only enrolled 50% of the students from the five primary schools. It was not uncommon that

6.4 The Local Context and Beyond

some students did not report to the schools when school began. The main reason for their absence was that they had been chosen by other schools in the same district or in neighboring districts that offered a higher quality education than their district.

Figure 6.1 shows the student mobility in Community A based on the interviews with the principals of School A and School B. The data also indicated that students who did not report to the schools assigned to them generally attended the schools in neighboring districts, such as *Chongwen* District, *Chaoyang* District, and *Xuanwu* District. A small number of students also chose the schools in *Dongcheng* District and *Haidian* District. Relatively speaking, those districts had more popular schools compared with *Fengtai* District (see Fig. 5.1 and Table 5.1).[32] The imbalanced distribution of education resources between districts intensified student mobility and *Zexiao* in Community A.

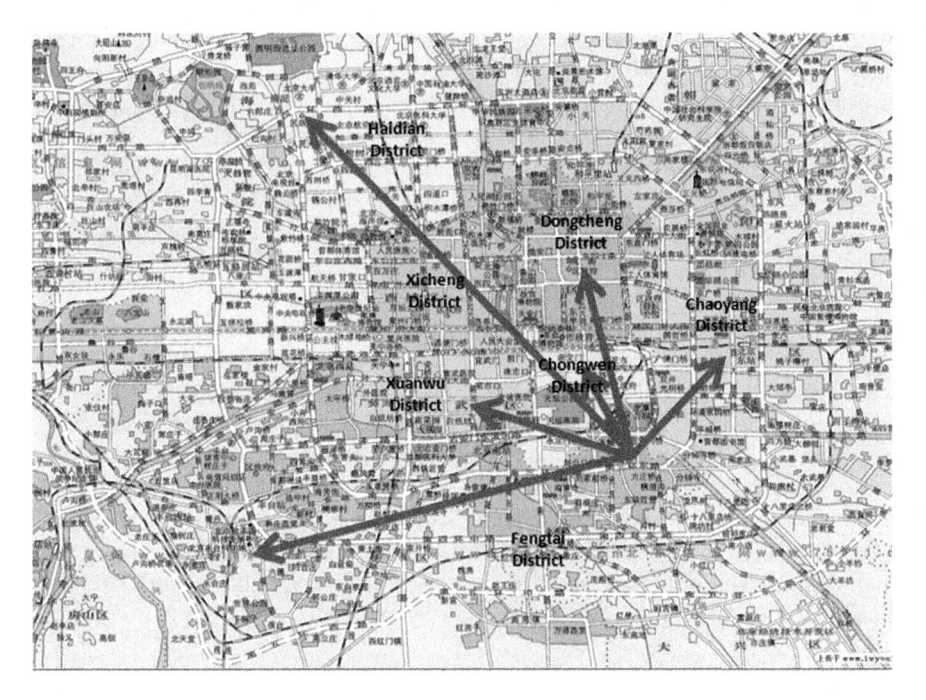

Fig. 6.1 Student mobility in Community A (Source: Compiled by the author based on information collected from interviews in Community A in 2011)

---

[32] The distribution of demonstration schools in Beijing is not in balance. According to the Beijing Municipal Education Committee, in 2010, there were 12 demonstration schools in *Dongcheng* District, 11 demonstration schools in *Haidian* District, and 7 demonstration schools in *Chaoyang* District. In contrast, there were only four demonstration schools in *Fengtai* District. Retrieved from http://www.bjedu.gov.cn/publish/portal0/tab40/, accessed on June 3, 2012.

6.4.1.2 The Gap Between Schools in Community A

As noted earlier, the interviews with respondents also showed a big gap between public junior high schools within Community A. The gap can be analyzed in the aspects of school facilities, student distributions, and teachers' salaries.

In terms of the gap between school facilities, the interviews with the principals of School A and School C illustrated the gap in school facilities between the two schools. Although the Beijing education authority had already made the decision to separate the junior high school department from "demonstration schools," it is interesting to find that School C, as a "demonstration school," just established a new junior high school department with government support in 2010. On the one hand, this confirmed the existence of conflicting policies between the district and city levels, as described by the ex-vice principal of School B. On the other hand, it showed the attempts of the education authority in *Fengtai* District to attract more quality students to stay in their own district. According to the principal of School A, the *Fengtai* District government invested about 140 million yuan building a new campus for School C.[33] Although School A was continuously receiving government investment as a "weak junior high school" between 2006 and 2011, the government investment for School A was much less than what was given to School C. There are differences in terms of the two school facilities. School C has teaching buildings, student dormitories, laboratory buildings, a library, and other facilities. In contrast, School A only has one building. The government investment in favor of key schools led to an imbalanced distribution of educational resources among public schools in the same district and in different districts.

The collected data confirmed the existence of a student distribution gap between schools. The interviews with respondents indicated a big difference in terms of school admission between School A and School C in Community A. The pro-key school admission policies broke the balance of student distribution within this area. According to the interview with the principal of School A, School A is an ordinary junior high school and was not authorized to enroll students by school recommendation or special talent students. In contrast, School C was a demonstration school that had the privilege to select well-developed students in the community and communities within the district. Therefore, School C had better quality students than School A. As the principal of School A complained:

> With the establishment of a junior high school department in School C, the district education authority gives them the privilege to select better-performing students in eastern *Fengtai* District.... This approach badly affected the opportunity for School A to enroll better-performing students. The students we have are called 'three without students'. That is, they are considered having no special talents, poor academic performance, and no other choices for school admission. (Interview conducted on April 18, 2011, translated by the author)

---

[33] This information can also be identified on homepage of School C, retrieved from http://bj18.schoolwires.net/domain/14, accessed on June 4, 2012.

6.4 The Local Context and Beyond

The ex-vice principal of School A agreed that the establishment of the junior high school department in School C might help *Fengtai* District keep better-performing students within the district. Nevertheless, she also believed that the policy had already negatively affected student distribution in School A. Since School C had the privilege to select well-performing students, School A experienced more difficulties in attracting quality students. Also, the interviews with the current principal of School A showed that the change of student quality in School A had deteriorated teachers' motivation for teaching. As a result, some teachers left for other schools. Meanwhile, the aggravated student quality directly affected School A's reputation at the district level.[34]

The gap of teachers' salaries was another factor that affected School A. The interviews with the school principals from both Schools A and B showed the imbalance of government investment in human resources, especially in teachers' salaries, between public schools in different districts and within the same district. The data collected revealed that the best teachers often left low-salary schools for high-salary schools. Consequently, it affected teacher retention and intensified the gap between public schools. The vice principal of School B confirmed that because of the salary gap, quality teachers in *Fengtai* District left for other districts where they received higher salaries, which seriously affected parents' decisions on which schools to choose. The ex-vice principal of School A defined her school as a "teacher training center for key schools." According to her, because of the difference in teachers' salaries, many quality teachers in School A left for key schools in *Fengtai* District after gaining enough experience.[35] The interview with the retired principal of School A showed that in the past 10 years, ten veteran teachers of School A left for key schools in the same district or in other districts.[36] In contrast, School C (a demonstration school at the city level) was able to offer teachers higher salaries by charging students tuition.[37] Quality teachers were often attracted by higher salaries, and they preferred to work in popular schools.

---

[34] The interview with ex-vice principal of School A was conducted on April 18, 2011.

[35] According to an ex-vice principal of School A (on April 18, 2011), teachers in their 30s are the most transferring group. A story of teacher's leave for a famous key school was given in the interview. The leave for the key school to gain higher salaries, which are often several times more than their salaries in School A. At the same time, the training subsidy for teachers in that key school was much better than the ones in School A. Teachers were encouraged to go abroad for studying. They were also given subsidies for buying laptops. These benefits are not provided to teachers in School A. There is a huge gap of teachers' benefits between schools and districts.

[36] Interview with an ex-vice principal of School A was conducted April 18, 2011.

[37] According to *Opinions on the Implementation of Rectifying the Charge of Unauthorized School Fees* (Ministry of Education et al., 2003), *Zexiao* is allowed at the public upper secondary education level. However, the school admission of *Zexiao* students should follow "three restrictions," including the restriction of numbers of *Zexiao* students, restriction of *Zexiao* fees (maximum 30,000 yuan in Beijing), and the restriction of academic achievement (minimum line). According to an interview with an ex-vice principal of School A, since there is an official standard for the charge of *Zexiao* fees at the senior high school level, people take for granted *Zexiao* fees at the junior high school level by following the standard at the junior high school level (the interview was conducted on April 18, 2011).

Accordingly, the gaps between Schools A and C in the aspects of school facilities, student distribution, and teachers' salaries became the key factors which affected parents' involvement in their kids' admission to public junior high schools in Community A.

6.4.2 Parents' Aspirations

The case study of Community A showed parents' involvement in *Zexiao* was inspired and affected by a conformist Chinese mentality that "My children should not be left behind at the starting line." Parents had their own definition of good quality schools which inspired them and affected their decision on school selection for their children. The interviews with parents indicated that sending children to Olympic math classes, English classes, and pre-admission training classes was stimulated by the conformist mentality. For example, some parents sent children to Olympic math class and successfully enrolled their children in popular junior high schools. Therefore, other parents followed and did the same. No parents wanted their children to be left behind. The parents in Community A shared the same view. As Parent 12 from School A said:

> In fact, you know, the purpose of taking Olympic math is not to have him left behind at the starting line... (laughing)... you know, just like many parents,...we did think Olympic math might help our son to go to a good school since we have heard many successful stories about it. We started Olympic math from G1. (Interview conducted on May 5, 2011, translated by the author)

Parent 16 from School A also said that she believed her child should go as well since everyone sent their children to Olympic math classes.[38]

The interviews with parents showed that parents' were inspired to send their children to popular schools and the education transition ratio of each school was the main criterion parents used to decide which school their children should attend. Parent 5 from School B pointed out that:

> the current education resources in Community A are not in balance. School A and School C are totally different. You know, one is considered a key school; the other is not. Then I think people will choose! People believe key schools receive more support! Therefore, I still choose School C for my daughter even though these two schools have the same education quality. Normally, parents just look at the education transition ratio!... if School A's education transition ratio is better than School C for three years, then I think parents will plan to send their children to School A! (Interview conducted on May 13, 2011, translated by the author)

To conclude, like many parents in urban China, parents in Community A had a high aspiration for their children's education. On the one hand, they were pushed by a conformist mentality to provide their children with quality education. On the other hand, they created their own criteria for choosing "quality schools" for their chil-

---

[38] The interview with Parent 11 from School A was conducted on May 11, 2011.

dren. It seems that the key school system and exam-driven education greatly affected parents' aspirations and decisions on their children's school admission. Consequently, these all fostered *Zexiao*.

6.4.3 Systematic Power Exchange

The interviews with the principals of Schools A and B did not show any power exchange for co-founding students or memo students introduced in Chap. 1. However, the interviews with parents in Community A showed the power exchange for schooling outside of school settings. As mentioned earlier, *guanxi* and *hukou* largely determined who could attend popular schools.

The interviews with parents showed *guanxi* was linked with the evaluation of school recommendation students. Parent 5 from School A believed that the evaluation of school recommendation student had been considered as an exchange between *guanxi* and good quality education resources. Parent 5 also added that people in the *guanxi* network would benefit through the exchange.[39]

Interviews showed that *guanxi* provided parents with greater assurance that their children would ultimately gain access to the popular schools. According to Parent 5 from School B, before getting recommended by School B to the key school in *Fengtai* District, Parent 5 utilized her *guanxi* to find access to key schools in other districts. She honestly confessed that:

> We just wanted to send my child to a school which was as good as possible. Without *guanxi*, it is almost impossible to enter into good quality schools even when you have money. Based on *guanxi*, a key school in *Xuanwu* District agreed to enroll us. Since the *guanxi* we had was not that reliable, we could not get access to the key school we preferred in *Dongcheng* District.... In my kid's class, the majority of students just looked for schools by the assistance and networks of their parents. (Interview conducted on May 13, 2011, translated by the author)

Nevertheless, *guanxi* did not guarantee the success in *Zexiao* sometimes. Whether *guanxi* was reliable and powerful enough or not became more important for the result of *Zexiao*. Parent 6 from School A told her unsuccessful story by using *guanxi* to take part in *Zexiao*. She said that:

> We had some friends who could help us to send my daughter to a popular junior high school in *Chaoyang* District. We paid 20,000 yuan to the middle man to negotiate the education transition. However, it was said that the principal of that school was sued and investigated by the local government due to the charge of the unauthorized fees.... As a result, the middle man could not make it and returned 20,000 yuan to us.... You know, we depended

---

[39] According to Parent 5 from School A, his daughter used to study in a key school (9-year school includes both primary education and lower secondary education) in *Xicheng* District. There were 18 students in his daughter's class, including 10 local students and 8 students without local *hukou*. These eight students without local *hukou* were grandsons of leaders in neighboring provinces. And except his daughter, other local students were children of leaders at the city or district levels in Beijing (the interview with parent from School A was conducted on May 4, 2011).

on this *guanxi* too much. More seriously, we did not prepare for other options.... Otherwise, we could have more options than that. (Interview conducted on May 4, 2011, translated by the author)

Interviews also indicated that *hukou* became another type of *guanxi* for parents to utilize for *Zexiao*. Since *hukou* is considered a basic condition to go to public schools in Beijing, *hukou* in popular school districts became an advantage for *Zexiao*. Local parents who have relatives in the good school district have the advantage to use this special *guanxi* to change children's *hukou* in order to enroll children in popular schools. Parent 4 from School A had relatives in *Chongwen* District where they have relatively more popular schools than *Fengtai* District. Therefore, she transferred her son's *hukou* into *Chongwen* District by borrowing her relatives' household registration. This approach provided an option for Parent 4 to send her son to good schools in *Chongwen*. As Parent 4 pointed out, even the school assignment-based admission by the local education authority in the new *hukou* area could provide access for her child to a school which was much better than School A. This case showed *hukou* as a tool for parents to look toward for good quality schools for their children. *Hukou* became an advantage for local parents to take part in *Zexiao*. Meanwhile, the approach excluded families without access to change their children's *hukou* for *Zexiao*.

6.5 Mapping *Zexiao* in Community A

Despite the survey result showed 70% of *Zexiao* students were in key schools in Beijing,[40] the interviews with parents in Community A indicated that parents from regular schools (e.g., School A) also actively took part in *Zexiao*. The study also showed that parents' participation in *Zexiao* in Community A is deeply influenced by "parentocracy" rather than meritocracy. Although parents from School A did not succeed in *Zexiao*, the interviews showed that parents had tried diverse approaches in order to send their children to popular schools. As shown in Fig. 6.2, *Zexiao* in Community A was categorized into two types, including *Zexiao* for local parents (in blue arrows) and *Zexiao* for migrant parents (in red arrows). The two types of *Zexiao* were pre-separated by *hukou*-based school admission policies made by the local education authority.

Firstly, as Fig. 6.2 shows, there are six approaches for local parents and students to take part in admission to junior high schools. Besides the school assignment approach, which meant the proximity-based school admission, other approaches required diverse preconditions for parents and students to prepare for. Although academic achievement was one of the most important factors for participation in diverse options in *Zexiao*, the success of *Zexiao* was closely dependent on some "parentocracy" factors, such as parents' *guanxi*, *hukou*, and financial condition. In

---

[40] See Hu, Lu, and Xue (2008).

6.5 Mapping *Zexiao* in Community A

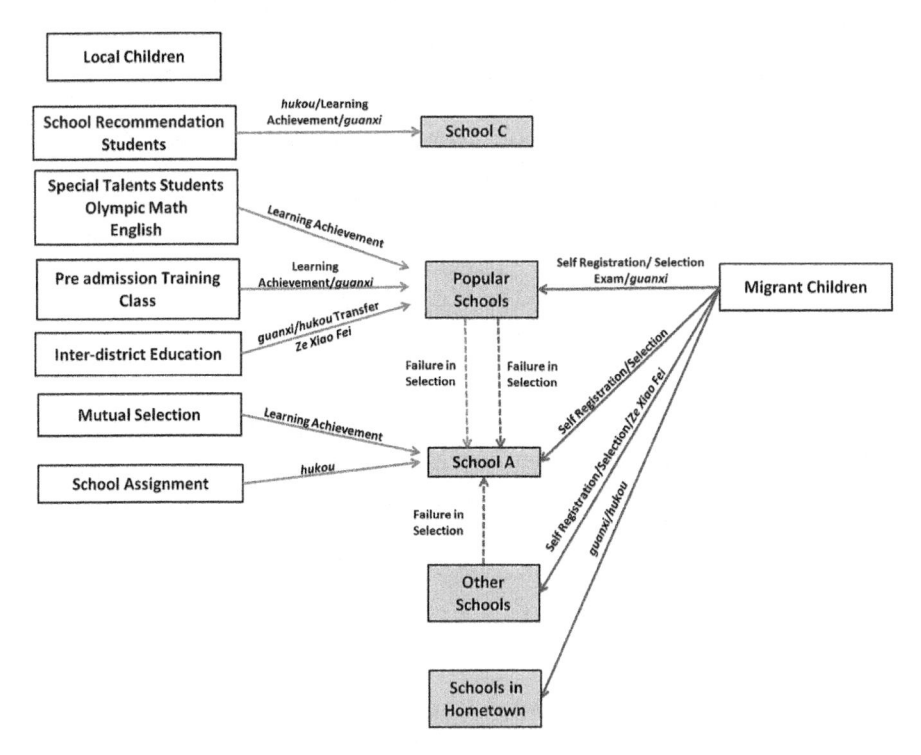

Fig. 6.2 Mapping *Zexiao* in Community A (Source: Author edited. Note: Dotted line means that parents sent children to School A after they failed in sending their children to other schools)

other words, the meritocracy-based competition for access to popular schools was stratified by parentocracy factors. Although the majority of parents involved in the interview took part in *Zexiao*, most of them failed in the student selection due to the mismatch between their conditions (such as parents' socioeconomic status, *guanxi*, and *hukou*) and the selection criteria made by schools. In general, admission by assignment to School A was the last choice for parents and children. The parentocracy-based channels for school admission did not reflect equality in public school admissions. Consequently, they intensified competition and exclusion in admission to public junior high schools in Community A. In addition, preparation for admission to popular schools had become a very costly and lengthy process. Only those parents who had time and money were able to participate in *Zexiao* and send their children to private tutoring, special talent studies, and pre-admission training classes.

Secondly, under the public admission policies by the local education authority, migrant parents and their children were excluded from the mainstream public school admission to junior high schools because they did not have *hukou* in Beijing. Thus, their participation in admission to junior high schools mainly depended on *guanxi* and affordability for *Zexiaofei* in Beijing. Migrant parents sent children to School A after their attempt to gain admission to their desired schools failed. Moreover, migrant parents who had *guanxi* in hometown also had advantages and were able to have their children admitted to popular schools there. As a result, other children might be excluded from admission to key schools.

Similar to the findings in the analysis of public discourse on *Zexiao*, *Zexiao* in Community A was also shaped by multidimensional forces, including diverse official and unofficial school admission channels, the local context of the imbalanced development of local public education, parents' aspiration, and the systematic power exchange for quality education resources. Those issues intensified *Zexiao* in Community A. The case study showed that the diverse public school admission policies at the district level did not reflect equality and fairness in public school admission. Moreover, the public school admission became more "parentocracy" dependent rather than "meritocracy" dependent, because the processes such as student selection and admission criteria led to the exclusion of vulnerable groups such as migrant families from public junior high school admission to quality junior high schools. More seriously, it intensified the inequality in public school admission in Community A.

References

Brown, P. (1990). The 'Third Wave': Education and the ideology of parentocracy. *British Journal of Sociology of Education, 11*(1), 65–85.

Hu, Y., Lu, K., & Xue, H. (2008). Zhongxiaoxue *Zexiao* wenti de shizheng yanjiu-jiyu beijingshi zhongxiaoxue de diaocha (The empirical study on school choice-based on the survey of elementary and secondary schools in Beijing). *Jiaoyu Xuebao* (Journal of Education Studies), *4*(2), 74–78.

Ministry of Education, National Development and Reform Commission, State Council Office for Rectifying, Ministry of Supervision, Ministry of Finance, National Audit Office. (2003). *Opinions on implementation of rectifying the charge of unauthorized school fees*. Beijing, China.

Chapter 7
Admission to Public Lower Secondary Schools as Social Closures

Abstract Having analyzed *Zexiao* at the policy, school, and family levels, in this chapter the author will interpret admission to public lower secondary education as social closures by elucidating the power relationship behind the interaction among government, schools, families, and other related stakeholders in public school admission to junior high schools in Community A of Beijing as a case study. The author will examine how rent-seeking, privileges, and social disparities formulated stakeholders' participation in public school admission to junior high schools. Moreover, the author will illustrate an interactive social closure constituted by diverse interactions between the advantaged and the disadvantaged to interpret further and discuss the diverse and stratified powers in urban China.

The past three chapters interpreted and visualized the formation of inequality in *Zexiao* for admission to public lower secondary education at the policy level and school and family level. This chapter summarizes the diverse interaction among stakeholders in admission to public junior high schools by applying social closure theory in order to visualize interactive social closures constituted by the advantaged and the disadvantaged at government, school, and family levels. This will allow us to further interpret and discuss the diverse and stratified powers shaping the inequality in admission to public lower secondary education in urban China.

I borrowed the two directions (exclusion and usurpation) of social closure as a conceptual framework to explore and present interaction between the advantages and disadvantages in *Zexiao* at the government, school, and family levels. Meanwhile, the analysis aims at summarizing how rent-seeking, privileges, and social disparities formulated stakeholders' participation in public school admission to junior high schools in urban China.

7.1 *Zexiao* as Social Closures

The concept of social closure that includes both exclusion and usurpation is inequality (Murphy, 1984; Parkin, 1979). The exclusion in downward and upward directions fostered the development of inequality in public school admission to junior high schools. More importantly, the analysis of channels for *Zexiao* indicated that the inequality in public school admission to junior high schools is constructed by exclusion and usurpation at multiple layers among stakeholders. Linking the analysis of case study of school admission to public junior high schools Community A in Beijing, this chapter explains how admission to public lower secondary schools can be designated as social closures.

7.1.1 Policy Level

The analysis indicates an upward social closure of district educational administrations to compete with other districts for well-performing students by strengthening popular schools in the district which have less quality educational resources. The well-performing students became a quality educational resource for public schools to compete for. District educational administrations took action to keep more well-performing students in one district. With the imbalanced development of public education among districts in Beijing, districts with more quality education resources attract more parents and students for quality schooling. The case study of Community A showed how the *Fengtai* District, a district with less quality educational resources, took action to strengthen the popular school in the community to attract more local well-performing students to continue their education in this district. The case study indicated that many parents of the community took part in *Zexiao* to look for schools in other districts with more popular schools. Facing the loss of well-performing students in junior high schools, the *Fengtai* District decided to strengthen and expand the popular school. As a result, School C received a large investment to build a new campus and upgrade school facilities. More importantly, the district educational administration authorized School C to establish a new junior high school department in order to attract well-performing students to stay in the district by utilizing the name of the school.

7.1.2 School Level

The analysis of case study in Community A presents both downward exclusion and upward usurpation at the public school level. In terms of school development, a key school system is considered a downward exclusion in the public school system. Although the key school system has been already abolished in the late 1990s, the case study showed that the district authority was still distinguishing public schools by providing development priority to the traditional demonstration school. School C received more investment for school infrastructure as well as more training opportunities and better welfare for teachers. On the other hand, School A was excluded from these investment opportunities and resources. More importantly, School C, as a key school, was given authority to select well-performing students of the community through school recommendation and special talent approaches. In contrast, School A was only allowed to enroll the remaining local and migrant students after School C's selection. The gap of student quality between these two schools also forced parents to be willing to send their children to School C instead of School A.

The analysis of the case study of School A shows an upward usurpation toward the downward exclusion by the pro-key school policy. The regular public school was forced to select migrant children in order to keep the quality of students to meet their minimum standard. Although School A has no authority to select well-performing students, they held screenings and interviews for the migrant children to select those who could meet their standard. The school principal admitted that they had to conduct quality control of the enrolled students despite it being against the government's basic principle of compulsory education. They even charged additional tuition for the migrant children who could not meet their enrollment standard.

7.1.3 Parent Level

There are diverse downward exclusion and upward usurpation in admission to public junior high schools in Community A at the parent level. Firstly, *hukou*, as special capital in Chinese society, became an approach for institutional exclusion in school admission. It became a ticket for access to public schools in the community which the *hukou* was registered. In contrast to local parents who have *hukou* or have the privilege to change children's *hukou* to good school district, migrant children without local *hukou* were excluded from the access to good public schools, such as School C in Community A. Secondly, parents' practice in *Zexiao* for sending their kids to a better school is considered an upward usurpation toward the current school admission policy. As access to quality public schools was limited to children with good academic achievement, parents whose children did not have good academic achievement started to utilize their diverse resources to compete for the limited access to good schools inside and outside of Community A. The analysis of case study in this community indicated that parents who had enough economic resources took part in the practice of paying additional admission fee to enroll their children in their target schools. More importantly, *guanxi*, as a social network of parents with the society in Chinese culture, was considered another important resource for them to be able to get access to pay the additional admission fee. Parents with money and the strong social network could guarantee access to good public schools for their kids. Moreover, parents without *guanxi* and enough money chose to send their kids to private tutoring classes to study Olympic math or English to join the competition for selecting students with the required capacity in these studies through the collaboration between the key schools and private tutoring institutes.

Although migrant children were excluded from the regular admission to public junior high schools in Community A, analysis of case study in Community A presented that there was upward usurpation by migrant parents to explore the possibility of enrolling their children in public schools in Community A and or in their hometown. Migrant parents who had been working and living in Beijing established their own business and made their own social network. They utilized these resources to send their children to good public schools in Beijing. Furthermore, even though they could not enroll their kids in public schools in Beijing, they could send their children to good schools in their hometown by paying additional admission or buying an apartment located in the community which had good schools.

The analysis above applied social closure theory to interpret interaction among stakeholders at different levels in admission to public junior high schools in Community A. It showed diverse downward exclusion and upward usurpation which presented the interactions between the advantaged and the disadvantaged in admission to public junior high schools in Community A. Meanwhile, it indicated that the district with more quality education resources; key schools or demonstration schools; local parents with economic, institutional, and social resources; and migrant parents with money and *guanxi* could dominate the process of *Zexiao* for admission to public junior high schools in Community A. In short, the diverse downward exclusion and the upward response from the excluded can be categorized into "institutional exclusion," "market exclusion," and "culture exclusion." First, the imbalanced development of public junior high schools between districts and within district, the pro-key school admission policy, and the strict admission requirement for migrant children are considered the "institutional exclusion" in *Zexiao*. *Hukou* as an "institutional exclusion" officially closed the door for migrant children without local *hukou* to take part in admission to public junior high schools. Second, the payment of *Zexiaofei*, the training for competition in school admission provided by private tutoring institutes, can be defined as "market exclusion." It means only those who can afford the cost or who can compete and win the exchange in the educational market can get access to good schools. And last, *guanxi*, as social and culture capital in Chinese society, became "culture exclusion" which kept parents without *guanxi* away from access to quality education.

7.2 *Zexiao*: As Educational Inequality and Social Reproduction

Nevertheless, the diverse approaches for *Zexiao* did not guarantee the success in public school admission to junior high schools. As argued by Wu (2012), parents' participation in public school admission became more dependent on "parentocracy." In other words, parents' socioeconomic status and had an important role in children's school admission. *Zexiao* became a competition among parents for children's positions in public junior high schools. As indicated in school choice cases of the

7.2 *Zexiao*: As Educational Inequality and Social Reproduction

UK and the USA, competition between parents for schools disadvantaged those families who are inclined to enter the competition but who are not well placed to exploit the market to their advantage (Andre-Bechely, 2005; Gewirtz, Ball, & Bowe, 1995). In other words, parents who were willing to compete for school position for their children may not be capable for the competition due to their disadvantages for such competition. Although the case study in Beijing showed parents' inclination to enter the competition for children's school admission, the rules of the competition disadvantaged parents whose capacity didn't meet the needed economic, cultural, and social capitals. Therefore, parents in School A finally failed in *Zexiao* and had to accept the authorized school assignment to enroll their children in regular schools. Consequently, parents without affluent economic, cultural, and social capitals can only enroll their children in the regular school. *Zexiao* became a process of social reproduction in admission to public junior high schools. And this type of social reproduction should be seen in the stratification order of Chinese society.

Next, in Chinese society, which is heavily constituted by *guanxi*, the combination of economic capital and cultural capital may not guarantee success in sending children to popular schools (Wu, 2012). Therefore, *Zexiao* is relatively dependent on how to mobilize social capital by economic capital. Parents' social capital tends to keep consistent with parents' social class (Horvat, Weininger, & Lareau, 2006; Lareau, 1989). Relatively, it would be more difficult for parents in lower social class to find *guanxi* for children's school admission. According to the analysis of the negotiation on *Zexiao* and case study in Community A, without *guanxi*, even for parents who have economic capital and cultural capital, it was still difficult for parents to enroll children in popular schools. However, similar to the conversion of social capital to economic capital demonstrated by Bourdieu (1986), the case study in Community A also indicated that parents mobilized their economic capital into *guanxi* for achieving *Zexiao*. Accordingly, success in *Zexiao* depended on whether parents had enough capacity to mobilize adequate resources to the social network for *Zexiao*.

Then, as introduced in Chaps. 3 and 4, when it comes to talking about *Zexiao* in urban China, it is necessary to pay attention to local social, political, institutional, and economic factors which may influence negotiation on *Zexiao* and the practice in *Zexiao* among stakeholders in urban China. Beijing, as the capital of China, has a responsibility to accommodate needs from central governments, headquarters of the army, other government institutions, and big-scale state-owned enterprises (21st Century Education Research Institute, 2011). These work units have capacities and advantages to cooperate with popular public junior high schools to have the privileges to provide good education environment for children of their employees. Sometimes, the agreement of co-founding relationship between these work units and popular schools or even memos from these work units to local education authority and public schools became the privilege for parents to send children to popular schools. In recent years, such approaches, considered as "legalized privilege in public school admission," were receiving concerns in the public. The privileges of parents' work units were converted to parents to compete for school positions for children. It represents another social reproduction in public school admission in urban China. It absolutely intensified the inequality in compulsory public education in urban China. And it should be abolished without hesitation.

Lastly, although migrant children's participation in *Zexiao* was not widely given concerns by the mainstream public discussion, the case study in Community A in Beijing illuminated the involvement of migrant families in *Zexiao*. Mainly, migrant parents paid *Zexiao* fees or mobilized their *guanxi* in Beijing for sending children to public junior high schools in Beijing. Besides money and *guanxi*, what mostly excluded migrant children from public school admission was *hukou*. Because of *hukou*-based compulsory education, migrant children were "legally" excluded from public school admission to junior high schools by local education authority and public junior high schools. Meanwhile, parents without capacities in enrolling children in public junior high schools in Beijing had to send their children back to hometown for secondary education. However, this is also a concern as their return may stimulate the competition for *Zexiao* in their hometowns where affluent migrant families will use their money and *guanxi* to choose schools for their children. As a result, it may intensify education inequality and social reproduction in these children's hometowns.

This chapter visualized diverse social closures in *Zexiao* for quality education in admission to public junior high schools in urban China. It also interpreted how stakeholders' involvement in admission to public junior high schools were shaped by the diverse and stratified powers in the current Chinese society. In this process, each stakeholder did their best to negotiate and exchange benefits to achieve their goals. Since *Zexiao* has been recognized as inequality in public education in Chinese society, the government has been making various efforts to eliminate educational exclusion and inequality to provide a free and quality for all. The following chapter will introduce and investigate the ongoing practices of Beijing in recent years to establish equitable and quality public lower secondary education for all at the local level.

References

21st Century Education Research Institute. (2011). *Beijingshi "xiaoshengchu" Zexiaore de zhili: luzaihefang?* (Where is the way for alleviation of *Zexiao* fever in transition to junior high schools?). Beijing, China: 21st Century Education Research Institute.

Andre-Bechely, L. (2005). *Could it be otherwise? Parents and the inequities of public school choice*. New York: Routledge.

Bourdieu, P. (1986). The forms of capital. In J. G. Richardson (Ed.), *Handbook of theory and research for the sociology of education* (pp. 241–258). New York: Greenwood Press.

Gewirtz, S., Ball, S. J., & Bowe, R. (1995). *Markets, choice and equity in education*. Buckingham, UK: Open University Press.

Horvat, E. M., Weininger, E. B., & Lareau, A. (2006). From social ties to social capital: Class differences in the relations between schools and parent networks. In H. Lauder, P. Brown, J.-A. Dillabough, & A. H. Halsey (Eds.), *Education, globalization & social change* (pp. 454–467). Oxford, UK: Oxford University Press.

Lareau, A. (1989). *Home advantage: Social class and parental intervention in elementary education*. Philadelphia: Falmer Press.

Murphy, R. (1984). The structure of closure: A critique and development of the theories of Weber, Collins, and Parkin. *The British Journal of Sociology, 35*(4), 547–567.

Parkin, F. (1979). *Marxism and class theory: A bourgeois critique*. London: Tavistock Publications.

Wu, X. (2012). School choice with Chinese characteristics. *Comparative Education, 48*(3), 347–366.

Chapter 8
New Solutions for *Zexiao*

Abstract From 2014, China has been entering into a new stage of economic development with moderate economic growth and progressive social and political reform for establishing a harmonious society. The governments at different levels have already recognized that it is necessary to promote appropriate reforms in social development to match the demands for economic development adjustment. In the public education sector, both the central government and local governments in China have already been taking actions to terminate privileges and balance resource distribution for public secondary education. This chapter will investigate the ongoing practices of Beijing as new solutions in establishing equitable and quality public secondary education at the local level to uncover opportunities and challenges for stakeholders in this process. It will map out a policy framework at the local level for reconstructing an equal and balanced development of public lower secondary education in urban China in order to best meet the needs of Chinese society.

> Equality and justice are the basic features of socialism. Educational equality is the important foundation for social equality. We need to consider more approaches for achieving educational equality, to pay more practical efforts, to review the existing education system from the perspective of educational equality, to re-evaluate the policy implementation, and to continuously improve educational equality through regulation adjustment and system innovation. – By Mr. Guiren Yuan, Minister of Education, in the National Education Conference 2014

In the era of establishing a harmonious society to fulfill the Chinese dream of the great rejuvenation of the Chinese Nation, equality and balance have already been taken as the two major issues in China's educational development by the government. With the economic growth became more moderate, quality, balance, and equity are receiving more focus than the speed of the economic growth. As emphasized by the minister above, by facing the emerging inequality in admission to public primary and lower secondary education in urban China, the government at different levels has already been taking various actions to alleviate the inequality which was caused by imbalanced educational resource distribution, institutionalized, commercialized persistent privileges, and powers. A nation-wide survey on citizens' satisfaction with balanced development of compulsory education in the 19 major cities[1] showed the efforts paid by the government brought a positive change of the imbalanced development of public schools in urban China although the change is limited. The survey presents that 37.26% of respondents in 2015 believe there is a clear gap between public schools and private ones. In comparison to 40.64% in 2010, when there were fewer people who believed there was a clear gap between public schools. Meanwhile, respondents who believe there is no gap between public schools increased from 0.80% in 2010 to 3.38% in 2015 (Zhang, 2016, p. 214). This chapter provides a review of efforts made by Beijing Municipal Government to use alternative approaches to balancing distribution of educational resource in public lower secondary education to best accommodate the needs for quality education from the society. It begins with a brief introduction to a recent policy flow for balancing development of public education at the central government level as background. Additionally, it presents some ongoing practices of Beijing Municipal Government to construct quality public education with balance and equity in recent years. Furthermore, it provides analysis of strengths and challenges of the construction of equal and quality public lower secondary education in Beijing to further discuss the possibilities for next steps of reform.

8.1 Policy Flow for Balancing Development of Public Education

The year 2014 is considered a milestone of the policy change regarding admission to lower secondary education at the central government level. The Ministry of Education released two policies which gave the most detailed regulation regarding the admission to junior high schools. These are considered to be the clearest interpretation of the admission process by the Chinese government. *The Implementation Opinions of Furthering Free and Proximity-Based School Admission at Primary and Junior Secondary Schools* gives details on how to decide the admission area, confirm the admission objects, regulate admission procedure, and keep the transparency along with other explanations regarding admission channels and how to balance educational development (Ministry of Education, 2014a). *The Notification of Furthering Free and Proximity-Based School Admission to Compulsory Education in Major Cities* gives detailed road map and schedule to further improve practices in admission to junior high schools. The ministry required the major municipalities to make plans for implementing admission to schools in compulsory education between 2014 and 2017. Additionally, as Fig. 8.1 illustrates, the central government sets up annual goals and criteria of proximity-based school admission for these

---

[1] Major cities refer to the municipalities, the sub-provincial cities, and the municipalities with independent planning status. The major cities include Beijing, Tianjin, Shanghai, Guangzhou, Chongqing, Harbin, Changchun, Shenyang, Dalian, Jinan, Qingdao, Xian, Nanjing, Ningbo, Hangzhou, Wuhan, Xiamen, Shenzhen, and Chengdu (Ministry of Education, 2014b).

8.1 Policy Flow for Balancing Development of Public Education

2014
To further improve and standardize plan for implementing a free and proximity based compulsorry education

2015
Degisnated area based admisstion to junior high school: 90%
Proximity based admission to junior high school: 90%

2016
Special talent based enrollment: less than 5%

2017
Degisnated area based admisstion to junior high school: 95%
Proximity based admission to junior high school: 95%

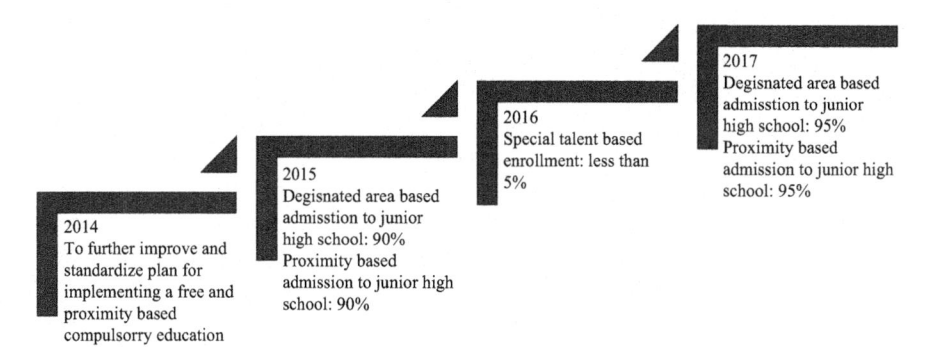

Fig. 8.1 Goals of reform for school admission in compulsory education in major cities (Source: edited by author)

municipalities from 2014 to 2017 (Ministry of Education, 2014b). It likewise shows that the central government planned to gradually expand the scale of proximity-based school admission to junior high schools to 95% in 2017 and limit the ratio of special talent-based school admission to junior high schools to less than 5% in 2016.

Of course, this target cannot be achieved in one day. A review of policies on balancing development of public education at the central government level indicates that the initiatives have been undertaking for more than a decade. In 2005, the government announced a systematic guideline about how to narrow down the gaps of compulsory education development between urban and rural areas, between different regions, and between public schools in the same region (Ministry of Education, 2005). It gives emphasis on further empowering the less developed schools. Moreover, it highlights an educational resource sharing mechanism to improve the quality of education in the less developed schools. The policy also shows the importance of terminating the key school system and the prohibition of conversion of well-performing public schools to *minban* schools.[2] In 2006, the amendment of *Compulsory Education Law* re-declares the abolishment of the key school system in compulsory public education and shows a negative attitude toward competition among public schools for school admission at compulsory education level (National People's Congress, 2006). In 2009, the central government launched *The Outline of National Medium and Long-Term Education Reform and Development Plan (2010–2020)*. In the plan, the government emphasized the importance of the balanced development of compulsory education in national education development and gave more detailed solutions, such as standardization of school construction, a balanced distribution of education resources and human resources among public schools. Furthermore, they also provided solutions for narrowing gaps among public junior high schools in the same area. The solutions include district-based rotation of school leaders, teachers, and assignment of admission slot of quality senior high schools (The State Council of China, 2010). In 2010, the Ministry of Education (2010)

---

[2] *Minban* schools refer to schools run by people but not the government in Chinese context (Liu, 2015b, p. 444).

shared their opinions about eliminating gaps between public schools in compulsory education. They accomplished this through an education resource sharing mechanism and teacher and principal rotation system. In 2012, to further eliminate the imbalance in the development of compulsory education at the regional and school level, the government introduced an assessment standard regarding the development of an equality compulsory education (Ministry of Education, 2012). In 2014, the Ministry of Education actively promoted other initiatives, such as the school district reform, the teacher and principal rotation system, and the school alliance system with the aim of expanding the scale of quality education resources (Ministry of Education, 2014a; National People's Congress, 2015). In 2016 the Chinese government integrated the construction of free, equitable, and quality public education as the first target of SDGs to the action plan for implementation of the 2030 agenda (Ministry of Foreign Affairs, 2016). To strengthen the implementation of the proximity-based school admission to compulsory education, in 2017, the Ministry of Education encouraged local education administrations to apply alternative approaches to school admission in the areas which have not achieved a balanced distribution of public education resources (Ministry of Education, 2017).

8.2 Policy Integration in Beijing Municipal Government

Policy integration in Beijing includes both construction of balanced development of public education and reform in admission to public schools. On the one hand, the municipal government systematically built a platform for balancing development of public education. They established an education resource sharing mechanism to strengthen balance at the school level. On the other hand, the government took action to firmly implement diverse approaches in admission to public junior high schools to further promote proximity-based school admission and eliminate privileges and powers in the admission process.

8.2.1 Construction of Balanced Development of Public Education

There are two stages of constructing a balanced development of public education in Beijing. In the first stage, the government launched a standard of school construction and management. And they built an education resource sharing mechanism among public schools in the second stage (Xi Zhang, Gong, & Zuo, 2012). The former stage aims at establishing a standardized school building, making school district-based management mechanism, and strengthening characteristics of public schools as precondition for a balanced school development. The later stage is to promote education resource sharing among public schools to narrow down the gap between public schools and achieve public education with balance and quality for all.

In the first stage, the government built standards of the school building, assessment of quality education, and content of core competencies of teachers in primary and junior high schools (Beijing Municipal Government, 2007). Moreover, the district governments introduced the school district-based management mechanism to strengthen education resource management, financial management, pedagogy reform and management, and teacher training. They also took the school district as a unit for management in sharing education and human resources (Gu, 2010; Liu, 2016; Xi Zhang et al., 2012). Schools within the same school district can share education resources, host joint teacher training programs, and organize class preparation to achieve mutual support in teaching and school management. Additionally, the municipal government provided an assistant for public schools at the compulsory education level to make school programs with unique characteristics to enrich the educational resources of public schools (Zhang et al., 2012).

The district education administration, in the second stage, established a mechanism to enlarge the education resource service scale and improve the quality of education to strengthen the fulfillment of the first stage. There are diverse approaches for sharing quality education resources among public schools. The major approaches include a school consortium system, school alliance, and nine-year school. The school consortium system is a widely applied approach for promoting devolution of education management and further sharing quality education resources among member schools of the consortium in a designated area. One well-performing school in the appointed area as a core member is assigned to take initiatives to support low-performing schools included in the cooperation group (Zhao & Zhang, 2015; Zhao, 2015, January 15). The school alliance is another popular approach for promoting education resource sharing between two public schools at the same education level and in the same school district. The partnership between two public schools provides a platform for them (including one well-performing school and one low-performing school) within the same school district to share education resources efficiently and promote school cooperation regarding teaching, learning, and school management (Cao & Zhao, 2014, January 8). This approach links different public schools in the same school district and enables them to share education and human resources (including school facilities and teachers) and experiences in teaching, learning, and school management. There are two types of nine-year school, including independent nine-year school and an education partnership with both junior high school and primary school in the same area. This approach aims at promoting school resource sharing and strengthening nearby school admissions (Cao & Zhao, 2014, January 8, p. A4).

8.2.2 Reform in Admission to Public Junior High Schools

In contrast to the policies of past years, the Beijing Municipal Government launched new measures in the policy of admission to junior high schools in 2014 to better implement the proximity-based school admission to junior high schools and improve equality in the admission process. Meanwhile, the government showed firm opposition to abusing of privileges and powers in admission to public junior high schools. The new measures include the following categories.

8.2.2.1 Introduction of Two Electronic Platforms

The Beijing Municipal Government put emphasis on the importance of student management in school admission. They constructed an electronic student management system and a registration system for admission to junior high schools. The former system assigns each G1 student an ID as the only code for proximity-based admission to primary schools. The latter system tracks and records each G6 student's status in the process of admission to junior high schools. It is helpful for local educational administration to handle the number and distribution of G6 to be enrolled in junior high schools. In particular, it provides a means of collecting detailed information of the migrant children in their school age for junior high schools. Also, it can monitor the interdistrict school admission to further guarantee the implementation of the principle of proximity-based school admission.

8.2.2.2 Definition of Proximity-Based School Admission Area

In order to further implement proximity-based school admissions, the municipal government ordered each district to redefine the service area of each school district. This resulted in the implementation of a one-school-to-designated-service-area or plural-schools-to-designated-service-areas, which guarantee the implementation of proximity-based school admissions. The one-school-to-designated-service-area is a direct school admission approach. It means one junior high school is designated to enroll all G6 students in the specific service area. The plural-schools-to-designated-service-areas depend on the application of students. Schools which receive fewer applications than the plan can enroll all students who applied in this school. Enrollment in schools which receive more applications than the plan depends on the result of computer lottery result.

8.2.2.3 Prohibition of Co-founding

The policy of 2014 in Beijing abolished co-founding as a channel for admission to junior high schools. As introduced in Chap. 1, co-founding-based school admission is one of the channels for admission to popular junior high schools in urban China. It is considered a privilege for the limited advantaged groups to get access to the limited quality education resource. The prohibition shows the government's effort to end the privilege and inequality in public school admission in Beijing.

8.2.2.4 Standardization of Enrollment of Special Talent Students

Following the national target to limit ratio of enrollment of special talent students, the Beijing Municipal Government limits the enrollment of special talent-based admission to intradistrict-based practice to cool down the interdistrict admission by special talent channel.

8.2 Policy Integration in Beijing Municipal Government

8.2.2.5 Computer Lottery-Based School Admission

In contrast to regular computer lottery-based school admission, in 2014, the Beijing Municipal Government encouraged district education administration to adjust the distribution of education resource and proximity-based school admission. In general, there were two types of computer lottery-based school admission in each district. The first one is similar to the school recommendation-based school admission. Since it is based on comprehensive evaluation of each student, only the well-performing students can be selected and get the access to the public schools with high-quality education. The second one is the regular computer lottery-based school admission for the rest who cannot get enrolled in the first round.

8.2.2.6 School Admission for Non-Beijing *Hukou* Children

The school admission policy for children without Beijing *hukou* did not change. Moreover, the stratification in school admission for these kids still existed. According to the policy, the kids can be divided into three groups. The first of which includes children with official certificates that prove their parents are Taiwan citizens, post-doctoral scholars from Beijing, army officers, and overseas Chinese. This group can be considered as children with local *hukou* and who take part in school admission as local children. As for the second group, children whose parents are overseas talents invited to work in Beijing or are working for the Beijing railway system can be enrolled in public schools by relevant agreements. In the last category, other children can be arranged to go to public schools even if their parents are working in Beijing and can submit the five certificates. Those of which include receiving a certificate of employment in Beijing, certificate of registered living address in Beijing, household registration account, temporary resident card in Beijing, and letter approving the difficulty in fulfilling guardianship in household registered place.

8.2.2.7 Measures for Preventing Irregularities

In contrast to previous years, in 2014, the Beijing Municipal Government elaborated clear measures for preventing irregular activities in school admission which are against the government's policy. It is considered the strictest school admission policy in Beijing which stated prohibition of *Zexiao* in compulsory education. Under the anti-corruption campaign which started from the 18th National Congress of the Communist Party of China in 2012, the municipal government released *The Certain Regulations on Strictly Following Discipline in Implementation of Admission to Compulsory Education* to prevent from abusing privileges and power in school admission (Li, 2014).

Consequently, with the strict implementation of the policy in 2014, stakeholders, especially the parents, showed a positive attitude toward the changes in admission to junior high schools in Beijing. According to a survey conducted by Beijing Education

Committee in 2014, 76.82% of G6 students were enrolled in junior high schools based on proximity-based school admission. In the urban areas of Beijing, this data was 74.01%. Comparing to 57% in 2011, the proximity-based school admission is becoming the major approach to school admission to public junior high schools. A survey shows that more than 63% of the respondents felt the positive change of admission to junior high schools in Beijing in 2014. More than 43% of the respondents are satisfied with the admission results of their kids as well. Nevertheless, the majority of parents were still not sure about the effect of the implementation of the new policies and the reform for enlarging the service scale of quality education. The survey presents that only 23% of the respondents who accepted the reform brought positive effect on enlarging the service scale of quality education resource and fostering quality schools. 45.1% of the respondents pointed out there still was an exam-based selection for school admission, and about 42% of the respondents showed concern on the right of education for migrant children in Beijing. In addition, about one-third of the respondents worried about the rising price of school district housing (21st Century Education Research Institute, 2014; Liu, 2015a).

8.3 Emerging Challenges

Obviously, the Beijing Municipal Government showed a firm attitude toward a full implementation of proximity-based school admission to junior high schools by applying policies of the central government to the construction of the balanced development of public education and the new measures for school admission to public junior high schools in Beijing. The data above indicates positive effects of these efforts for building a balanced development of public education with quality and equity in urban China. However, the new policies showed some limitation in dealing with the privileges and powers in school admission. Also, stakeholders are facing diverse barriers against the ongoing construction of balanced development public school in urban China.

8.3.1 Influence on the Well-Performing Schools

The full implementation of proximity-based school admission and the education resource sharing mechanism has positive effects on the regular public schools. They could receive more well-performing students than the past. And the change of quality of students motivated teachers and the schools to make further efforts for teaching and learning (Liu, 2015a). In contrast, the new reform brought challenges to the well-performing schools. Without selection, to some extent, the well-performing schools received more diverse students with different levels of achievement. The diversity of students pushed teachers in such schools to reconsider how to take actions to accommodate the change and diverse needs. Teachers who've adjusted to teaching well-performing students may face such challenges in teaching not only well-performing students but also those left behind. Moreover, the reform also gave pressure to well-performing schools to adjust their education focus in daily teaching and learning in order to fully meet the diverse needs from students.

The prohibition of enrolling interdistrict special talent students also caused difficulties for the well-performing schools. This policy may limit the selection of special talent students for the well-performing schools which are authorized to enroll special talent students. Meanwhile, with the start of the abolishment of special talent students in the coming years, these schools will lose another important platform for them to select well-performing students in admission to junior high schools.

8.3.2 Persisting Privileges in School Admission

The most successful change of policy of admission to junior high schools in Beijing in 2014 was the prohibition of co-founding-based school admission. The change received a positive welcome from the society. However, privileges in school admission still existed on the policies. As introduced above, most district education administration still left loopholes for the privileged to enroll their offspring in well-performing schools. Each district established a new category of admission named "Policy adjustment based school admission" for the privileged. It showed that there are still special interest groups in the process of admission to public junior high schools, such as offspring of diplomats, civil servants dispatched to remote areas, and army officers. It seems it still needs more time, wisdom, and courage to end the privilege-based school admission in Beijing as a city full of economic and political interest conflicts.

8.3.3 Education Exclusion in Admission for Migrant Children

Similar to migrant families' experience in Community A, the new policy did not change the situation of admission of migrant children to public junior high schools. On the other hand, the situation may become worse for these kids' education in Beijing. In 2014, the Chinese government abolished the dual *hukou* system which broke China into rural and urban areas. And they launched a new reform of *hukou* system aiming at establishing a unified *hukou* system to gradually accommodate the rise of internal migration with the rapid urbanization. The policy gives loosely controlled *hukou* relocation from migrants' original place of residence to small- and medium-sized cities. It allows these migrants to enjoy the same public services as the local residence. However, the reform clearly states that the *hukou* relocation in megacities as Beijing, Shanghai, and Guangzhou should be strictly controlled (State Council, 2014). With the pressure of the rising population in Beijing, the Beijing Municipal Government has already launched plans for strictly implementing population growth control in this city (Beijing Municipal Commission of Development and Reform, 2014). Under this circumstance, the municipal government started managing education as a measure of population control. Consequently, they released plans for migrant children's post-compulsory education in Beijing (Beijing Municipal Education Committee, Beijing Municipal Public Security Bureau, Beijing Municipal Commission of Development and Reform, & Beijing Municipal Human Resources and Social Security Bureau, 2012). The plan limits access to post-compulsory education for migrant children to vocational training and education with the conditional requirement of their parents' socioeconomic status (Chen, Wang, & Zhou, 2016; Liu, 2015a).

8.3.4 *Barriers for Construction of Balanced Development of Public Education*

Besides reform of admission to public schools, the government at different levels has been taking initiatives to balance the development public education. Most of the initiatives give emphasis on expansion of service scale of quality education resource by establishing school collaboration partnership. The partnership could expand service scale of quality education resource to more students and more teachers. On the other hand, there are existing conflicts among partners within the collaboration which may become barriers for the construction of balanced development of public education. With a long-term imbalanced development between public schools, schools within the same collaboration partnership hold different foci priorities on education. The difference may become barriers once the partner schools start joint teaching. Moreover, the differences in school management and leadership style may also cause misunderstanding and conflicts among schools in the collaboration. In addition, the different incentive environment for teachers and school leaders, such as a gap of income and training opportunities, may discourage teachers and school leaders to be fully involved in the reform. It is necessary to implement a further systematic policy reform to break the barriers of the reform to accommodate the construction of school-to-school collaboration for school improvement and balanced development of public education in urban China.

8.4 Discussion

This chapter introduces some new trends in the policy change of admission to public lower secondary education and the application of the policies to local practices in Beijing. The analysis shows that the new solutions for constructing equitable and quality public lower secondary education include two perspectives. On the one hand, the government at both central and local levels recognized the importance of

8.4 Discussion

balancing development of public schools and expanding the service scale of quality education. The establishment of education resource sharing cooperation has become a well-known model. There are diverse approaches which are formulated by the local context. Collaboration between well-performing schools and regular schools is widely promoted in the reform. The collaboration, to some extent, can accommodate needs for quality education from parents and the society. However, it is necessary to further promote the exchange among the partner schools in terms of teaching, school management, leadership empowerment, teacher training, monitoring, and assessment. Meanwhile, it is important to pay attention to the protection of the school culture in a sustainable way. More importantly, it is necessary for policy makers to consider the reform in a wider policy context which can support the school collaboration. It needs a further systematic policy reform to break the barriers in the reform.

On the other hand, they took initiatives to introduce new measures and approaches to admission to public junior high schools. These new solutions accommodate the current social context of urban China. Meanwhile, it reflects negotiation and compromise among different interest groups in admission to public junior high schools. Under the anti-corruption campaign, the abuse of privileges and power is strictly banned and monitored by the government and the society. It leads to a positive change of the reform of channels of admission to public junior high schools at the local level. The analysis of the reform in Beijing reveals that the co-founding-based school admission has been officially prohibited. It abolished the abuse of privilege and power exchange between the state-owned enterprises and popular public schools. However, the new solution presents a new round of negotiation among stakeholders which left a loophole for the advantaged in school admission. Although the government abolished co-founding-based school admission, there was "Policy adjustment based school admission" for the privileged on the school admission policy of Beijing in 2014. Moreover, the government has been making efforts to improve education for migrant children in urban China in the past decade. However, they will have limited options for the post-compulsory education for migrant children in the major cities as the government is implementing a strict population control to push temporary residents out of the center of these megacities. The policy of school promotion for migrant children has become a tool for population control. Coupled with *hukou* system, population control is becoming a new barrier which excludes migrant children from continuous education in urban China.

It is obvious that the new solutions brought some positive progress in constructing a balanced development of public schools with quality and equity. The efforts paid for expanding the service scale of quality education resources did provide more access for all to experience quality schooling. Moreover, the prohibition of privileges in the admission to public junior high schools shed light on the attitudes of the government toward socially and institutionally stratified public education. Notwithstanding, with the further promotion of the reform, it is necessary for the policy makers to consider a wider policy context which can support the ongoing reform to construct a quality education for all with balance and equity in urban China.

References

21st Century Education Research Institute. (2014). *Beijingshi "Xiaoshengchu" Gaige Pingjia Baogao 2014* (Evaluation report on reform of public school admission to junior high schools in Beijing 2014). Beijing, China: 21st Century Education Research Institute.

Beijing Municipal Commission of Development and Reform. (2014). *Report on the implementation of the 2013 plan for national economic and social development and on the 2014 draft plan for national economic and social development*. Beijing.

Beijing Municipal Education Committee, Beijing Municipal Public Security Bureau, Beijing Municipal Commission of Development and Reform, & Beijing Municipal Human Resources and Social Security Bureau. (2012). *Plan for school promotion in post-compulsory education for children living with rural migrant workers in Beijing*. Beijing.

Beijing Municipal Government. (2007). *The decision on implementation of capital education development strategy to take the lead for education modernization*. Beijing.

Cao, Y., & Zhao, P. (2014, January 8). Docheng Datong Jiaoyu Tongdao Quanmian Pojie *Zexiao* (Dongcheng District: Breaking through education path, fully eliminating school choice). *Xiandai Jiaoyu Bao* (Modern Education), A4–A17.

Chen, J., Wang, D., & Zhou, Y. (2016). Education for population control: Migrant children's education under new policies in Beijing. In Y.-K. Cha, J. Gundara, S.-H. Ham, & M. Lee (Eds.), *Multicultural education in glocal perspectives* (pp. 153–166). Singapore, Singapore: Springer.

Gu, M. (2010). A blueprint for educational development in China: A review of "The National Guidelines for Medium- and Long-Term Educational Reform and Development (2010–2020)". *Frontiers of Education in China, 5*(3), 291–309.

Li, R. (2014, May 21). Beijing "Shishangzuiyan*Zexiao*jinling" fabu (The Strictest Prohibition of Zexiao Prohibition published in Beijing), *Modern Education*, p.A01.

Liu, J. (2015a). Beijingshi "Xiaoshengchu" Ruxue Zhengce de Gaige (Policy reform of admission to lower secondary education in Beijing). In D. Yang (Ed.), *Annual report on China's education (2014)* (pp. 80–90). Beijing, China: Social Sciences Academic Press (China).

Liu, J. (2015b). Understanding inequality in public school admission in urban China: Analysis of public discourses on *Zexiao*. *Asian Education and Development Studies, 4*(4), 434–447.

Liu, J. (2016). School district reform for "Free, equitable and quality" public education in Urban China: Achievements and challenges. *NORRAG NEWS*. Retrieved January 16, 2017, from http://www.norrag.org/fileadmin/Full%20Versions/NN54.pdf

Ministry of Education. (2005). *Opinions on further promoting balanced development of compulsory education*. Beijing.

Ministry of Education. (2010). *Opinions on applying the scientific outlook on development to further promotion of balanced compulsory education development*. Beijing.

Ministry of Education. (2012). *Interim measures of monitoring and evaluation of the balanced development of compulsory education at county level*. Beijing.

Ministry of Education. (2014a). *Implementation opinions of further better doing free and proximity-based school admission at primary and junior secondary schools*. Beijing.

Ministry of Education. (2014b). *Notification of further better doing free and proximity-based school admission to compulsory education in major cities*. Beijing.

Ministry of Education. (2017). *Notification on implementation of school admission to compulsory education*. Beijing.

Ministry of Foreign Affairs. (2016). *China's National plan on implementation of the 2030 agenda for sustainable development*. Beijing.

National People's Congress. (2006). *Compulsory education law of the People's Republic of China*. Beijing.

National People's Congress. (2015). *The 13th five-year plan for economic and social development of the People's Republic of China*. Beijing.

State Council. (2014). *Opinion on further promoting hukou system reform*. Beijing.

The State Council of China. (2010). *The national guidelines for medium- and long-term educational reform and development (2010–2020)*. Beijing.
Zhang, X. (2016). Monitoring results and evaluation of balanced development of compulsory education in 19 major cities. In D. Yang (Ed.), *Annual report on China's a (2016)* (pp. 207–221). Beijing, China: Social Sciences Academic Press (China).
Zhang, X., Gong, X., & Zuo, H. (2012). Yiwujiaoyu Junhenfazhan de Beijing Moshi Yanjiu (Beijing Model of Balanaced Development of Compulsory Education). *Kecheng Jiaoxue Yanjiu (Journal of Curriculum and Instruction), 12*, 11–15.
Zhao, X., & Zhang, Y. (2015). Xuequyitihua Guanli Tezheng Yu Lujing (Features and Pathways of Integration of School District). *Journal of The Chinese Society of Education (Chinese), 6*, 32–37.
Zhao, Y. (2015, January 15). Xi Cheng: Jiaoyu Jituan Jinnian Jiang Zengzhi Qige (*Xi cheng* District: Education Group grew to Seven in 2015). *Xiandai Jiaoyu Bao* (Modern Education), p. A5.

Chapter 9
Conclusion

Abstract This final chapter summarizes the research findings based on the analysis of discourses and practices in the development of competition for a school position in public lower secondary education in urban China. Discussion on how to further understand the phenomenon of *Zexiao* was provided, as well as implications for the theoretical debate, the new solutions, and future research.

This book offered a comprehensive construction of an understanding of *Zexiao* in public school admission to junior high schools as social reproduction in urban China by investigating what people said about *Zexiao* and how *Zexiao* is understood and practiced in the context of urban China. It gave a critical definition of *Zexiao* by contrasting a global discussion on school choice. It uncovered continuities and changes in discourses on *Zexiao* shaped by diverse forces in public lower secondary school admission within the social transformation from a profit-driven society to a more inclusive and equitable society in China. It visualized power relationships among stakeholders in public school admission by analyzing their interplay in the process. More importantly, it exposed how current socioeconomic, institutional, and educational systems and culture are shaping the stratified engagement of stakeholders in the public school admission process to lower secondary education in urban China. It also presented some ongoing new solutions and challenges to constructing a more balanced development of public secondary education with quality and equity in urban China.

9.1 Summary of the Findings

In this section, I report the findings, including meanings of *Zexiao*, a trajectory of public discussion on *Zexiao* from the 1980s to the 2000s, interactions among stakeholders in admission to public junior high schools at policy, school and family levels stratified by socially and institutionally structured power relationships, and the new solutions and challenges for constructing a balanced development of public lower secondary education with quality and equity in urban China.

9.1.1 Zexiao ≠ *School Choice*

This book gave a systematic interpretation of choosing school practices in the context of urban China. It expanded the understanding of school choice and diversified general meaning of school choice in a global context. As discussed in Chap. 2, *Zexiao* does not 100% present the meaning of school choice discussed in a Western and neoliberal context despite its literal meaning is choosing schools. Firstly, in contrast to a top-down policy of school choice in the Western context, *Zexiao*, as a bottom-up phenomenon, is against the government's stance demonstrating a free, no selection, and proximity-based admission to public primary and junior high schools. On the other hand, as *Zexiao* could generate additional financial resources to supplement the limited educational investment by the government, the local government in urban China left loopholes and distributes privileges to key schools to allow mutual selection between key schools and individual families. Secondly, there is a big difference regarding basic concept between school choice in general and *Zexiao*. School choice in the Western context is based on an emphasis on efficiency of public education, freedom of consumers in the education market, and right for quality education. In contrast, *Zexiao* in the context of urban China is conditioned by elitism and rent-seeking to foster the most necessary human resources for the country's development and to generate fund for a supplement of limited public education investment. Thirdly, in contrast to subsidy-based school choice in general, *Zexiao* in China's context depends more on the socioeconomic status of parents and learning capacity of children. Finally, although both school choice and *Zexiao* caused educational inequality, school choice promoted diverse education for all in the Western context, while *Zexiao* compounded exam-driven education and competition in the education sector.

9.1.2 *Trajectory of Public Discourses on* Zexiao

The findings of this study indicated that stakeholders' negotiation on *Zexiao* in the context of public school admission to junior high schools was driven by multidimensional forces, for example, the paradoxical attitudes of the government toward *Zexiao*, the imbalanced distribution of resources for public education, parents' aspiration, diverse public school admission policies, and systematic issues in social and educational system. Moreover, the discursive development of negotiation on *Zexiao* in urban China took place in two stages: "the 1990s" and "after 2000." The public discussion in the first stage has the theme of the unauthorized collection of school fees. In this stage, firstly, *Zexiao* was mainly discussed as the result of the lack of government investment in education. It was taken as a tool for public schools to generate education fund from parents for school admission to popular schools. Secondly, the gap between public schools intensified *Zexiao*. With the emergence of elite education from the 1980s, the government's pro-key school education policy

9.1 Summary of the Findings

reinforced the advantages of key schools in public school admission. It intensified the gap between public schools and stimulated the competition for limited access to the key schools. Thirdly, with the abolishment of the entrance exams to junior high schools, there was no reliable approach to guarantee access to popular schools in secondary education. Therefore, paying an additional fee to buy access to popular schools became widely accepted approach, and it intensified *Zexiao*. Fourthly, parents' aspiration is stimulated by the traditional understanding of education and pressures from competitions in school admission. And the One Child Policy also played an important role in forcing parents to invest their kids' education by *Zexiao*. Moreover, in contrast to the government-dominated negotiation and discussion on *Zexiao*, little was heard from parents and schools.

In the second stage "after 2000," with the emphasis on the construction of harmonious society and the focus on alleviation of social inequality by the leadership shift to Hu Jintao, *Zexiao* was, mainly, negotiated in the theme of imbalanced education development. As a continuity of the understanding of negotiation on *Zexiao* in the first stage, public discussions that took place in this stage highlighted that the negotiation on *Zexiao* developed due to the government's limited investment in education, the gap between schools, parents' aspiration, and the diversification of inconsistent policies on school admissions. On the other hand, there were newly emerged focuses on each dimension compared to public discussion in the 1990s. For example, the focus of the discussion shifted to the imbalance in distributions of the limited government investment in education instead of criticizing it in the 1990s. Also, the diversification of public school admission approaches at the local level after 2000 was considered an emerging force that intensified *Zexiao*. Besides by admission to children's academic performance at schools and by paying unauthorized school fees, admission processes became more dependent on children's participations and achievement in after-school curriculum, private tutoring, and special talent contests. In addition to the forces mentioned above, the public discussion on *Zexiao* after 2000 gave more attention to the influence of the issues related to the educational and social systems in urban China on school admission to secondary education. To be more specific, those issues included the mismatch between the economic development and the education development (for instance, how to accommodate diverse demands for education with the rapid social change?); the exchange between privileges, power, and education resources (memo students and co-founding students); and the limited government's capacity (lack of monitoring system for alleviation of *Zexiao*). In contrast to the government-dominated public discussions on *Zexiao* in the 1990s, there were diverse voices about *Zexiao* from both the central and local perspectives. More importantly, the negotiation on *Zexiao* after 2000 was influenced by increasing arguments regarding the role of the central and local governments and their attitudes toward the alleviation of *Zexiao*. The study also found that the negotiation on *Zexiao* was significantly influenced and shaped by the following factors: (1) some social, political, economic, and institutional factors at the local level, (2) the political position of Beijing and the rapid urbanization, and (3) the privileges of parents as employees of the central and municipal governments, PLA, state-owned enterprises, and other prestige organizations in Beijing. Moreover, the increasing demands for quality education from families of permanent residents and migrant families outpaced the government's capacity to accommodate those demands that influenced the negotiation on *Zexiao* in Beijing. Moreover, the analysis of the public discourses on *Zexiao* presented a framework of multilayered inequality and stratification of stakeholders' participation in *Zexiao*. I used the framework to show how policies, school system, and family socioeconomic status shaped stakeholders' participation in *Zexiao* in the 1990s and after 2000 in Chaps. 4, 5, and 6.

9.1.3 Multilayered Inequalities in Zexiao

This book, in Chaps. 4, 5, and 6, interpreted how inequality in admission to junior high schools was shaped by stakeholders at policy, school, and family levels. These unveiled multilayered inequalities in *Zexiao*.

9.1.3.1 Policies Matter

The loopholes of policies left in the policy making and implementation in the process of admission to public junior high schools between the central and local governments affected provided a policy space for local educational administration and public schools to innovate different channels for accommodating diverse needs for admission to public junior high schools in urban China. Both the central government and local governments kept the same tone regarding a full implementation of proximity-based admission to public junior high schools between the 1990s and the 2000s. Nevertheless, the local education authorities and public schools could give relevant stakeholders diverse advantages through the delegation of educational administration to the district level. With the concept of elitism, key schools were authorized to select students they preferred. With the process of commercialization of public education, these schools were allowed to charge *Zexiaofei* to enroll students to the schools. Moreover, the rising education market made a collaboration between key schools and private tutoring institutes for school admission possible to satisfy mutual selection between key schools and parents. As a result, the loopholes did provide convenience for the district educational authority, public schools, parents, and private tutoring institutes. On the other hand, the policy spaces encouraged stakeholders to abuse their privileges and advantages to break the equality in admission to public junior high schools.

9.1.3.2 Imbalance Between Public Schools

The key school system stratified public schools into "good schools" and "bad schools." It was established by the elite-oriented concept and the pursuit of economic efficiency. Because of this system, "good schools" received more educational investment, development priority, and human resources with higher qualification. In an efficiency-oriented Chinese society in the 1980s and 1990s, this system was considered a cradle for fostering the most needed human resource for the economic development of China. However, the system caused the imbalanced development of public schools and forced parents to compete for enrolling their kids in the "good schools." Although the system has been abolished in the late 1990s, its conversions kept or even enlarged the gap between public schools. These schools, as pushing factors, are still driving parents to be involved in the competition for their kid's quality education. Moreover, with the commercialization of public education, the key schools were utilized as a fund generator for the poor public education through charging additional tuition fees from parents who are eager to enroll their kids in "good schools." In recent years, to keep the equality in admission to public schools, the government prohibited student selection by the key schools through exams and charging additional fees. Nevertheless, some of them established a close collaboration with private tutoring institutes to consign these institutes to host exams or training organized for their student selection. The practices pushed the rich families to compete for sending their kids to after-school training, while it excluded the poor families and their kids from the competition for quality education. Also, the collaboration stratified students with different achievements to "good schools" and "bad schools." It further deteriorated gap between public schools.

9.1.3.3 Competition of Family Background

The case study on parents' engagement in admission to public junior high schools in Community A indicated that a "parentocracy"-based admission to junior high schools presented a reproduction of social inequality in public school admission to junior high schools. Besides students' academic achievement, the admission channels to public junior high schools in Community A are significantly dependent on parents' socioeconomic status and some legalized social and institutional exclusion of the disadvantaged, such as *hukou* system. My interviews with parents in Community A showed that, in conjunction with *Zexiaofei*, *guanxi* was an extremely important precondition for parents to successfully have their children accepted by popular schools. The study also found that parents' practice in *Zexiao* heavily relied on both social capital and economic capital of parents. That is, children from the families who had money, power, and social network (*guanxi*) were more likely to be enrolled in key schools than others. Moreover, the institutional barriers, such as key school system and *hukou*, forced the disadvantaged groups, such as the lower-income urban families and migrant families, to give up the positional competition for public schooling in urban China.

More interestingly, the analysis of parents' participation in competition for admission to public junior high schools in Community A unveiled interaction among the advantaged and the disadvantaged in school admission. Although this process has been stratified socially, economically, and institutionally, the case study of school admission in Community A showed a clear upward response from the disadvantaged to utilize their parentocracy (their available power and resource) to compete with the advantaged for the limited position of quality education for their kids. It provides us a new understanding of the complicated interplay of the social exclusion in urban China.

Moreover, the case study of practices in admission to public junior high schools of Community A in Chap. 7 indicated that "parentocracy," such as money and social network of parents, is interdependent in *Zexiao*. Chapter 2 introduced that there are three types of *Zexiao* in admission to public junior high schools in urban China, including money based, power (*guanxi*) based and achievement based. Nevertheless, the case study of Community A reveals that it is necessary for parents to have both financial capacity and social network for a successful *Zexiao*. Without access to the key person who decided student selection in the admission process, it is still difficult for parents to enroll their kids in the good schools. Also, without financial power, it is difficult for parents to send their kids to the after-school education programs to equip their children the necessary knowledge to win the selection for *Zexiao*. Therefore, achievement-based *Zexiao* also depends on parents' financial capacity. It is necessary for parents to comprehensively utilize their financial capacity and social networks for a successful *Zexiao* in admission to public junior high schools.

9.1.4 New Solutions and Challenges

Entering into the twenty-first century, with the rapid economic growth and the rise of social inequality, the Chinese government has been forced to give continuous attention to alleviate the various inequalities in Chinese society. Construction of an equal and quality public education with balance became a means for establishing a harmonious society and fulfilling the Chinese dream of a great rejuvenation of the nation by the government. The newly launched sustainable development goals by the global community are providing China a new platform to explore alternative approaches to balance development of public education and construct an equitable and quality public education for all in China. The analysis of the new solutions indicates that there are two major reforms for achieving these goals. On the one hand, the governments at different levels are taking initiatives to balancing the distribution of educational resources to fill up the gap among public schools in urban China. The establishment of educational resource sharing collaboration in different shapes has become a widely recognized approach. It could enlarge the scale of service of quality education to more people in urban China. Nevertheless, it is still necessary for all stakeholders to consider the reform in a wider policy context which can break any barriers and further strengthen the school collaboration. On the other hand, the governments are making efforts to provide fair measures and approaches for admission to public junior high schools to terminate the abuse of privileges and powers. However, it seems that it will take more time for the stakeholders to adjust the interest conflicts in order to build a quality education for all with balance and equity in urban China (Liu, 2018).

9.2 Reconsidering *Zexiao*

The deconstruction of the formation of people's negotiation on *Zexiao* in this study elucidated that *Zexiao* no longer merely meant that parents enrolled their children in schools of their choices. Rather, the meanings behind the stakeholders' negotiation on *Zexiao* and the practice in *Zexiao* were institutionally, socially, and economically shaped by multidimensional forces. An emerging discussion illuminated that *Zexiao* was caused by series of systematic problems and mismatches between the social and educational developments in urban China. The findings of this study provided us a couple of new perspectives to understand *Zexiao* in China's context and to enrich the general international knowledge of school practice.

9.2.1 Zexiao: *As a Result of the Imbalanced Distribution of Education Resources*

The lack of governmental investment in education was considered as one of the main reasons for *Zexiao*. Due to limited education investment, public schools had no choice but charge additional fees. However, as Yang (2005, December 1) argued, the reason that school charge *Zexiaofei* was due to the imbalanced distributions of governmental investment in public education. Although the key school system was abolished in the late 1990s, the demonstration school system continued to exist, which affects the distribution of government investment in public education. The case study in Community A showed the imbalanced distribution of education resources between public schools within the same community. Both the gaps of infrastructure and human resources between schools gave parents no choice but to participate in *Zexiao*. Moreover, selection of well-performing students authorized to the key schools became a privilege for such schools to abuse to force additional *Zexiaofei* from parents. These schools took their advantage as education resources for renting.

9.2.2 Zexiao: As a Loophole Left by the Policy Gap Between Central and Local Levels

As noted in Chap. 3, besides the imbalanced development of public schools, the policy gap between the national, municipal, and district levels in public school admission intensified *Zexiao*. With the delegation of authority in administration at the compulsory education level to the education authority at the district (county) level, public school admission policy became more dependent on local education authority (National People's Congress, 2006; Wang, 2009). The governments at any level showed a clear stance in alleviating inequality in admission to public schools. Nevertheless, the delegation left a loophole for local education authorities to accommodate the local needs for more diverse options in public school admission compared with the residence-based public school admission. Despite the Beijing Municipal Education Committee continuously urging the public to follow the proximity-based school admission policy in admission to junior high schools, education authorities at the district level in Beijing insisted on offering diverse admission approaches for public schools and parents. The diverse approaches pushed parents, schools, and private tutoring institutes to compete and collaborate for mutual benefits in admission to public junior high schools.

On the other hand, the diversification of school admission policy at local level presented a compromise of local education authority for diverse demands in public school admission. Firstly, diverse channels were innovated for responding to increasing demand for children's good education from parents. The various approaches provided parents more choices and possibilities to send children to popular schools they preferred. Secondly, competition among public schools, particularly among popular schools, intensified the demand from public schools to select students. In order to accommodate the demand for keeping advantages in competition among public schools, popular schools were officially or unofficially authorized to select students (through school recommendation) they prefer before the school assignment. Thirdly, besides school recommendation-based student selection, to further satisfy the appetite of popular public schools to select students, pre-admission training class, as collaboration among popular public schools and private tutoring institutes, was promoted and became popular in recent years. Since exam-based selection is not allowed in public school admission at compulsory education level, popular public schools selected students they preferred through selection exams held in pre-admission training classes. The selection intensified Olympic math fever and English certificates fever for primary school students in urban China. Meanwhile, it made public school admission more complicated and utilitarian.

9.2.3 Zexiao: *As Educational Inequality and Social Reproduction*

Nevertheless, the diverse approaches for *Zexiao* did not guarantee the success in public school admission to junior high schools. As argued by Wu (2012), parents' participation in public school admission became more dependent on "parentocracy." In other words, parents' socioeconomic status and wishes of parents had important role in children's school admission. *Zexiao* became a competition among parents for children's positions in public junior high schools. As indicated in school choice cases of the UK and the USA, competition between parents for schools disadvantaged those families who are inclined to enter the competition but who are not well placed to exploit the market to their advantage (Andre-Bechely, 2005; Gewirtz, Ball, & Bowe, 1995). In other words, parents who were willing to compete for school position for their children may not be capable for the competition due to their disadvantages for such competition. Although case study in Beijing showed parents' inclination to enter the competition for children's school admission, the rules of the competition disadvantaged parents whose capacity mismatched the needed economic, cultural, and social capitals. Therefore, parents in School A finally failed in *Zexiao* and had to accept the authorized school assignment to enroll their children in regular schools. Consequently, parents without affluent economic, cultural, and social capitals can only enroll their children in the regular school. *Zexiao* became a process of social reproduction in admission to public junior high schools. And this type of social reproduction should be seen in the stratification order of Chinese society.

Next, in Chinese society, which is heavily constituted by *guanxi*, the combination of economic capital and cultural capital may not guarantee the success in sending children to popular schools (Wu, 2012). Therefore, *Zexiao* is relatively dependent on how to mobilize social capital by economic capital. Parents' social capital tends to keep consistent with parents' social class (Horvat, Weininger, & Lareau, 2006; Lareau, 1989). Relatively, it would be more difficult for parents in lower social class to find *guanxi* for children's school admission. According to the analysis of the negotiation on *Zexiao* and case study in Community A, without *guanxi*, even for parents having economic capital and cultural capital, it was still difficult for parents to enroll children in popular schools. However, similar to the conversion of social capital to economic capital demonstrated by Bourdieu (1986), the case study in Community A also indicated that parents mobilized their economic capital into *guanxi* for achieving *Zexiao*. Accordingly, success in *Zexiao* depended on whether parents had the enough capacity or not to mobilize enough resources to the social network for *Zexiao*.

Then, when it comes to talking about *Zexiao* in urban China, it is necessary to pay attention to local, social, political, institutional, and economic factors which may influence negotiation on *Zexiao* and the practice in *Zexiao* among stakeholders in urban China. Beijing, as the capital of China, has a responsibility to accommodate needs from central governments, headquarters of the army, other government institutions, and big-scale state-owned enterprises (21st Century Education Research Institute, 2011). These work units have capacities and advantages to cooperate with popular public junior high schools to have the privileges to provide good education environment for children of their employees. Sometimes, the agreement of co-founding relationship between these work units and popular schools or even memos from these work units to local education authority and public schools became the privilege for parents to send children to popular schools. In recent years, such approaches, considered as "legalized privilege in public school admission," were receiving concerns in the public. The privileges of parents' work units were converted to parents to compete for school positions for children. It represents another social reproduction in public school admission in urban China. It absolutely intensified the inequality in public compulsory education in urban China. And it should be abolished without hesitation.

Lastly, although migrant children's participation in *Zexiao* was not widely given concerns by the mainstream public discussion, the case study in Community A in Beijing illuminated the involvement of migrant families in *Zexiao*. Mainly, migrant parents paid *Zexiao* fee or mobilized their *guanxi* in Beijing for sending children to public junior high schools in Beijing. Besides money and *guanxi*, what mostly excluded migrant children from public school admission was *hukou*. Because of *hukou*-based compulsory education, migrant children were "legally" excluded from public school admission to junior high schools by local education authority and public junior high schools. Meanwhile, parents without capacities in enrolling children in public junior high schools in Beijing had to send their children back to hometown for secondary education. However, I show my concern on *Zexiao* in migrant children's hometowns which is caused by their return from urban areas. Affluent migrant families will use their money and *guanxi* to choose schools for their children in hometowns. As a result, it may intensify education inequality and social reproduction in these children's hometowns.

Besides these, when it comes to considering *Zexiao* in urban China, it is necessary to take culture and history of education in Chinese society into account. Traditionally, there is a consensus of *He who excels in the study can follow an official career (xueeryouzeshi)* in China. Education is considered one of the most important tools for climbing up the social ladder and achieving social mobility in Chinese society. Hundreds of years ago, individuals spent years to become government official through government's civil examination. Even until now, entrance exams to college in China is still considered, comparatively speaking, the fairest way for people to access to higher education for an upward social mobility in Chinese society. Therefore, to change children's lives and fortune of the family, parents were willing to sacrifice everything they had to create any opportunity for children's education. A well-known story of *Mencius' mother, three moves (mengmusanqian)* tells parent's aspiration for children's education by selecting good education environment in ancient China. Similarly, the competition among parents for buying apartments within areas having good quality public schools indicates the same wishes and motivation of parents in contemporary society of urban China. In other words, it is essential and necessary for the

9.3 Implication for Theoretical Discussion

This book applied theory of social closure to frame the analysis of interaction among stakeholders in admission to public junior high schools in urban China. The analysis of two directions of social closure in *Zexiao* has the potential to enrich the discussion about social closure and provide a detailed analysis of multilayered and dynamic interactions among stakeholders involved in social exclusion and usurpation. It not only revealed the rounds of social exclusion and usurpation in admission to public junior high schools but also presented rounds of interactive social exclusion and usurpation at multilayered levels shaping inequality in public education of urban China. On the one hand, it visualized a top-down social exclusion of the disadvantaged in the admission to the good public education resources by the advantaged. On the other hand, it presented the disadvantaged did not accept the exclusion only until they admitted their limitation. As a bottom-up usurpation, they tried to fully utilize their limited power and resources to compete with the advantaged for their interests in admission to public junior high schools rather than silently accepting the exclusion in the beginning. Moreover, the findings of the book presented that such interactive exclusion and usurpation among stakeholders happened at multilevels, including policy, school, and family levels in admission to public junior high schools. Besides parents with different socioeconomic statuses, public schools and local education authorities with different resources also experienced interactive exclusion and usurpation at their levels in admission to public junior high schools. The analysis of case study in Chaps. 6 and 7 provided a new perspective to understand dynamics of social exclusion and usurpation from both the disadvantaged and the advantaged.

Moreover, the phenomenon of *Zexiao* in the context of urban China gives a new interpretation of parental choices in the context of the public education sector. As introduced in Chap. 2, parental choice has been understood from the perspective of choice for basic human needs and the perspective of choice for educational consumers. As basic needs of the citizens, the government should provide public education with equal access and quality to fully accommodate the basic educational needs for all. The service should be in the same (or similar) standard as it is in public goods. In other words, the government has the responsibility to provide a public education service with the same access and in the same quality to best meet the basic needs for education from both the advantaged and the disadvantaged. In China's case, the basic needs have not been met as there is an exclusion regarding equal access to educational services. And there are gaps regarding the quality of educational services for all. On the other hand, the promotion of competition between public schools and private sector is seen as a force to push public schools to improve quality and efficiency of their educational service in the global debate on parental choices. In contrast to the parental choice-based competition between public schools and private schools in the Western context, as shown in Chap. 5, there was a collusion between public schools and private tutoring institutes which intensified the competition for student selection for the popular key schools and caused inequality in admission to public junior high schools. It showed few effect of the collusion on the improvement of quality or efficiency in public education. Rather, it caused stratification of public schools and educational exclusion in the public education sector. Besides the basic public education service, it is necessary to construct more alternative options for accommodating diverse needs for education. Such alternative educational service can be provided as educational products for exchanging in the educational market between parents and service providers. However, with a public school-dominated education sector in China, parental choices have the potential to boost collaboration between public schools and private sector to best accommodate the needs for public education in the context of urban China. The government even can purchase the market-based educational service to best meet the needs for basic educational service.

9.4 Implication for Practice

Despite consistent government opposition to *Zexiao*, it has never been alleviated so far. In contrast, with the rapid economic and social change in China, the demand for *Zexiao* will definitely intensify. As Tsang (2003) addressed, it is not a matter of whether or not to allow *Zexiao*. What really matters is how to manage *Zexiao*. In other words, *Zexiao* itself has nothing wrong; the problem is the rules that governed it. Based on the analysis of negotiation on *Zexiao* and the practice in *Zexiao*, I made the following policy recommendations for the policy makers and practitioners.

9.4.1 Balanced Education Development

As government recognized, the imbalanced educational development in China is one of the most important reasons for *Zexiao*. On the one hand, there is still ample room for raising "public finance rate"[1] to strengthen government investment in compulsory education. On the other hand, since the gap between regions, districts, or schools still exists, it is necessary for governments at a different level to take action to make the government investment in compulsory education more reliable and sustainable. Furthermore, considering the differences across the country, the state policy should keep the basic principle and allow the local adaptation.

---

[1] According to Tsang (2003, p. 189), the "public finance rate" refers to total government revenue from tax and nontax sources as a percentage of gross domestic product.

Secondly, it is necessary to further enhance the educational resource sharing collaboration in diverse shapes to expand service scale of quality education for all in urban China. On the one hand, the local education administration should continuously balance distribution of quality education resource in urban China to best meet the needs for demographic change and the rise of needs for quality education. On the other hand, to further enhance the collaboration, it is necessary for policy makers to reconsider how to make relevant reform in a wider policy context to redress the mismatch between this policy reform, the current education system, and social and cultural norms. For example, in order to adjust the imbalance in human resource distribution to public schools, standardization of teacher welfare system, such as a recently implemented performance-based pay system for teachers in public schools at city level, should be fully promoted and implemented. The gap of income between public schools in the same city should be reduced gradually. Meanwhile, in order to further balance the teaching team in public education system, a reliable and fair teacher-principal relocation system at city level should be established.

Thirdly, it is necessary to give concern on the balanced development of both public and private education. It would be impossible to alleviate *Zexiao* in public education system without the development of private education. Since most private schools just re-emerged from the late 1990s, it is still difficult for them to compete with popular public schools (key schools or demonstration schools) in terms of financial capacity, human resources, reputation, and education quality (Lin, 2006). Therefore, it is difficult to follow the principle which addressed "Public schools do not enroll *Zexiao* student. Go to minban schools for *Zexiao*" by the Ministry of Education. Apparently, policies which assist the development of private education should be discussed, released, and implemented. The renationalization of converted schools, in fact, should be given reconsideration. The development of the converted schools in the past decade showed the possibility to make good schools in private sectors. And I support the idea which suggested keeping the converted schools independent and staying in private education sector. With the gradual empowerment of private schools at compulsory education level, affluent families could be attracted to choose schools for children from public sector to private sector. Then, *Zexiao* in public schools could be solved.

9.4.2 Does Balanced Education Development Work?

As analyzed in this book, the central government took the strategy of balanced education development as the major solution for alleviating *Zexiao* in urban China. In contrast, there were increasing concerns which doubted whether this solution could really cool down the positional competition in admission to junior high schools for children. I argue that it would be difficult to deal with *Zexiao* without solving the systematic problems in social and educational system in urban China.

Firstly, it is necessary for Chinese society to reconsider the question: Compulsory education for what? As discussed in this book, if compulsory education is still linked with the preparation for entrance exam to popular junior high school, popular senior high school, and the key universities, then *Zexiao* at compulsory education level, which represents one of the steps in the preparation for the entrance into the key universities, is almost impossible to be alleviated. Compulsory education has been taking too many social responsibilities. It has been closely linked with the post-compulsory education and children's future career. The pressure for children to climb up their social ladders has been shifted down to compulsory education or even earlier. In order to deal with *Zexiao*, it is necessary to simplify function of compulsory education and to unlink it with post-compulsory education by establishing "independent exam system" for children's school promotion to post-compulsory education. In my opinion, compulsory education should not be responsible for children's school promotion to senior high schools. If the exam result for the upper secondary education of children has nothing to do with the evaluation of junior high schools and teachers, then it may be possible to solve the positional competition at compulsory education level. For parents as the major participants in *Zexiao*, it would be better if public schools and public media could provide parents additional instruction to lead them to calm down to reconsider what kind of education is more appropriate for their children instead of considering what is the best education their children should have.

Secondly, abolishment of privileges in public education can be considered as the key to solving *Zexiao* in urban China. Apparently, the analysis in previous chapters showed there were diverse privileges for *Zexiao* in urban China. At public school level, privileges were authorized to the key schools, demonstration schools, and the converted schools in terms of distribution of government investment, distribution of human resources, and the priority in student selection. Without abolishing these privileges, it is almost impossible to reduce the gap between public schools and to solve *Zexiao*. At family level, the privileges parents received were socially constructed. Parents' personal socioeconomic status and the strength of their work units deeply influenced the options they chose for *Zexiao* and the result of *Zexiao*. Moreover, *hukou* as another important factor which "legally" excluded migrant children from public school admission in urban China intensified the inequality in public education of urban China. Accordingly, on the one hand, with the improvement of the balanced development in public education system, proximity-based school assignment should be followed without hesitation. And the collaboration between powerful work units and popular schools should be completely abolished. Meanwhile, a third-party-based monitoring system for public school admission to junior high schools should be established. Although it is still difficult to change the *hukou*-based school admission, it is possible to establish a more flexible school admission system at compulsory education level for migrant children. If the government could establish a system to open an account for every school-aged child in China, then the cost of migrant children's compulsory education in urban China could be transferred through this system from their hometown to the receiving areas. And the uncovered part could be paid by the central government.

9.5 Implication for Future Research

Although I did my best to involve diverse participants in this study, what I could not analyze in detail was the experiences of parents from popular schools in *Zexiao*. The discourse on their experiences in *Zexiao* will illuminate more details in terms of the "parentocracy"-based public school admission and the formation of *Zexiao* in urban China. Meanwhile, although I argue the conflict of public school admission policy at city and local level intensified *Zexiao* in Beijing, I could not provide in-depth analysis of discourse on *Zexiao* from government officials. The analysis of this perspective may strengthen the interaction on the alleviation of *Zexiao* between the government and the public. Moreover, this study has already identified the important role of social, economic, political, and institutional factors at the local level in shaping the development of *Zexiao* in Beijing. Therefore, it would be necessary to include areas with more popular schools in order to explore additional forces which shape the development of *Zexiao* in urban China. Meanwhile, this point also raised the question as to how the case of *Zexiao* in Beijing is applicable to other parts of urban China. Analysis of discourse on *Zexiao* shows *Zexiao* became a nationwide phenomenon in public school admission. It also briefly introduces the commonalities and differences in terms of channels in *Zexiao* in different cities of urban China. Obviously, the case in Beijing cannot fully represent the whole situation of *Zexiao* in urban China. However, the analysis of *Zexiao* in Beijing elaborated the necessity of taking local characteristics into consideration. Therefore, considering the diverse characteristics of cities in China, a comparative study on the development of *Zexiao* between cities would be useful for further comprehensively interpreting the dynamics of the phenomenon in urban China. Moreover, a comparative study between China's case and cases in Asian and other parts of the world may further diversify the mainstream discussion on school choice at the global level. In addition, to further clarify the deeper structure and order of educational stratification in current Chinese society in rapid market transition, it would be worthy to conduct district-based or city-based surveys to further testify the relationship between inequality in public schools and institutional change of urban China.

Through the deconstruction of knowledge on *Zexiao*, I reconstructed the ongoing phenomenon of competition in the admission process to junior high schools in urban China. The interpretation of *Zexiao* can be considered as a puzzle-solving and puzzle-making process. As long as *Zexiao* continues in urban China, further interpretation of this phenomenon is expected to identify more forces which shaped *Zexiao* as a phenomenon of educational inequality in urban China as a socialist state in market transition. Moreover, it will be more interesting if the future study can give special focus on interaction among stakeholders in the emerging new solutions for constructing a balanced development of public education with quality and equity in urban China (Liu, 2016, 2018). Stakeholders who have already taken *Zexiao* for granted in the past decades may have difficulties in the reforms of balancing education development in urban China. The analysis of these new practices can provide not only the updated understanding of social power relationship in current Chinese education reform and social change but also new references for the global community to construct quality education for all as a part of the Sustainable Development Goals of 2030. Moreover, as a limitation of the book, the future study can be conducted from a comparative perspective between China and other Asian countries which have similar school choice phenomenon through juxtaposing school choice policies and practice. Such effort has potential to construct a new understanding of school choice in the Asian context and allows us to contrast to the ones in the Western context which have been already widely discussed.

References

21st Century Education Research Institute. (2011). *Beijingshi "xiaoshengchu" Zexiaore de zhili: luzaihefang?* (Where is the way for alleviation of *Zexiao* fever in transition to junior high schools?). Beijing, China: 21st Century Education Research Institute.
Andre-Bechely, L. (2005). *Could it be otherwise? Parents and the inequities of public school choice.* New York: Routledge.
Bourdieu, P. (1986). The forms of capital. In J. G. Richardson (Ed.), *Handbook of theory and research for the sociology of education* (pp. 241–258). New York: Greenwood Press.
Gewirtz, S., Ball, S. J., & Bowe, R. (1995). *Markets, choice and equity in education.* Buckingham, UK: Open University Press.
Horvat, E. M., Weininger, E. B., & Lareau, A. (2006). From social ties to social capital: Class differences in the relations between schools and parent networks. In H. Lauder, P. Brown, J.-A. Dillabough, & A. H. Halsey (Eds.), *Education, globalization & social change* (pp.454–467). Oxford, UK: Oxford University Press.
Lareau, A. (1989). *Home advantage: Social class and parental intervention in elementary education.* Philadelphia: Falmer Press.
Lin, J. (2006). Educational stratification and the new middle class. In G. A. Postiglione (Ed.), *Education and social change in China* (pp. 179–198). Armonk, NY: M.E.Sharpe.
Liu, J. (2016). School district reform for "free, equitable and quality" public education in urban China: Achievements and challenges. *Norrag News, 54,* 59. Retrieved January 14, 2017, from http://www.norrag.org/fileadmin/Full%20Versions/NN54.pdf
Liu, J. (2018). Constructing resource sharing collaboration for quality public education in urban China: Case study of school alliance in Beijing. *International Journal of Educational Development, 59,* 9–19.
National People's Congress. (2006). *Compulsory education law of People's Republic of China.* Beijing, China: National People's Congress.
Tsang, M. C. (2003). School choice in the People's Republic of China. In D. N. Plank, & G. Sykes (Eds.), *Choosing choice* (June 2001 pp. 164–195). New York: Teachers College Press.
Wang, L. (2009). *Basic education in China.* Hangzhou, China: Zhejiang University Press.
Wu, X. (2012). School choice with Chinese characteristics. *Comparative Education, 48*(3), 347–366.
Yang, D. (2005, December 1). Huifu yiwu jiaoyu de gongyixing, pingdengxing, gongzhengxing (The return of publicity, equality, and equity of compulsory education). *Nanfang Zhoumo,* p. A2.

Appendices

Appendix 1: Interview Protocol for Principals

Junior High School

- School information in details (school history+ current situation)Student number/teacher number/teachers' qualification/student performance/facilities/others
- Admission changes from the late 1980s
- Current admission

    1. Government policies/school policies
    2. Admission-related documents/application forms
    3. From when to when is the general admission?
    4. School choice lottery system/admission criteria and process/proportion in total enrollment
    5. School choice students/admission criteria/admission process/proportion in total enrollment
    6. Cost for parents
    7. Are there any activities organized by school side regarding admission for parents?
    8. Is there a collaboration with other stakeholders? Please give details.

- What is the proportion of students enrolled through lottery system and through other approaches? Who are they? How are their family backgrounds?
- What is the benefit/lost from current admission for school? Why do you think so?
- What is the benefit/lost from current admission for students? Why do you think so?
- What is the benefit/lost from current admission for parents? Why do you think so?

- What is the benefit/lost from current admission for the community? Why do you think so?
- How do you think of parents' position in the process of *Zexiao*?
- What does *Zexiao* mean to you? And why?
- How does *Zexiao* influence the admission to junior high schools?
- How do you think of the discussion that *Zexiao* caused to social inequality? Why do you think so?

Primary School

- School information in details (school history+ current situation)
- Student number/teacher number/teachers' qualification/student performance/facilities/others
- Changes of admission to junior high school from the late 1980s
- Current admission
  1. Government policies/school policies
  2. Admission-related documents/application forms
  3. From when to when is the general admission to junior high schools?
  4. How is primary school involved in the school choice lottery system?
  5. What is the proportion of student enrolled in key schools?
  6. What is the proportion of students involving in school choice lottery system? Who are they? And how are their family backgrounds?
  7. What is the proportion of students involving in other school choice approaches? Who are they? And how are their family backgrounds?
- Have you ever organized any activity for parents regarding admission for children to junior high school? If yes, what kind of activity did you organize? And why?
- How do you think of parents' position in the process of *Zexiao*?
- How do you think of the current admission system to junior high schools? And why do you think so?
- Regarding the discussion on *Zexiao* which causes social inequality, how do you think? And why do you think so?

Appendix 2: Interview Protocol for Educational Administrators

1. Could you please introduce public school admission policy in your district?
2. Could you specify the public school admission approaches in your district (e.g., school recommendation student, special students, lottery system, etc.)?
3. How do you understand *Zexiao*?
4. What caused *Zexiao*?
5. How do you think of the charge of *Zexiaofei* for public school admission?
6. What caused the charge of *Zexiaofei*?
7. How do schools charge *Zexiaofei*? Could you explain the internal relationship between public school, local education authority, and parents in terms of charge of *Zexiaofei*?
8. What did the government do to tackle the charge of *Zexiaofei*?
9. How to understand balanced education development?
10. What is the situation of balanced education development in Beijing and in your district?
11. What is your suggestion for the balanced education development in Beijing and in your district?

Appendix 3: Interview Protocol with Scholars

1. Could you please recall your experience in school admission to junior high school? How about your children's experience? And how did public school admission to junior high schools changes?
2. How do think of *Zexiao* in urban China and in Beijing?
3. What's your opinion of the key school system or demonstration school system? And how do you think of their relationship with *Zexiao*?
4. How do you understand diverse approaches/choices for children's school admission to junior high schools? Could you clarify your opinions on school recommendation student approach and special talent student approach?
5. What caused *Zexiao*?
6. Why did the government failed in alleviating *Zexiao*?
7. How to deal with *Zexiao*?
8. How do you understand balanced education development? What is the relationship between *Zexiao* and balanced education development?
9. Do you think through achieving the balanced education development we can alleviate *Zexiao*? Why?

Appendix 4: Interview Protocol with Manager of Private Tutoring Institute

1. Could you introduce your private tutoring institute (such as number of branches, number of students, number of teachers, types of classes, the fees, etc.)?
2. Why did private tutoring institutes become popular in recent years? What is the relationship between *Zexiao* and private tutoring institute?
3. How do you think of *Zexiao*?
4. What caused *Zexiao*?
5. How do you understand balanced education development? What is your opinion on key school systems/demonstration schools and the gap between these schools and regular schools?
6. Could you specify Olympic math and English training classes in your institute? Are they popular among students, and why? How do think of this fever? And why do you think so?
7. Do you have pre-admission training class? How does it work?
8. What is your relationship with popular schools, in terms of public school admission?
9. How do you think of government policy on unlinking the pre-admission training class and public school admission to junior high schools? Why do you think so?
10. What's your opinion on the alleviation of *Zexiao*?

Appendix 5: Interview Protocol with Parents

Parents' Background

(a) Age/birth of place/your parents' information
(b) Household registration (*hukou*); if without local *hukou*, then when did you come to Beijing, and why did you come to Beijing?
(c) How is your living place/living condition/home-moving experience, and why did you move? Have you ever considered another move? If yes, where? Why? How do you decide where to live?
(d) Why did you choose to live there? What is the evaluation of the community where you are living in? How are your relations with neighbors? How is the distance to your workplace?
(e) Education background/education experiences: How did you like school? How was your school like? How do you think of your education level? Have you ever planned to go further? Are there any barriers?

- Compulsory education: admission process/admission criteria/cost
- Post-compulsory education: admission process/admission criteria/cost

(f) How do you think of education? And why?
(g) Working experiences:

- Occupation: How did you come to work at this job? How long have you been working on this job? How many times did you change your job? And Why?
- Income
- Working hours
- Job satisfaction

Children's Education

(a) Birth of place/age/*hukou*. Have you had change of *hukou*? When and why?
(b) Are they living together with you? If not, where and with whom do they live?
(c) How difficult is it to have a child in school? Provide examples.
(d) Schooling: school name/school location/distance from home/school's information/grade. Does he have any school transfer experience? When and why does he transfer?
(e) What is your expectation for her/his education? How far do you expect him/her to go? Why?
(f) How is your involvement in her/his education?
(g) How is her/his schooling going on? Which subject is his/her favorite and which is not?
(h) What are the problems/challenges for her/his schoolings? What are the reasons for those problems/challenges?
(i) Are there any after-school activities, like *Juku* or others? Why do you send them to study and how many times per week? How long does it take for once, and what is the cost?

Appendices 207

(j) Is there any other investment in children's education? Why? What is the cost?
(k) How important do you think compulsory education is for your child? Why?

Choosing School

For G7 Students' Parents

(a) How did you choose a school for your child?
   1. In the admission policy to junior high school, how much did you understand?
   2. How much do you understand on the principle of proximity and school choice lottery system?
   3. Do you follow the principle of proximity or not? Why?
   4. **For parents who chose school choice lottery system:**
   - What was the application process like? Could you explain? Are there any documents?
   - Are you having any problems or challenges in this process? What are they? How did you deal with them?
   - Are you satisfied with the system and the result? Why?
   5. **For parents who chose other school choices**
   - The process of choosing the school your child is attending now:
   - From where/whom do you gather information?
   - With whom are you talking about schools?
   - Are you visiting schools?
   - Application process
   - Application forms
   - Application criteria: especially from junior high school side
   - Are there after-school programs for application for junior high schools? What were they? How were they? Did you let your child attend? And why?
   - Cost: time/money
   - Others: what is the role of private education institutions in this process? How is your experience?
(b) Why did you choose the school which your child is attending now? Do you have any standard?
(c) Have you ever got any help from primary school side regarding your children's promotion to junior high school? What were they? How did you feel?
(d) How did you feel the process? Are there any problems/challenges?

For G6 Students' Parents

How are you preparing for choosing a school for your child?

1. Are you clear about this year's policy regarding promotion from primary school to junior high school? Could you explain? Where do you get the information? How do you think of this year's policy? And why?
2. Do you have any questions regarding this year's policy or any documents distributed by schools/governments or others? Could you explain in details?
3. Which way will you choose, following the principle of proximity or others? And why?
4. Do you have any preference for child's junior high school? And why do you prefer that school?
5. What kinds of information regarding school do you care about? Why?
6. How do you collect information regarding child's promotion to junior high school?
7. To whom do you talk about child's school choice? What do you talk?
8. What is your situation now regarding child's school choice? Which stage are you in? How do you feel?
9. Are there any problems/difficulties?
10. Have you ever got any help from primary school side? What are they? How do you feel? Is there any additional help you need?
11. How do you feel about the information provided by the key schools regarding admission?
12. How do you think of the admission criteria made by the key schools or the school you prefer?
13. Have you ever attended the activities organized by private education institutes? And why did you attend or why not? How do you feel?
14. What other activities do you and your child attend regarding the child's admission to junior high school?

About *Zexiao*

(a) What is your understanding of *Zexiao*? In other words, what does *Zexiao* mean to you?
(b) How do you think of *Zexiao*? Why?
(c) How do you think of public schools (key schools and non-key schools), *minban* schools, and private schools? Which type of school did you/do you plan to enroll your child? And why?
(d) How do you think of current admission process? Why?
(e) How do you think of principle of proximity? Why?
(f) For parents who did not /do not plan to follow principle of proximity, why do you participate in *Zexiao* or why not?
(g) Do you think *Zexiao* can cause social problems? What are they? Why do you think so?
(h) Regarding the current admission to public schools, do you have any ideas for improvement? What are they?

Appendix 6: Interview Protocol with Journalist

1. Could you please recall your experience in public school admission to junior high school? How different it is from current public school admission as you know?
2. How do you understand *Zexiao*? And how do you interpret it?
3. How did *Zexiao* occur? Could you please share your idea of the background?
4. Could you please analyze the reasons for *Zexiao*?
5. Regarding *Zexiao*, what kind of issue did you concern in the past years? Could you specify?
6. What kind of issues did you give special attention in terms of *Zexiao*? And why?
7. Could you introduce the approaches of *Zexiao* you found in your reports? Which is the most popular approach? And why?
8. Could you share the attitudes of parents, schools, and governments toward *Zexiao*?
9. How do you think of the policies related to *Zexiao*? Do they work? And why? What is your opinion on the improvement?
10. How do you understand the balanced education development? What is the relationship between the balanced education development and *Zexiao*?

Appendix 7: Socioeconomic Status of Parents

		Education		Occupation	
Parent no.	*Hukou*	Father	Mother	Father	Mother
Parents_20110510_ Shijingshan01_FW1	Beijing	PhD	PhD	Associate professor	Assistant professor
Parents_20110513_ Shijingshan02_FW1	Beijing	Master	Master	Associate professor	Civil servant
Parents_20110518_ Dongcheng01_FW1	Beijing	Bachelor	Bachelor	IT engineer	Teacher
Parents_20110503_ School A01_FW1	Beijing	Lower secondary	Upper secondary	Policeman	Accountant
Parents_20110503_ School A02_FW1	Beijing	Bachelor	Bachelor	Artist	Doctor
Parents_20110503_ School A04_FW1	Beijing	College	College	Policeman	Policeman
Parents_20110504_ School A05_FW1	Beijing	Vocational school	College	Designer	Bank staff
Parents_20110504_ School A06_FW1	Beijing (transfer from Henan)	PhD	College	Scientist	Post office staff
Parents_20110504_ School A07_FW1	Beijing	Lower secondary	Vocational school	Worker	Sales
Parents_20110505_ School A09_FW1	Beijing	Lower secondary	Lower secondary	Worker	Underemployed
Parents_20110505_ School A10_FW1	Beijing	Lower secondary	Lower secondary	Underemployed	Catering
Parents_20110505_ School A15_FW1	Beijing	Upper secondary	Upper secondary	Company staff	Company staff
Parents_20110510_ School B02_FW1	Beijing	Bachelor	Bachelor	Company staff	Teacher
Parents_20110511_ School A16_FW1	Beijing	Upper secondary	Upper secondary	Company staff	Company staff
Parent_20110513_ School B05_FW1	Beijing	Upper secondary	Upper secondary	IT	Businesswoman
Parents_20110502_ School A03_FW1	Henan	Lower secondary	Lower secondary	Worker	Worker
Parents_20110504_ School A08_FW1	Hebei (transfer in process)	Vocational school	Upper secondary	Construction company	Housewife
Parents_20110505_ School A11_FW1	Jiangsu	Upper secondary	Upper secondary	Construction company	Housewife
Parents_20110505_ School A12_FW1	Henan	Upper secondary	Upper secondary	Private business	Company staff

(continued)

Parent no.	Hukou	Education Father	Education Mother	Occupation Father	Occupation Mother
Parents_20110505_School A13_FW1	Henan	Upper secondary	Upper secondary	Private business	Private business
Parents_20110505_School A14_FW1	Shandong	NA	Lower secondary	NA	Private business
Parents_20110510_School B01_FW1	Hebei	Bachelor	Bachelor	Company staff	Teacher
Parents_20110512_School B03_FW1	Shandong	Lower secondary	Lower secondary	Private business	Private business
Parents_20110512_School B04_FW1	Shandong	Upper secondary	Upper secondary	Private business	Private business
Parents_20110513_School B06_FW1	Jilin	Upper secondary	Upper secondary	Private business	Private business

Source: Author edited

Appendix 8: Global Comparison of School Choice Policy

Country	Characteristics	Patterns	Objectives
Australia[a]	Private sector-centered choice, quality, equity	Public subsidy to both Catholic private schools and other non-Catholic private schools	Maintain private school sector and raise standards, political motive
UK[b]	Public sector centered. Self-managed school (from cost-effectiveness to quality control), competition, cooperation	Open enrollment	More freedom and choices for parents
		Linking school funding with enrollment	To stimulate motivation of school side
		Grant maintained school	More autonomy to schools
		City technology college	More choice/specialization
		Public support for poor pupils to private schools	More choice
USA[c]	Public sector centered. Social justice, competitiveness of public schools, academic achievement	Alternative programs/magnet school	Desegregation
		Charter school	Autonomy
		Education voucher	Access for disadvantaged students to private schools
		Inter/inner district choice/home schooling	More choices
Japan[d]	Public sector centered. Liberalization of education: diversity and quality improvement	Free choice, block choice, neighboring area choice, specially approved school, and specific area choice system	Increasing demand from parents according to social issues (bullying, school violence, etc.), dissatisfaction with the quality of teacher and school leadership, dissatisfaction with standardization, limited capacity of public schools

Source: Author
[a]Forsey, 2008; August, 2003; D. Hirsch, 2002, OECD, 1994; Potts, 1999
[b]Brown, 1990; Hirsh, 2002; OECD, 1994; Walford, 2008
[c]OECD, 1994; Andre-Bechely, 2005a, 2005b; Chubb and Moe, 1990; Ladd, 2003; Levin, 1992; Witte and Rigdon, 1993; Lubienski, 2008
[d]Fujita, 2000; Yoshida, Kogure, and Ushijima, 2008; Dierkes, 2008; Hayase, 2009

Appendix 9: Brief Introduction of *Zexiao* in Big Cities in Urban China

Guangzhou

According to 21st Century Education Research Institute (2011), there are two types of *Zexiao* in Guangzhou in 2010: first, to take part in entrance exams held by *minban* schools or public schools and, second, to take part in a test for special talent-based school admission. The special talents mainly refer to talents in sports, arts, Olympic math, and English. Sponsor fee to public education (educational donation is another official title of *Zexiaofei*) is allowed in public school admission. In 2010, it was said that the city as a whole collected 1.1 billion yuan as *Zexiaofei*. Moreover, although Olympic math-based student selection has been alleviated in Guangzhou, English-based selection became popular in this city recently.

Chengdu

According to 21st Century Education Research Institute (2011), about 70% of primary school student in Grade 6 follow the principle of proximity to go to junior high schools. And 30% of Grade 6 students in primary schools go to junior high schools by using other channels. Mainly, these students are memo students and fee-charged students. The *Zexiaofei* in Chengdu is from 30,000 yuan to 50,000 yuan. About 20% of the charged fees is redistributed to the schools which charged fees. And the rest is used for reconstruction of the left-behind schools.

Nanjing

According to 21st Century Education Research Institute (2011), the school admission policy at lower secondary education is "Free, no entrance exam, and proximity"-based in public schools; No entrance exam-based in *minban* schools." One characteristic of *Zexiao* in Nanjing is that *Zexiao* mainly happens among *minban* schools. *Minban* schools enroll students through two approaches, including school lottery and school-based admission. School-based admission leaves loophole for *minban* schools to select students at compulsory education level through their own criteria. The same as *Zexiao* in other cities, "Three excellence student", achievements in various types of contests and competitions are the channels for *Zexiao*. The collaboration between *minban* schools and private tutoring institutes in terms of student selection is also reported. Since the popular *minban* schools in Nanjing are mainly established by popular public schools, the relation stipulates the "legalization of *Zexiao*" in compulsory education.

Xianan

According to 21st Century Education Research Institute (2011), five public schools at secondary education level are the main focuses for *Zexiao* in Xianan. Interestingly, these schools both have *minban* junior high school department and public senior high school department. Moreover, three out of five popular schools are affiliated to local universities. Olympic math became an important criterion for student selection. It is reported that 70% of primary school students in Grade 3 to Grade 4 are studying Olympic math in Xian.

Shanghai

According to 21st Century Education Research Institute (2011), public school admission in Shanghai mainly depends on school lottery system. Public schools have two school-based admission approaches, including special talent-based and school recommendation-based. These types of enrollment share 5% of the total enrollment in public schools. In Shanghai, *minban* schools do not follow the principle of proximity. They collaborate with primary schools and private tutoring institutes for student selection. It is reported that Olympic math is still important criterion for school admission in *minban* schools. Moreover, the pre-admission training classes are becoming popular in recent years.

Appendix 10: School Admission Schedule in School B

2011届六年级毕业工作内容及时间安排

时间	工作内容	责任人	备注
4月13—17日	打印毕业生复核单交由学生复核，本人及家长签字，并上网修改各项错误。	钱鹏、班主任、学生、家长	
4月19～20日	带齐"8种人"有关材料（证明），到招办集中办理审查手续。	钱鹏、班主任、家长	Document submission for migrant children with "Green Card"
4月22日	小学启动推荐入学工作。	学校	
4月28日8:00—29日17:00	各小学登录考试中心小升初网站（http://ftks.org），网上填报推荐人选并打印名单。	学校	School Recommendation
5月4—5日	小学为回外区户籍就读的毕业生打印申请表。【5月4日学校打印申请表，下午家长携带学生户口（或家庭实际居住地房产权证明）原件到校，领取并填写。】	学校、钱鹏、家长	Document submission for children who go back to study in hukou registerred
5月5日17:00前	小学上交本校毕业年级正式生名册（从小升初智能平台http://ftks.org打印，加盖公章）。	学校、钱鹏	
5月5日17:00前	小学持本校申请表、学生户口（或家庭实际居住地房屋产权证明）原件到区考试中心中招办办理转出手续。	学校、钱鹏、家长	
5月5日	各小学上报本校推荐名单（网站打印）和推荐学生综合材料（学生自荐表、学校推荐表等）。以上材料以推荐初中校为单位区分，加盖校章。	学校	School Recommendation
5月6日	小学将通过审批的申请表等材料发给对应学生。（请家长到校领取。）	学校、家长	
5月8—9日	回外区户籍就读的毕业生到接收区县办理转入手续，完成后将申请表交回原小学。	家长	
5月11—12日	小学登陆考试中心小升初网站，按要求生成毕业生上网用户名及密码，发给对应小学毕业生。	钱鹏、班主任	
5月14—15日	体育、艺术、科技传统项目校受理小学毕业生报名，正式生须带本人上网用户名及密码，借读生等学籍卡复印件。	家长	Special talents students / Children without local hukou can apply for special talents student
5月17日8:00—18日17:00	小学毕业生上网填报（http://ftks.org）片内双向选择志愿。	钱鹏、班主任、家长	Mutual Selection

时间	工 作 内 容	责任人
5月19—20日	小学打印毕业生志愿确认单,交由学生及家长签字并收回,月底前统一交招办..	学校、钱鹏、班主任、家长
5月21日 14:00-15:00	对报名的体育特长生进行特长测试(丰台体育中心14看台集中)。	家长
5月21日	对报名的艺术、科技特长生进行特长测试(上午 8:30-11:30,下午 1:30-4:30 在区少年宫进行)。	家长
5月21—22日	片内双向选择初中校到对应小学查阅参加双向选择的小学毕业生综合素质评价手册。	班主任
5月23日 8:00—27日 17:00:	小学登录考试中心小升初网站,录入本校毕业生毕业成绩(等级值)和评语。	班主任
6月1日	下发有关文件,小学初审合格的从小升初网站(http://ftks.org)打印申请表。	学校、钱鹏
6月3日前	小学上交有关纸介材料。注意时间,过期不再办理。	班主任、钱鹏
6月1—6日	小学毕业生上网查询部分初中校前期初录结果。	学校、家长
6月26—27日	回外区学生户籍就读的毕业生持申请表和学校打印的初中入学登记表去接收区县办理接收手续。	家长
7月6日起	小学上网查本校毕业生录取去向。	学校
7月7—10日	小学毕业生上网查询录取结果。	学校、家长
7月8日起	中小学开始发放入学通知书。	学校、班主任
放假前	小学毕业生完成离校刷卡工作。	钱鹏、班主任
开学前	小学毕业生持录取通知书到录取校注册。	家长

Special talents student Test

Mutual Selection

Source:
Source: Collected from parent-teacher meeting in School A, April 27, 2011

Index

A

Academic achievement, 7, 57, 85, 146, 159, 162, 167, 189
Access, v, 3, 6–10, 15, 16, 20, 45, 57, 59, 61, 85, 86, 91, 99, 106, 107, 109–111, 117, 120, 133–135, 137, 144–147, 149, 151, 153, 154, 161–163, 167, 168, 176, 177, 180, 181, 187, 190, 194
Accountability, 2, 3, 31, 33, 62
Admission, v, vi, 1–3, 10, 12, 14–16, 20–22, 30, 37, 39, 44–46, 48, 52, 55–60, 62, 63, 71, 74, 75, 77–79, 85–91, 97–112, 118, 120, 123, 128, 131, 133–137, 141–156, 158–181, 185–195, 197–199, 201–206, 208, 209, 213, 214
After school training program, 190
Autonomy, 7, 31, 62, 212

B

Balance, 2, 22, 71, 75, 78, 79, 91, 104, 106, 118, 120–122, 129, 130, 132, 157, 158, 160, 171, 172, 174, 180, 181, 190, 197
Basic education, 1, 2, 60, 72, 81, 82, 97, 109, 133, 136
Beijing Municipal Education Committee, 19, 20, 58, 101, 104, 121, 122, 157, 180, 192

C

Capital, xvii, 5, 7, 8, 46, 63, 86, 167–169, 189, 193
Capitalism, 38

The Central Government, 13, 21, 55, 75, 97, 100, 103, 127, 172, 198
The Charter Schools, 32, 33
China, xvii, 1–4, 6, 8–9, 12–16, 21, 22, 29, 35–48, 51–55, 57–59, 62, 63, 71–79, 81–83, 85, 86, 88, 91, 97–100, 102, 108–112, 118–120, 123–129, 132–136, 149, 150, 153, 155, 156, 169, 171, 173, 176–179, 181, 185, 186, 189–191, 193–199, 213–214
The Chinese Dream, 35, 43
Class, 5, 7, 11, 18, 35–38, 41, 49, 55, 60, 73, 89, 90, 106, 108, 109, 111, 112, 124, 126, 131, 135, 136, 143, 148–152, 160, 161, 169, 175, 192, 193, 205
Co-founding student, 46, 54–56, 86, 187
Collusion, 22, 118, 134–137
Commercialization, 21, 91, 101, 113, 117, 118, 123, 128, 153, 188, 189
Communist Party, 6, 13, 40, 42, 43, 73, 77, 97, 125, 177
Communist Party of China (CPC), 13, 42, 43, 77, 105, 119, 125, 177
Competition, v, 1–5, 7, 10, 22, 30–33, 35, 41, 44, 45, 58, 63, 75–77, 79, 83, 84, 89, 90, 102, 107, 108, 117, 122, 133, 137, 142, 148, 151, 163, 167, 168, 170, 173, 186, 187, 189, 190, 192–194, 197–199
Compulsory education, v, 1, 3, 8, 14, 16, 21, 42, 45, 47, 53, 55, 57, 60, 62, 72–75, 78, 82, 83, 89, 91, 99, 100, 102–105, 107, 109, 112, 120, 124, 126, 128, 130, 132, 135, 144, 167, 170–173, 175, 177, 180, 181, 192, 194, 196–198, 206, 207, 213

© Springer Nature Singapore Pte Ltd. 2018
J. Liu, *Inequality in Public School Admission in Urban China*, Education in the Asia-Pacific Region: Issues, Concerns and Prospects 43, https://doi.org/10.1007/978-981-10-8718-9

Compulsory Education Law, 1, 3, 42, 45, 74, 87, 98, 100, 104, 105, 108, 112, 134, 142, 173
Computer lottery system, 105, 130, 131
Conflict, 5, 31, 35, 38, 89, 134, 148, 156, 199
Contest-based school system, 34
Converted schools, 14, 53, 101, 120–121, 128, 132–134, 197, 198
Cultural capital, 5, 169, 193
Cultural Revolution, 35–39, 41, 45, 101, 119, 120
Curriculum, 6, 42, 58, 73, 100, 110, 137, 151, 187

D
Decentralization, 9, 33, 98
Demonstration school, 18, 77, 90, 120–123, 125–128, 130, 132, 134, 137, 156–159, 168, 191, 197, 198, 204, 205
Demonstration senior high school, 20, 120, 124
Desegregation, 2, 30, 34
Disadvantaged, 3, 5, 7, 10, 22, 30, 33, 73, 91, 98, 109, 155, 165, 168, 169, 189, 190, 193, 195, 212
Discourse analysis, 12, 20, 21, 156
Distribution, 4, 7–9, 22, 30, 35, 48, 53, 77, 78, 87, 90, 104, 111, 121–123, 131–133, 156–160, 171, 173, 176, 177, 186, 190, 191, 197, 198
Donations, 3, 52, 55, 72–74, 88, 103
Downward, 10, 166–168

E
Education for All, 1
Educational administrators, 14, 16
Educational inequality, 2, 3, 8, 16, 78, 129, 168–170, 186, 193, 194, 199
Educational selection, 29, 34
Effectiveness, 7, 32, 212
Efficiency, 2, 3, 5, 21, 29–34, 39, 40, 62, 72, 74, 89, 91, 186, 189
Elites, 6, 34, 39, 120, 134
Engagement, 2, 21, 22, 185, 189
Enrollment, 19, 20, 37, 42, 52–58, 85, 88, 102, 104, 106, 108, 109, 119, 131–133, 136, 156, 167, 176, 201, 212, 214
Entrance exam, 3, 12, 45, 98, 100, 102, 107, 111, 133, 135, 143, 144, 152, 198, 213
Exam-driven education, 62, 63, 82, 89, 90, 186
Excellence, v, 21, 29, 33, 34, 57, 105–107, 146, 213
Exclusion, vi, 10, 11, 84, 91, 98, 137, 141, 144, 145, 147, 153, 154, 163–168, 170, 179–180, 189, 190, 195

F
Family background, 2, 8, 22, 63
Freedom, 5, 30–32, 62, 63, 186, 212

G
Gap between schools, 16, 187
Globalization, 5, 32, 33
Government, v, 1, 3, 6, 8–10, 12, 14, 16–18, 21, 22, 32, 35, 40–45, 47, 48, 52–56, 58, 62, 71–78, 80–83, 85–91, 97–103, 108, 111, 112, 120, 121, 123–131, 133–135, 137, 142, 149, 158, 159, 161, 165, 167, 169–181, 186–191, 193, 194, 196–199, 203–205
Grant-maintained schools, 33
Guanxi, 45, 54–57, 63, 84, 85, 90, 110, 142, 147, 152–156, 161–163, 167, 169, 170, 189, 190, 193, 194

H
Harmonious society, 22, 35, 42, 43, 77, 82, 171, 187, 190
History, 6, 8, 29, 36, 52, 119, 154, 194, 201, 202
Household registration system, 9, 36
Hukou, 3, 9, 17, 36, 83, 99, 108, 142, 143, 145–147, 155, 161–163, 167, 168, 170, 177, 179, 181, 189, 194, 198, 206
Human resources, 40, 62, 72, 76, 79, 82, 118, 119, 124, 127, 132, 159, 173, 175, 186, 189, 191, 197, 198

I
Ideology, 29, 31, 34, 35, 37, 39, 40, 42, 62, 74–76, 82, 87, 89, 127, 134
Imbalance, 9, 22, 53, 72, 74–79, 111, 122, 127, 130, 131, 133, 137, 174, 187, 189, 197
Imbalanced education development, 3, 16, 43, 71, 77, 79, 81, 129, 131, 196
Inequality, 2–4, 6–10, 16, 21, 34, 41, 42, 53, 56, 62, 63, 77, 91, 103, 118, 129, 137, 145, 147, 156, 164–166, 169–171, 176, 186–190, 192, 194, 195, 198, 199, 202
Institutional factors, 8, 9, 187, 199
Interactions, 2, 4, 10–12, 16, 21, 22, 71, 168, 185, 195

Index

International competence, 21, 29
Interplay, 2, 185, 190

J

Junior high schools, 3, 7, 10, 12, 14, 15, 17, 18, 21, 22, 44, 45, 47, 48, 53, 54, 57, 59, 60, 63, 71, 73, 76, 79, 84, 88, 90, 91, 97–103, 105, 107–112, 118, 119, 123, 124, 129, 131, 133, 135, 136, 141–145, 149–154, 156, 158, 160, 162–170, 172–179, 181, 185, 186, 188–195, 197–199, 202, 204, 205, 207, 213

K

Key schools, 14, 16, 19, 21, 45, 47, 53, 55, 57, 58, 61, 72–75, 77–79, 87, 88, 90, 91, 101, 102, 106–113, 117–120, 122–124, 126–132, 134–137, 146, 147, 153, 154, 158–162, 164, 168, 186–189, 191, 197, 198, 202, 208
Key school system, 21, 37, 39, 74, 75, 77, 78, 117–124, 126–128, 130, 134, 137, 161, 166, 173, 189, 191, 204

L

Language, 10, 12, 42
Leadership, v, 31, 35, 38, 39, 41, 124, 128, 180, 181, 187, 212
Local characteristics, 22, 199
Local education authorities, 2–4, 16, 31, 46, 63, 72, 80, 90, 91, 99, 102, 107, 127–128, 130, 134, 188, 192
Loophole, 73, 103, 106, 179, 186, 188, 192, 213

M

Market, 5–7, 31–34, 42, 62, 73, 74, 76, 77, 79, 84, 90, 91, 109, 111, 112, 125, 136, 168, 169, 186, 188, 193, 199
Market economy, 38, 74
Marketization, 6, 10, 32, 33, 112, 137
Mechanism, v, vi, 5, 7, 10, 88, 173–175, 178
Memo student, 46, 54, 55, 85, 187, 213
Migrant children, 19, 20, 81, 83, 90, 142–145, 147, 152–154, 156, 167, 168, 170, 176, 178–181, 194, 198
Migrant parents, 15, 83, 145, 152, 153, 162, 164, 168
Minban school, 50, 53, 77, 82, 90, 121, 123, 126, 129, 132–134, 142, 173, 197, 213, 214
Mobility, 6, 9, 33, 122, 156, 157, 194
Modernization, 38, 39, 62, 72, 76, 82, 119, 120, 124
Multi-layered, 21, 188, 195

N

Negotiation, 11, 12, 16, 91, 105, 169, 181, 186, 187, 191, 193, 196
Neo-liberalism, 5, 31–33, 62, 63
Networks, 4–6, 33, 153, 161, 190
New Normal, 43–44
New Public Management (NPM), 32
New solutions, 2, 22, 180, 181, 185, 190, 199

O

Olympic math, 46, 58–61, 87–90, 100, 102, 108–110, 136, 137, 167, 192, 214
Olympic school, 102
The One Child Policy, 20, 75, 79, 90, 144, 187
The Open-Door Policy, 38
Organisation for Economic Co-operation and Development (OECD), 3, 30, 33, 34

P

Parental choice, 7, 30, 31, 53
Parentocracy, 7, 141, 142, 145, 156, 162, 164, 168, 189, 193, 199
Parents, v, vi, 2, 3, 7, 12, 14, 16, 18, 20, 22, 30, 31, 41, 44–48, 51–53, 55, 58–63, 72–77, 79–85, 87, 89–91, 99, 105–112, 117, 120, 122, 126–137, 141–156, 159–164, 166–170, 177, 180, 181, 186–195, 198, 199, 201–203, 206–209, 212
Parents' aspiration, 16, 45, 53–54, 72–77, 79–80, 90, 108, 164, 186, 187
Participation, 3, 4, 8, 22, 36, 46, 60, 106, 133, 141, 142, 150–152, 162, 163, 165, 168, 170, 188, 190, 193, 194
Policy borrowing, 33
Popular schools, 2–4, 7, 15, 45, 47, 55–57, 59, 60, 73, 75, 77–79, 83–86, 90, 104, 106–108, 110, 111, 128, 129, 132, 134, 135, 137, 142, 146–149, 151–157, 159–164, 166, 169, 186, 189, 192–194, 198, 199, 205, 214

Population, 5, 8, 17, 36, 38, 122, 144, 179, 181
Power, v, vi, 2, 4–6, 10, 13, 16, 21, 22, 31, 35, 36, 43, 45, 51, 54–56, 61–63, 71, 77, 80, 83–86, 88, 90, 91, 130, 147, 156, 161, 164, 177, 181, 185, 187, 189, 190, 195, 199
Power exchange, 164, 181
Power relationships, 2, 21, 71, 185
Practice, vi, 5, 7, 11, 12, 20, 46, 48, 52, 54, 56, 57, 63, 85, 98, 102, 108, 112, 126, 131, 148, 167, 169, 176, 189, 191, 193, 196, 200
Pre-admission training classes, 3, 90, 111, 112, 134, 135, 137, 151, 152, 156, 163, 192, 214
Private schools, 2, 30, 31, 121, 126, 197, 208, 212
Private tutoring institutes, 2, 3, 12, 14, 16, 21, 57, 61, 63, 80, 90, 91, 108–113, 118, 134–137, 149, 151, 156, 168, 188, 189, 192, 205, 213, 214
Privatization, 10, 32, 33, 53
Privilege(s), 4, 6, 11, 20, 22, 45, 55, 73, 75, 77, 82, 86, 87, 90, 91, 99–101, 117, 128–134, 137, 158, 159, 165, 167, 169, 171, 174–179, 181, 186–188, 191, 194, 198
Programme for International Student Assessment (PISA), 33, 34
Proximity-based public school admissions, 3
Public discussions, 13, 16, 71, 75, 78, 102, 187
Public education, 3, 9, 10, 21, 22, 30–34, 44, 53, 62, 63, 74, 76, 79, 81, 83, 86, 89, 91, 97, 99, 101, 103, 113, 118, 123, 126, 128, 129, 132, 142, 144, 153, 164, 166, 169, 170, 172–175, 178, 180, 181, 186, 188–191, 195, 197–199, 213
Public English Test System (PETS), 58–60, 108–110
Public lower secondary education, 2, 21, 22, 98, 165, 166, 170, 172, 180, 185
Public schools, v, 1, 3, 7, 12, 14, 22, 30, 31, 45, 48, 52, 53, 61–63, 72–79, 82, 83, 85–87, 89–91, 97, 99–106, 108, 111, 112, 118–120, 122–134, 137, 142, 152, 153, 156, 158, 159, 162, 166–169, 172–175, 177, 178, 180, 181, 186, 188–192, 194, 195, 197–199, 208, 212–214

Q
Quality, 2, 3, 7, 18, 19, 22, 29, 31–33, 39–44, 46, 48, 56, 58, 61–63, 74, 76, 80, 82, 84–87, 90, 91, 104, 110, 111, 117–120, 124, 126–135, 144, 146, 147, 153, 154, 157–162, 164, 166–168, 170, 171, 173–178, 180, 181, 185, 186, 188–190, 194, 197, 199, 212

R
Redistribution, 6, 7
Reform, 5, 7, 9, 12, 19, 22, 29, 31–34, 38, 40–42, 53, 62, 74, 75, 83, 89, 98, 100, 107, 111, 118, 123–126, 129, 132, 133, 172, 174, 175, 178–181, 190, 197, 200
Regular schools, 14, 21, 45, 47, 61, 91, 117–119, 124, 131, 133, 134, 137, 162, 169, 181, 193, 205
Regulations, v, 2, 3, 10, 12, 21, 60, 97
Rent seeking, 22, 84, 90, 106, 165, 186
Rights, 4, 5, 29, 31, 32, 84
Rural-urban migration, 8, 18, 38

S
School assignment, vi, 48, 50, 61, 81, 169, 192, 193, 198
School choice, v, 2–5, 7, 21, 29–31, 33, 34, 62, 63, 168, 185, 186, 193, 199, 200, 202, 208
School lottery system, 45, 49, 58, 99, 214
School principals, vi, 14, 20–22, 73, 80, 89, 129, 130, 132, 159
School recommendation, 19, 49, 57, 58, 101, 103–107, 113, 133, 135, 142, 167, 177, 192, 214
Segregation, 7, 34, 120
Self-interests, 32
Social advantages, 5, 91
Social capital, 5, 169, 193
Social change, 9, 21, 29, 35, 71, 81, 91, 187, 196, 200
Social closure(s), vi, 10, 22, 165, 166, 168, 195
Social construction, 11, 12
Social constructionists, 11, 12
Social context, 8, 35, 181
Social interaction, 12, 22, 54
Social mobility, 34, 40, 194

Social reproduction, 3–5, 10, 169, 170, 185, 193, 194
Social transformation, 2, 185
Socialism, 6, 37, 171
Socioeconomic status, 3, 4, 7, 15, 17, 20, 33, 40, 44, 46, 106, 142, 150–152, 155, 163, 168, 180, 186, 188, 189, 193, 198
Special talents, v, 3, 4, 58, 101–105, 107, 108, 110, 113, 142, 143, 147, 148, 158, 173, 213
Sponsor fee, 45, 55, 72, 73, 85, 86, 213
Sponsor-based school system, 34
Stakeholders, v, 2–4, 10–12, 16, 17, 21, 22, 30–32, 35, 44, 46, 63, 71, 74, 76, 79, 87, 90, 91, 100, 103–105, 108, 113, 129, 130, 134, 141, 153, 165, 166, 168–170, 177, 178, 181, 185, 186, 188, 190, 191, 195, 201
Stratification, 2, 5, 6, 22, 36, 84, 117, 118, 123, 130, 169, 177, 188, 193, 199
Student placement, 21, 98, 112
Student selection, 22, 45, 57, 59, 61, 79, 90, 91, 100, 102, 104, 108–112, 117, 118, 122, 127, 130, 132, 134–137, 164, 190, 192, 196, 198, 213, 214

T
Theory of school systems, 34
Three excellence students, 57, 105–107, 213
21st Century Education Research Institute, 16, 45, 46, 48, 50, 51, 55–59, 61, 82, 86, 98, 99, 104, 169, 178, 194, 213, 214

U
Unauthorized school fees, 16, 52, 88, 89, 98, 126, 128, 187

Understanding, 4, 11–13, 16, 32, 35, 40, 76, 78, 79, 86, 185–187, 190, 199, 205, 208
Upward, 11, 34, 40, 166–168, 190, 194
Urban China, 2–4, 7–9, 12–16, 21, 22, 30, 36, 41, 44–46, 63, 78, 81–83, 89, 91, 99, 100, 103, 111, 112, 118, 120–123, 126–129, 132, 134, 141, 155, 160, 165, 169–171, 176, 178, 180, 181, 185–195, 197–199, 204
Urbanization, 18, 41, 83, 179, 187
Usurpation, 10, 165–168
Utilitarian doctrine, 82

V
Voucher, 30, 31

W
Work unit, 3, 54, 55, 63, 85, 86, 90, 169, 194, 198

Z
Zexiao, v, vi, 2–4, 10–17, 19–22, 29, 44–63, 71–91, 98–105, 108, 110–113, 118, 121–123, 125–135, 137, 141, 142, 145, 148, 152–157, 159–170, 177, 185–199, 202–205, 208, 209, 213–214
   achievement-based *Zexiao*, 51, 57–63, 104, 190
   money-based *Zexiao*, 51–54, 61
   power-based *Zexiao*, 51, 54, 56, 61, 63, 86, 90
Zexiaofei, 52, 53, 72–78, 83, 85, 88–90, 101, 104, 108, 127, 128, 163, 188, 189, 191
Zhankengban, 58, 61, 111, 112, 135, 136

Printed by Printforce, the Netherlands